THE
MOM
FACTOR

Other books by Henry Cloud and John Townsend

Boundaries
Boundaries Workbook
Changes That Heal (Cloud)
Changes That Heal Workbook (Cloud)
Hiding from Love (Townsend)
False Assumptions
False Assumptions Workbook
Safe People
Safe People Workbook

Dr. Henry Cloud
Dr. John Townsend

THE
MOM
FACTOR

Dealing with the Mother You Had,
Didn't Have, or Still Contend With

ZondervanPublishingHouse
Grand Rapids, Michigan

A Division of HarperCollinsPublishers

The Mom Factor

Copyright © 1996 by Henry Cloud and John Townsend

Requests for information should be addressed to:

ZondervanPublishingHouse

Grand Rapids, Michigan 49530

Library of Congress Cataloging-in-Publication Data

Cloud, Henry.
    The mom factor : dealing with the mother you had, didn't have, or still contend
with / Henry Cloud and John Townsend.
      p.   cm.
    ISBN: 0–310–20036–9 (hardcover : alk. paper)
    1. Parent and adult child. 2. Mother and child. 3. Mother and child—Religious
aspects—Christianity. 4. Adult children—Family relationships. 5. Mothers—Family
relationships. 6. Reconciliation. I. Townsend, John Sims, 1952–
II. Title.
HQ755.86.C56   1996
306.874'3–dc20   96–9487
                                                      CIP

This edition printed on acid-free paper and meets the American National Standards
Institute Z39.48 standard.

Published in association with Sealy M. Yates, Literary Agent, Orange, CA.

Printed in the United States of America

96 97 98 99 00 01 02 03 / ❖ DH/ 10 9 8 7 6 5 4 3 2 1

Contents

Introduction

Welcome to *The Mom Factor*. We hope it's helpful. Before you begin, however, we want to introduce you to what's behind this book and what you can expect from it.

The fact that you are reading this book indicates that you are curious or that you have concerns or struggles surrounding your relationship with one of the most important people in anyone's life: Mom. This may mean your own mother, or it could mean the mother of your spouse or a friend. God gave you a mother to protect, nurture, and mature you. She takes on part of his loving nature. Your mom, or some person in that role, was right there in the middle of your becoming you. Religious leaders, politicians, great thinkers, and artists often give glowing testimonies to the impact their mothers had upon their lives. Mothering is the most significant, demanding, and underpaid profession around.

Yet, for many, mom also means conflicts or problems. You may have haunting memories of bad experiences in the past, or you may have a difficult present connection with your mother. Yet, since as most of us love our mothers deeply, we have a hard time talking about our problematic feelings or issues with her. For example, you might have the following questions:

How can I have a better present-day relationship with my own, or someone else's, mother?

Which of my current relationships or work problems might have been influenced by my mothering?

What went right and wrong in my mothering, and how did that affect the connection between my childhood and my life today?

How can I get beyond my past mothering problems, so that I can get on with my life?

What's the best way for me to parent my own children?

These and many other questions aren't some act of disloyalty to mother. We strongly believe that God ordained the specialness and importance of mothering: "Honor your mother and your father" is a recurring theme throughout the entire Bible. Yet, we also need to be honest, tell the truth, take responsibility, heal, forgive, and grieve at the same time that we honor mom.

And this is why we wrote *The Mom Factor.* For many years as clinical psychologists, we have studied and seen how crucial mothering is. Much has been written about mothering on a professional level, yet very little addresses the problems and solutions on a general level. Even fewer writings show the spiritual side of mothering dynamics. We have seen so many people struggle for so long because they had no way to understand what to do about how they were mothered, for better or worse.

On a brighter note, we have also seen miracles happen. Many individuals we have known through our speaking or counseling have examined how they were mothered. A great number of these people have learned much, healed much, loved much, and now have more fruitful, more meaningful relationships with mom and others. It is to these people that we dedicate this book.

The organization of *The Mom Factor* is straightforward. Six "mom types"—the Phantom Mom, the China Doll Mom, the Controlling Mom, the Trophy Mom, the Still-the-Boss Mom, and the American Express Mom—explain how the mothering process breaks down in different ways, from emotional absence to problems in letting go of kids. Each mom type is presented in a pair of chapters. The first chapter will describe the problem and the needs that may not have been met. The second will provide the steps to meeting needs that were unmet and repairing whatever was broken. We finish the book with chapters on the unique issues that women and men have with mothers, including their own tasks as parents.

One important point: When we say "mother," we mean your real mother or anyone who played the role of mother in your life. Many people were not raised by their biological mother; for example, those who were reared by a grandparent, stepparent, or friend of the family. If this is your situation, mother for you is that most significant person.

We hope it becomes obvious that this is not a negative book about mom, but one designed to meet a great need today: *reconciliation*. We are all called both to ask and to give forgiveness, and, as a result, we can enjoy better lives and better connections. The first step of any reconciliation is to understand the problems. That's why understanding the mom types is so important.

A final note: You may be curious about why a couple of men, rather than women, are writing a book about mom. While we can understand the concern that a woman's perspective might not be included in a book about a womanly role, we didn't exclude anyone in writing this material. Here are a few reasons we felt qualified:

- Mothering issues involve a role and function that has been studied extensively in the clinical arena, by scientists and thinkers of both genders.
- We have had clinical training and experience, including many years of directing multiple outpatient and inpatient settings.
- Many men have played large roles in "mothering" their children, just as many women have done so in "fathering."
- We both had moms ourselves, and today have good connections with them!

In fact, we feel that the issue is more non-issue. Understanding mothering has much more to do with understanding God, people, and how we are to relate than it has to do with gender.

So we hope you learn some things about yourself, mom, and God in reading *The Mom Factor*. More than that, we hope you find yourself better and healthier as a result. Enjoy the book!

Chapter One

What About Mom, Anyhow?

Beth hung up the phone, frustrated, confused, and discouraged. She had just spent ninety minutes talking to her mother—ninety minutes of wasted time. As a working mother, Beth didn't have that kind of time to spare.

She had tried to explain to her mom that their vacation plans wouldn't include a visit to see her. "You know we'd love to see you," Beth said, trying to reason with her mom, "but this vacation we really wanted to see the Grand Canyon."

The silence that followed was too familiar to Beth. Hurt, distance, and coldness were the hallmarks of saying no to her mother. Beth tried to scramble and make some connection with her. "Mom, we'll make a real effort to see you on the next trip."

"That won't be necessary. I'm sure you'll be too busy for me then too." Her mother hung up, and the dial tone accented that ache in Beth's stomach that she knew too well. Again, she realized that her mother couldn't be pleased; Beth was always "not enough," or "too much" something. It was confusing: Was she really an ungrateful, selfish daughter, or did her mother have too many expectations?

Beth loved her mother deeply and desired more than anything to have a close, respectful relationship with her. She remembered the commandment to "honor thy father and mother," and thought, *This is impossible. If I honor her, I dishonor my family, and if I honor my family, I dishonor her.* She resigned herself to the way things always had been and went back to planning the vacation. However, emptiness now surrounded the entire project.

WHAT'S WRONG?

This scene repeats itself millions of times daily around the world. Every six seconds, another adult alternates between resentment, anger, guilt, fear, and confusion about ongoing interaction with a mother.

Most people want a comfortable, mutually satisfying friendship with that very significant person in our life—our mother. But the reality falls short of the ideal. You may experience "mother trouble" in several areas. You may feel:

- unable to communicate with her
- her lack of respect for your choices and values
- her refusal to accept your own family and friends
- a lack of freedom to have a separate life without losing her love
- disconnected from and misunderstood by her
- difficulty in saying no and confronting her
- you have to hide your real self and be perfect
- responsible to make her think that she is perfect
- guilt when you don't take care of her as she wants you to
- disillusionment and conflict over her interactions with your spouse
- guilt over not living up to her expectations and wishes
- sorrow that she can't seem to comprehend your pain
- childlike in her presence
- frustration over her seeming self-absorption
- like cringing when she treats your children in familiar hurtful ways
- discouraged that this list is so long

The list could go on, but it points to a fundamental truth: Our relationship with our mother either in the past or present hasn't left us where we want to be. You may wish you and your mom were closer. And you may wish she had better prepared you for other aspects of life.

For not only does the quality of your relationship with your mother dictate how things go between the two of you, it also drastically impacts all areas of your life. Not only do we learn our patterns of intimacy, relating, and separateness from mother, but we also learn about how to handle failure, troublesome emotions, expectations and ideals, grief and loss, and many of the other components that make up our "emotional IQ"[1]—that part of us that guarantees whether or not we will be successful at love and work. In short, the following two realities largely determine our emotional development:

1. How we were mothered
2. How we have responded to that mothering

Dave got out of the car in the flower shop parking lot. It was another apology bouquet day. His wife, Cindy, had been in tears last night when she had staged a special evening alone with him without the kids. Dinner had gone well, and she had been looking forward to an evening of intimacy and vulnerability. Yet when she looked into his eyes and asked him how he was feeling about their marriage and life in general, Dave had shut down inside. As usual he was at a loss for words and could not bridge the emotional gap between himself and his wife.

"Maybe I just don't deserve her . . . a husband is supposed to love his wife, so why don't I even desire this closeness that's so important to her? What's wrong with me?" he wondered, as he plunked down another bill for the flowers. "Are flowers the best I'll ever do?"

Dave's dilemma would seem at first glance to have little to do with mothering problems. He just knew he had a problem with his wife. But the reality is that Dave's pattern of relating was working exactly as God planned: we learn from our parents about relationship. In his relationship with his mother, Dave had learned that closeness could be dangerous. For example, when he was scared or hurt, his mother would become anxious and fuss over him to the point that he felt smothered. As a result, any time his wife moved toward him in an emotional way, his walls went up, and he braced himself against emotional overinvolvement. He found himself in a lose-lose situation.

While he did not like being cut off from his wife, he did not like being close either. Either position left his wife feeling unfulfilled. Until Dave dealt with his fears of intimacy, this pattern would continue.

Dave's struggle illustrates the major point of this book: What we learned in our relationship with our mother deeply affects every area of our adult life.

DOES IT HAVE TO BE THIS WAY?

Just as God's plan for us to learn patterns of relating from our mothers can end up wreaking destruction in our adult lives, so can his plan of repair bring change and growth.

As a single man, Mark had noticed patterns in his relationships similar to Dave's pattern with his wife: He couldn't sustain long-term, intimate relationships. He'd get close to an eligible woman, even consider marriage, and then inexplicably back off from the relationship, complaining that she was "too demanding," or "too serious," or "not serious enough," or whatever. For years he simply told himself that he just couldn't find the "right one," until a friend suggested that the problem might be *him.* In response to his friend's suggestion, Mark joined a support group that dealt with issues of intimacy and trust. It was hard work at first as those were the very dynamics in which he felt the most deficient. Yet, as he opened himself to the consistent nurturing and confrontation of the group members, something began to change in him. As they held him accountable for his own fears and deficits, *as well as gave him what he missed with his own mother,* he began to notice that he avoided intimacy less. In fact, he even began to long for it. And his long list of requirements for a partner became much more realistic.

As Mark continued on his growth path, he found "the right one." But in reality, Mark had become "the right one" because he had allowed his friends to provide the mothering he needed and thus learned the patterns of relating he had missed the first time around. When we aren't mothered perfectly, God will provide others to fill in the gaps. He can redeem our early experience, either building on the good our mother did, or providing basic essentials our mother may have missed.

TWO CONSIDERATIONS

Many people suffer under the delusion that their mother is the real problem. Many modern pop psychology approaches promote the following:

- blaming parents for all of the client's problems
- focusing only on dredging up "pain from the past" and "getting the pain out," thinking that catharsis cures
- identifying the client as a victim and commiserating with how bad "Mom" or someone else was
- excusing behavior, lack of performance, and failure in love or work because of what mother failed to provide
- encouraging the client to live more in the past than in the present
- arranging sessions with mom, thinking that reconciling with mom or having mom "own" how bad she was will finally fix the hole in the client's heart

This thinking focuses on the mother of the past, not on the process of mothering in the present. Thinking that resolution will come from blaming parents, trying to get them to change, or continuing to process the events of the past, they miss out on the necessary character change that leads to real healing.

While we believe that working out one's relationship with one's mother is very important in the growth process, it is not the whole picture. We must also look at the process of mothering in the present as well.

Therefore, the two considerations that we will be focusing on in this book are *your relationship with your mother* and *the process of mothering itself*. Let's look at each one of those issues for a moment.

YOUR MOM

When we talk about "dealing with the past," we aren't saying to "go back into the past." You cannot go back to 1950, 1960, 1970, or even yesterday to deal with mother. But, dealing with mother is possible because, whether you like it or not, she lives with you every day in the present.

Two very important issues are at work every day that result from unresolved aspects of our relationship with mother. The first issue has to do with the feelings we have for our mother, the injuries we felt from her, and the needs that she didn't meet. The second issue is the dynamics and patterns of relating that we learned in our relationship with mom. The first deals with how we feel today about the past; the second deals with how we repeat patterns from the past.

Leftover Feelings

Let's look at the first issue—the feelings that we have toward our mother.

Jim and Debbie were preparing for a trip. She was packing, and he was getting the car ready when Debbie suddenly remembered that it was time to change the oil in her car. She walked out into the garage. "Jim, did you get the oil changed?" she asked. Maybe he had remembered and taken the car in earlier in the day.

"Will you get off my back?" Jim screamed. "What do you think I am, an idiot? Of course I got the oil changed. I told you I would take care of the car, and you don't ever believe anything I tell you." He stared at her with such contempt and hatred that an icy feeling moved down her spine. Debbie, not ever knowing what to do when Jim reacted in this way, withdrew to her room and cried.

Debbie had asked an innocent question. But Jim reacted as if she thought he was an "idiot," and he was prepared to fight and defend himself against her.

Why? Jim grew up with a mother very unlike Debbie. A domineering and controlling woman, Jim's mother did not trust Jim to do things on his own, nor did she believe him when he told her he had done his jobs. He grew up trying to please her and at the same time resenting her.

One reason Jim had fallen in love with Debbie in the first place was because she was so unlike his mother. Although not consciously thinking about his mother at all, he was drawn to Debbie's warmth and lack of domination. He felt close to her almost from the first time they met. She was his ultimate fantasy woman.

As time went on, the relationship naturally deepened—and then the problems emerged. Jim began to lose his warm, tender feelings toward Debbie, and instead began to feel a growing resentment resulting in angry outbursts like the one above.

The sad thing was that Debbie hadn't changed. She was still the same warm, noncontrolling person he had loved.

What had happened? As Jim's attachment to his wife increased, his unresolved feelings about his mother began to emerge and interfere with how he experienced Debbie. His anger toward his mother and his feelings of being controlled, mistrusted, and dominated by his mother got displaced onto Debbie. He experienced Debbie as an adversary, as he had his mother. In reality, he could no longer even see Debbie for the woman she was, because of his feelings about his mother. He actually began to experience Debbie as if she were his mother.

Psychologists call this phenomenon "transference." It is our tendency to direct feelings toward people in the present that should really be directed toward people in our past. It's the old "burned dog dreads the fire" routine. If someone hurts us, and we fail to work through our wounded feelings, we will distort future relationships that appear even close in character to the one in which we were hurt. If we have unresolved feelings toward our real mothers, we need to deal with that relationship.

The Bible calls this process forgiveness. Forgiveness involves looking honestly at problems in a relationship, facing them, letting them go, and grieving our losses. It frees us from our past. We name what went wrong, look at it, feel the feelings, and let them go. The goal is to get to the place where we are "finished with mother" and ready to see people as they are.

Patterns of Relating

The second issue related to our mother has to do with *understanding the dynamics and patterns of relating that we learned in our relationship with mom.* Let's go back to Dave for a moment. He had learned some patterns in his relationship to his mother that he was exhibiting now with his wife. These patterns of relating, called "dynamics," are like maps laid down in our brains; they determine how we will operate in different kinds of relationships. Dave's map of closeness worked this way: When he became intimate, he feared he would be smothered and overwhelmed, losing himself. In order to regain his own space that he feared his wife (like his mother before her) was about to take away from him, he withdrew.

Dave is living out the *pattern of relating* that is familiar to him, and until he changes it, he will continue to "walk in the ways of [his] elders." The Bible tells us that we repeat unhealthy patterns of relating until we take ownership of them and work through them (see Mark 7:8–9). Dave needs more insight into the patterns that he had learned in his relationship with his mother, so that he can turn from them and begin to create healthier ones with his wife.

We need to look at the patterns that we learned in our relationship with our mother. Patterns of avoidance, control, compliance, dominance, passivity, aggressiveness and overcontrol, mistrust, and a host of others can get hardwired into our brains. We were made to take in those patterns and to live by them. That is what parenting is about. We internalize the ways of our parents, and then live by them.

Thus, we are destined to repeat troublesome internalized patterns of relating or performing until we become aware of them and change. In this way, our relationship with mom needs more than forgiveness: We need to become aware of dynamics and patterns and change them into more helpful ones.

THE MOTHERING PROCESS

Jordan was a diligent mother of two, and she loved her children very much. But her children were disorganized, as children often are; they would leave their toys lying around and generally create chaos. When this happened, Jordan would grow more and more irritated, until finally through clenched teeth, she would yell, "Put your toys away." Fearing her blowups, her children were beginning to show signs of anxiety. Whenever she would yell at them, or respond harshly, she would feel like a "horrible mother" and be overcome with guilt.

Jordan began to talk to a trusted friend, Susan, about her problem; it was the first time she had ever openly shared a shortcoming with a friend. Susan responded with empathy and understanding, so Jordan began to admit other imperfections.

Over time, Jordan began to notice the difference between Susan and some of the other women she hung around with. The others talked about their wonderful lives, their successful children, and their incredible spiritual growth. There was nothing wrong with sharing successes, but these women never shared failures. Susan was open not only to the good things Jordan had going but also to her struggles.

Jordan was changing. As she continued to share all of herself— the good and the bad—with Susan, she was becoming a more relaxed person. The little things she did not have "all together" did not bother her as much. And she found she was less bothered by what her children were doing. She found that she was able to just be with them in their imperfections in a whole new way. Susan's acceptance of her was being passed on in her mothering.

What was happening here? Jordan was getting restored to the *process of mothering*. Susan was providing Jordan with empathy and containment, a basic aspect of mothering Jordan had not received from her own mother. For us to become comfortable with ourselves, all of ourselves, we need someone with whom we can be ourselves. We need acceptance and understanding, so that we can contain and integrate all parts of ourselves. A good mother does this. She listens to and accepts the negative, contains it, and helps her child not feel overwhelmed. She is comfortable with her child's imperfections. The child takes her comfort into his personality, and he becomes comfortable with imperfections as well. The mothering process of acceptance integrates the child.

Some people, however, do not receive this empathy and understanding from their own mothers. They experience the "uncomfortable with imperfections" mothering that Jordan first gave to her children. This was the kind of mothering she had received from her own mother, and the only kind she knew how to pass on to her children. Her mother had failed to give her empathy and understanding, and so she did not have it inside to give to herself and to her children.

God has designed several ingredients into the growing up process that a "good-enough mother" provides. Our aim here is to help you understand that you may not have received everything you needed from your mother, and only when someone gives you those ingredients can your life work correctly. This is what Susan did for Jordan; she gave her what her mother failed to give her. This is what friends do for each other every day. This is what it means to be restored to the mothering process.

So, not only do we need to resolve things with one real person in our past as we mentioned above, but we must get from others what we did not get completely from our mother.

In the rest of the book, we will outline the major aspects of the mothering process so that you can understand why some areas of your relationships and your performance are not working, and so you can know what you need for it to change. Just as Jordan discovered that she lacked empathy and was restored to that aspect of mothering through Susan, you will find what it is that you have missed.

RESPONDING TO MOTHERING

Remember the two issues we identified above that determine who we are as people: (1) the kind of mothering we had—both from our own mothers and from our significant relationships since then—and (2) our response to the mothering process.

When we have gotten negative mothering, we can begin a pattern of mistrusting for the rest of our lives. We hide our needs and vulnerability. We become combative and aggressive. To show that we can't be controlled, we control others. And the list goes on. We respond to mothering in defensive and reactive ways, as did Jim, which, in turn, like Jim above, prevents us from getting what we need, thus perpetuating our own problems.

Jordan had not received the acceptance that she needed from her mother. As a result, she had also developed a pattern of avoiding the acceptance that was available to her later in life. Others, even before Susan, would have listened to Jordan and accepted her. But she was so caught up in her efforts to be perfect that she was not responding to the good mothering that was around her at all times.

Jordan's rejection of good mothering is in contrast to what the Bible calls responding to the light. Things of light—like honesty, vulnerability, trust, responsibility, acceptance, forgiveness—are around us all the time. Our part is to open up and respond to them.

OUR ASSUMPTIONS

In this book, we are making three assumptions:

Our first assumption is that there is no such thing as the "good child" and the "bad mom." Sometimes people in recovery and psychological movements encourage "parent bashing"; every negative thing is the fault of one or both parents. Mothers do fail in being all that they need to be. Some fail in being almost anything that they needed to be. Still others do a pretty good job and just leave a few things undone or in need of fixing. But, children have defensive and inappropriate responses as well, and as adults they often continue in inappropriate patterns. Consequently, adult children need to shoulder much of the responsibility.

As you begin to see and understand the missing elements in the mothering you received, your responsibility is to grieve and forgive so that way you may be healed of whatever your mother might have done wrong. Then, as you see and take responsibility for your side of the problem, you will be able to receive what you did not get, gain control, and change those areas where life has not worked for you thus far. In this twofold process of forgiveness and responsibility, you will find unlimited growth.

Our second assumption is that there are preordained tasks of mothering and responses to mothering. We will outline the universal and predictable process that all children need to go through with their mother. We will take you through that process and help you understand how that process relates to you, your history with your mother, and your current life. We will start with basic issues like the importance of making emotional connections and proceed to leaving your mother and cleaving to your spouse.

Our third assumption is that you need love and limits along each step. Your mother needed to be loving so that you learned to bond with others, and your mother needed to set limits so that you learned to shoulder your own responsibilities. If your mother neglected to provide love and limits, or if she provided one but not the other, you will need to find a way of completing what is missing.

So, join us on the wonderful, difficult, and challenging process of dealing with mom and mothering.

Chapter Two

The Phantom Mom

I (Dr. Cloud) was speaking one evening, and I asked the audience which words came to mind when they thought of "mothering." They answered: *nurture, care, bondedness, cookies, trust.* These are normal responses to the word *mother.* It is mother who gives birth, who gives life to the infant. It is in her arms that we learn safety and trust and that we are not alone in the world. Indeed, for most of us, mothering has something to do with a caring connection.

The psalmist said it this way: "Thou didst make me trust when upon my mother's breasts."[1] For as long as humankind has been on the earth, we have associated mothering with trust and nurture. Yet many have not received nurture and trust from their mothers. Instead of connecting safely to their mothers, they have found an emptiness and a void.

Keith recalled his childhood with vivid imagery: "I remember feeling a comfortable numbness much of the time. Our house was big, and when I was small it seemed like it went on forever and ever and had a sort of darkness to it, even in the daytime. It's funny, when I think of being in my house, I don't even see anyone else there. It's empty.

"I know that my mom was there a lot, though. I just can't remember interacting with her. When I can picture her, I see her reading or working in the kitchen. She always seemed so busy when she was up and around. If I try to picture talking to her, I really don't come up with anything.

"There are other memories too. I remember her being in bed a lot. She seemed to just lie there sometimes for hours. Dad would tell me to leave her alone, that she wasn't feeling well. I would usually go outside and make up games or create imaginary worlds. It's kind of funny because I don't really remember feeling what you would call lonely. In other words, I didn't really feel as though I was wanting something and wasn't getting it; it's more like I just felt a sort of darkness or emptiness.

"When she would come home from work, she seemed a little put out by the day. She was kind of irritated almost, but not really with anything that I had done. It was more of a mood that left her a little unapproachable. I just didn't feel like I wanted to be around her. But she would take care of dinner, and we would all eat together most of the time. I just can't remember much of a warm feeling.

"Then, as I got older, I just mostly stayed away from home. I wasn't thinking that I was avoiding home or her. I guess I just didn't want to be around the emptiness. It's funny. She is a pretty neat person. I just don't understand why it was so emotionally empty."

Keith looked up at me at this point. "Does that have anything to do with why I struggle in relationships?" I just nodded, not knowing how else to express my agreement.

KEITH'S LIFE SINCE THEN

Keith was gifted academically, athletically, and socially. Most people found him warm and engaging, and he had a lot of friends. In close relationships, however, he was cool and aloof. His girlfriends felt that he did not need them; they felt emotionally unfulfilled. He vacillated between being in relationship and being alone for long periods. In addition, in his day-to-day interactions he could be harsh and sarcastic.

He continued this way well into adulthood until he finally saw his pattern of broken relationships and significant depression. That is when he came to see me and began to discover the emotional void he had carried around for a lifetime.

What was going on? Keith had experienced a Phantom Mom—a mother who was detached and absent. His mother had not abused him, but she had not been emotionally available. Thus Keith never learned how to connect and be intimate with others. In many instances, the Phantom Mom is a lot different than Keith's. He experienced a Phantom Mom who didn't connect but did not abuse.

Following are some of the many variations on the Phantom Mom theme:

- overt abuse that makes connection impossible
- control issues that block true connection
- perfectionistic demands that leave the real self alone
- abandonment that makes trust too dangerous
- difficulties in the mother's life that take her away from the child
- reactive mothers with whom the child cannot freely share for fear of upsetting her

The common and unfortunate scenario in all of this is that the child cannot develop an attachment to his mother that fosters his emotional ability to become a truly relational person.

THE NEED THAT WON'T GO AWAY

What is the need that Phantom Moms are not fulfilling? What is it that an absent and detached mother is not doing? A child—and later an adult—has five basic needs that must be met by a mother.

1. Safety

As little people, we experience the world as dangerous. We feel alone. We don't have love inside—we have overwhelming needs and feelings. This is painful. You can see this pain on the face of any infant who needs to be picked up or of the child who is terrified of something in her imagination. *The child does not have safety inside but danger. Safety can only be found in the mother—or in whoever is providing the mothering.*

Safety comes in the form of a person who is predictable, stable, and danger-free. This kind of mother creates a foundation for all the other tasks of mothering. Without this person, the child remains in a state of panic or anxiety, unable to love or learn. The mother's consistent, caring, and soft and understanding attention gives the child a safe place to turn; she transforms the dangerous world into a place of safety.

2. Nurture

Webster says that to nurture is to "feed or nourish." A mother's nurture is fuel for the soul. Good mothers pour care into the souls of their children much like sunlight and water pour nutrients into a plant. Our souls flourish when we are being nurtured and cared for. We grow, develop, and change according to the way we were designed.

Without nurture we wither. The "failure to thrive" syndrome and many other childhood problems are directly related to a lack of nurture. In some cases, institutionalized babies have even died from maternal deprivation and a lack of nurture. We were created with needs that go deeper even than our physical need for food. We need the immaterial and spiritual requirements of relationship in order to live.

3. Basic Trust

Basic trust is the ability to invest oneself in a relationship. We must first experience many instances of trustworthiness before we can truly trust others. We aren't born trusting; trust is learned. Trust enables us to reach out, to depend, to need, and to see others as the source of good things. We can depend on our caretaker—when we reach out, she will be there and she will respond to our needs.

When we trust someone, we invest something of ourselves and hope for a good return. If we invest our money, we want safety and dividends. With a good mother, we invest our hearts and our being and find a good return, which leads us to invest again and again in relationships. Trust nurtures our ability to *need* and to *depend*, which allows us to grow and develop relationally. We need to need, and we need to feel comfortable with dependency. A trustworthy mother develops those abilities in us. Healthy people let themselves need and depend on others without fear.

4. Belonging and Invitation

We all have a need to belong to someone and to something bigger than ourselves. Belonging and love are at the root of our humanness. The foundation of our existence is relationship, and we cannot provide that for ourselves. The Bible tells us to be "rooted and established in love."[2] If we are rooted and grounded with God and others, we belong; we feel nurtured, secure, and free from the universal experience of isolation. And it is our mother's responsibility to rescue us from alienation and isolation and to usher us into the world of relationship.

Mothers, through their love and care, make us feel wanted, which transfers into later feelings of worth and confidence in relationships. We have worked with countless people who feel "unlovable" or "unwanted," when in reality lots of people love and adore them. It's obvious that they have failed to receive good mothering.

The sense of feeling wanted and loved is not an intellectual exercise that we can do for ourselves. It comes through the experience of being invited into relationship with another person. You may know intellectually that you are loved, but if you never felt loved by your Phantom Mom, your feelings won't match up with what you know intellectually. When we experience being consistently wanted early in life, we move easily into other relational settings later, never wondering if we belong or not.

5. Someone to Love

Emotional development comes not only from the mother's investment in the child but also from the child's investment in the mother. A mother provides someone for the child to love—she is a good "object of love." In order to develop emotionally, physically, intellectually, and socially, we need not only *be* loved but *to* love. Love fills us up, and colors our outlook on others and the world in which we live, so that we view life with hope and optimism. We have a basic need to love people, and that requires someone to love. If mother is safe, we love her. If she is not, we either are overwhelmed by isolation or we are filled with hatred.

These needs are universal and documented by research, clinical experience, people's experiences, and the Bible. If mother or the surrogate mother provides safety, nurture, trustworthiness, belonging, and lovability, then the child is on his way to healthy development.

RESULTS OF THE PHANTOM MOM

Keith's life of detachment is a fairly common one. We have seen what this life looked like after he left home. What other signs of Phantom mothering show up in adult life?

Relational Problems

An unavailable mother causes devastating consequences to her child later in life. You might ask, "So why does our past have to determine our future? So Keith's mother didn't connect. Can't he just connect her later?" The answer is no, not unless he is open to healing and change.

We are talking here about the development of a child's relational equipment. We can relate this process to the manufacturing of a car. The car will only run in 1996 if all the cylinders were installed in the engine in 1960. It does not matter that the car was built so long ago. *What matters is whether or not all the parts were installed.* This is how early development affects later life: **It leaves us with or without ability**. If we lacked good mothering, our ability to relate well to others in the present must still be built. If we experienced good mothering and we respond, we possess the ability to relate well to others.

Here are a few other relational problems that people with a Phantom Mom may experience:

Shallowness in relationships. These people experience shallow relationships—they can't get "below the surface." Their partners complain of a lack of satisfaction in trying to connect.

Aloofness. These people are "in the world of relationships" but are removed. They are distant with others. They may hold themselves emotionally apart from their family, leaving their spouse to emotionally care for the rest of the family members.

Withdrawal. The natural "seeking" parts in these people don't function. Instead of seeking out others during painful times, they withdraw into themselves, often to the disappointment of those who love them.

Mistrust, hostility, and aggression. These people use a pattern of aggression and hostility to keep others away. They distrust others and will attack and fight off anyone who tries to get close.

Overvaluation of relationship. These people search for significant others in adult life to "fill the void" left by a Phantom Mom. They expect a friend or lover to fill all that their mother failed to give them. They see their spouse as a prince or princess who will transform their empty experience to a life of wonder. But a spouse will never be able to live up to such high expectations and demands. Unhappy single people who think that getting married will make them happy are often looking for maternal love.

Negative relationships. These people enter into negative relationships that are the result of an insecure start in life. A secure start in life with a good mother is what we need to sustain us during the loneliness of waiting for a good relationship in our adult life.

Theresa belonged to a support group in which she was asked over and over again why she chose to continue dating George. This man was not anything like what she needed. She'd come from a home with little love, and she had chosen a man with little love to give. An angry person, George hurt her in many ways and very infrequently did he do loving things. Finally, one day after he had hurt her again and the group had asked again why she put up with him, she replied in tears, "Because if I break up with him, I won't have anyone."

Because of her disconnected relationship with her mother, Theresa had severe problems with abandonment. When a relationship would end, she would go into such a painful state of loss that she would return to the relationship, no matter how bad it had been. She was so afraid of being alone that she would rather be in an abusive relationship than in no relationship at all. This is often why, when someone like Theresa gets close to ending an abusive relationship, she finds that she can't do it; she is terrified of the aloneness in between relationships.

Functional Problems

If our mother was emotionally unavailable, our ability to function in other areas is affected. Studies have shown that health, physical development, and learning are all affected by the quality of our early attachments. When we lack the basic security that an attachment with mom provides, we often avoid risk, are devastated by failure, are unable to take criticism and solve problems, suffer from devastating guilt, and feel estranged from our talents. To function well, we need the basic security that comes from mothering.

Randy, a bright financial manager, had achieved much success in his field. As chief financial officer for several companies, he was valued for his ability to forecast a company's financial needs. But whenever someone questioned his decisions or opposed him in any way, he could get vicious. He had a knack for turning normal conflicts into win-lose confrontations; matters of simple disagreement quickly became adversarial. His basic orientation was "for" and "against." If someone questioned him, he assumed that person was "against" him, and he began to mobilize his defenses to fight off the "attack."

Randy's pattern of insecurity interfered with his ability to keep a job. He would do well for a while in a company, his strengths shining and the CEO generally pleased with his accomplishments, until his adversarial mode of operation would divide the management team. Lines would be drawn until finally the president would figure out what was going on and let Randy go. Randy's insecurity came from a lack of basic trust at his core. Without a mother's love inside, Randy experienced the world as a hostile and dangerous place. His role in this world was to defend himself.

Our ability to function well in the world does not depend on aptitude, intelligence, or talents alone. All of these are only useful to the person who has resolved the question of whether or not the world is a safe place, and only good mothering provides that kind of safety.

Spiritual Problems

The writer of Psalm 22 learned to trust at his mother's breast. We quoted him earlier, but in a different translation the verse reads this way: "Yet you brought me out of the womb; you made me trust *in you* even at my mother's breast."[3] The idea of trust in God is connected with learning trust in our earliest relationships. This idea of a connection between how we experience God and how we experience people permeates the Bible. The two are interrelated.[4]

If we believe in a personal God, then we will relate to God as a person. He might be very different than what we have experienced with humans, but we often have expectations for him to be the same. Those who did not learn to trust at their mother's knee have difficulty trusting God.

Marty got interested in spiritual things in college. He began to attend church and fellowship groups and was very excited about building a spiritual life. Somewhat mystical and aesthetic, Marty liked the idea of developing a personal relationship with God.

However, Marty soon got into trouble with his new spiritual life. As he read the Bible, he became more and more confused about God because everything he read seemed to condemn him. He was afraid that God thought he was "bad" and was about to "get" him in some way. His guilt and fear increased until he finally decided he must be headed for hell.

He went to see a couple of pastors associated with the school, and even though they explained to him that he had misunderstood the Bible and that God really loved him, he could not *feel* God's love. Fear continued to paralyze his spiritual walk for a long time.

He finally received some in-depth counseling and discovered that his spiritual problems were linked to his lack of an emotional connection with his mother—he felt unwanted at a deep level. Through the love and acceptance of some friends and his counselor, he gradually began to trust God and others. But the impact of his early life on his spiritual walk took a lot of work to overcome.

Our early relationships have a significant impact on our ability to enjoy the spiritual life. They affect our view of God and our ability to integrate spiritual development into the whole of life. Specifically, our relationship with our mother affects our ability to trust and to love and receive love. The way that we experience security, freedom, healthy self-esteem, and a mystical connection with God is strongly influenced by the kind of mothering we received.

Emotional Problems

In the movie *Manhattan*, Woody Allen was dismayed because his wife had left him for another woman. He was particularly upset about his son's living in such an arrangement. At one point, he voiced his dismay over his son's having two mothers. "Nobody ever survives one!" he said.

Sadly, many people feel this way. The relationship that should provide the bedrock of emotional security too often ends up providing just the opposite—the seeds and paths of emotional insecurity. Following are a few of the emotional consequences of the Phantom Mom:

Depression. Many kinds of depression stem from something that happens, such as the death of a spouse. But the person who has no "good mother" inside feels a sense of perpetual loss. This depression comes from deep inside. If we miss out on a sense of connectedness early in life, we live in a state of emotional emptiness that translates into a deep, dark feeling of depression. It is often triggered in adult life when we lose a significant relationship and are forced into the deeper feelings of not having someone to love.

Feelings of emptiness. Emptiness is one of the most intolerable emotional states known to humanity. We are unable to stand emptiness for long, however, and usually will try to do something to fill the void felt inside. The feeling often has to do with early mothering patterns. The child, and later the adult, is "filled up" inside by his own feelings of responsiveness to the love and nurture of his mother. As adults, we often think that someone's love "fills us up," and we will often hear empty people wanting someone's love to "fill the void inside."

But in reality, it is our response to love that "fills us up." It is our own loving feelings inside that provide a feeling of "being full." As we are loved, we love back, and that response is fulfilling. We would have a problem if no one were there to consistently "love back." Having no one to love and attach to sets a child up for feelings of emptiness that continue into adulthood. Detached mothers— Phantom Moms—create detached children who grow up into detached and empty adults.

Addictions. The word *addiction* is used loosely these days as we speak of being addicted to everything from food to work to sex. Traditionally, we reserved the term to refer to enslavement to alcohol or other drugs. But as people now think of addiction as a mood-altering behavior, addiction can certainly have its roots in the search for mother. It is a way to deal with the emptiness that we saw above; a substance or a behavior is used to avoid the feeling.

Thinking problems. While emotional attachment is a primary process, thinking is a secondary process. We must be nurtured before we can begin to think and use language. This is why babies begin talking in the second year of life, after they have received a lot of nurture. In this way, thinking rests on a bedrock of safety and security so that it is relatively unhampered by the need for love.

The thinking of people without early security rests on the sand— on feelings of being unloved, and feelings of suspicion and lack of trust. These people entertain suspicious thoughts, paranoid thoughts, mistrustful thoughts, negative thoughts about themselves and others, negative evaluations of their performance, and negativity about the world at large. Generally, these thoughts attack the connection in some way or another. Either someone does not love them, or they don't find the other one lovable. This is why some efforts at positive thinking fail. The problem is not with the thinking, but with the lack of love underneath. Insecure people think insecure thoughts.

The most extreme example of thinking problems is "psychosis," when someone loses his or her ability to know what is real and what isn't. This is experienced in differing degrees by people with very early developmental attachment problems.

Hopelessness and meaninglessness. Hope is one of the most important virtues that can be instilled in our soul. Many people think that hope has to do with the future, when in reality it has to do with the past. We develop hope as we experience pain transformed into comfort. When this happens enough, we begin to have faith that our pain will not do us in and that comfort is on its way.

Mothers are crucial to this process. When babies or young children are upset, their only comfort is the secure safety of a loving mother. When they are hurting, and a loving mother offers comfort, their misery is transformed to safety and gratitude. When that happens literally thousands of times, they come to expect an end to their pain, and they develop the virtue we call hope—the expectation that good will come eventually, no matter how bad things are right now.

Finding meaning in life is similar. Love and relationship with God and with other people are the true meaning of life. If we did not have a mother to connect to and did not get a good relational start in life, we lose the whole picture. We do not find the true meaning of life but look for meaning in places other than fulfilling relationships, such as work, achievement, or materialism.

WHY ME?

People with mothering problems often ask, "Why me?" They wonder why their mothers did not or could not love them in a way that helped them. Why couldn't mom be "good enough"? They may even feel as if mom singled them out on purpose.

But nobody really knows why. If your mother found it difficult to feel or express love, it could be for any number of reasons, few, if any, having to do with you. These problems are often carried down generational lines. She may not have felt loved or nurtured herself, and she couldn't give away what she didn't have. So, an understanding of her situation is very helpful as you work through your feelings toward her.

Here are some possible reasons for her limitations:

- She lacked the connection and nurture she needed as a child.
- She was abandoned or hurt in the past and was unable to allow herself to attach deeply to anyone, even her own child.
- She was emotionally empty.
- She feared intimacy—knowing and being known.
- She was depressed and did not have the emotional energy to give.
- She had marital pain and was being torn apart.
- She was ill or had various other difficulties.

Like the old proverb, if we have not walked in someone else's shoes, we have no idea what that person is dealing with or what it is like to be that person. If we look at various times in our own lives and think what it would have been like to be a mother of a young child with "all of that going on," it can lead to greater understanding. We just don't often know.

Another possible answer to why your mother couldn't be all that you needed her to be is that she chose the selfish path. Everyone, no matter what their past dealt them, makes choices that they are responsible for. No matter what was done or not done to your mother, she is still responsible for how she responds to the truth. "Not good-enough" mothers are rarely evil people. They are often just too caught up in themselves and their own concerns to see the needs of another. Children are used only as objects to meet their needs. This is the basic sin of selfishness: they believe the world revolves around them. Jesus invited all of us to treat others in the way that we would want to be treated.[5] In this case, these mothers chose not to heed his invitation.

We are all responsible for our own selfishness and lack of response to the light of God, who invites us into the life of love. So, the answer to "why?" is probably a mixture of what was done to your mother as well as how she responded to what was done. The first should move us to compassion and the second to forgiveness, as we understand that we, too, are selfish and in need of forgiveness. We will look at the process of healing in the next chapter, but for now, it is important to know that the reason your mother failed to love you the way you needed to be loved had much more to do with her than it did with you.

WHAT IT LOOKS LIKE NOW

We have looked at some of the results of the Phantom Mom in a child's life, but what about mom now? What goes on between the adult child and the detached mother? What does this look like in adult life? Here are some common scenarios:

Please Love Me

Maria looked forward to her parents' visit. She hadn't seen them for about a year and relished the thought of sitting down and talking with her mother.

Maria's most recent visits with her mother had not gone well. Not that they had argued; that was not Maria's style. Arguments were the style of her sister, the "black sheep of the family." Maria's style was to be "nice." But, even without overt fights, something didn't feel right. Maria usually came away from her mother feeling empty.

She was twenty-eight now, and though visits with her mother had been without conflict, she longed to feel a closeness with her mother. She wanted to share what was going on in her life, her plans and dreams, her pain, and all the things she treasured in her heart now that she was an adult.

But when Maria attempted an intimate connection with her mom, she experienced frustration. Her mother just could not connect with her feelings and more intimate parts. She would immediately start talking about her own life, or the life of a friend, and it would usually be something of less depth. Her interests seemed so shallow to Maria, so petty and image-conscious.

But each visit Maria would try again. She would long to see her mother, and before the visit, they would talk on the phone as if it were going to be so glorious. And for her mother, it usually was, for she did not know what had not happened. But for Maria, it was another unsuccessful attempt to get her mother to love her in a way she could feel. She found herself performing—listening, cooking, and sight-seeing. She bent over backward to show her the kind of life she had created for herself, so her mother would be proud. And she was. But pride did not fill Maria's soul. And if she would have been objective, she would have seen another disappointing trip on the horizon—before it happened.

Where Did the Family Go?

In Maria's case, the kind of detached relationship she'd always had with her mother simply continued on. In other situations, the lack of relatedness tends to go to its logical conclusion. The parties have less and less contact, and the relationship just seems to go away. I treated one young man in his early thirties who had a Phantom Mom. I asked him one day how his parents were doing, for he hadn't mentioned them in a long time.

"I guess we really don't have a lot to say to each other anymore," he told me. "I just don't talk to them." This kind of separation is always sad, but in reality it had always been there. As he'd grown into adulthood, he'd found some people with whom he could really connect, but this made him more aware of the separation from his parents that had always been. While sad, a lack of connection that comes to the forefront like this can be a time of great growth and reconciliation, as we will see later.

I Hate You, Don't Leave Me

In this scenario, the adult child covers up his longings and feelings of disconnectedness with anger. But rarely is the anger directed toward what is really wrong: the lack of connection. Quarreling and bickering in the family is usually over lots of little things—wrong kinds of presents, plans for who is or is not going to visit whom, how one person is choosing to live, or a whole host of other distractions.

The real issue, of course, is the lack of connection that the adult child feels. The tendency to pick fights is generally a sign that we want something from someone; the quarrelsome adult is most likely still wanting the connection and finding it difficult to face it directly. In all of this, a clear tie of "don't leave me" is evidenced by the inability to let go. Anger may be the language, but the need for love is the strong message.

THE SAD REALITY

You can see that there are many different versions, sizes, and shapes of scenarios of adult children with Phantom Moms. The longing for connection may cause one person to move toward mother and try to please her; this pattern of "mother pleasing" can go on for decades, like Maria's case. Or the adult child can move away from mother, avoiding the relationship and the lack of relationship all together, like the patient I mentioned who never talked to mother. An adult child may express anger to cover up the longing for connection. These dynamics go on in a variety of ways, but the salient message is that "we are not finished yet."

And that becomes our question. If we are not finished, either with mother or mothering, how do we complete the process? We have seen what detached and absent mothering looks like, what it causes, what the need is, and how it can set up a painful pattern of relating even in adulthood. The need that God programmed into us for good mothering just does not go away until it is met. In the next chapter, we will explore how that happens and how this kind of healing will help you relate to your detached or absent mother in a more satisfying way.

Chapter Three

Rebuilding Your Connection

Val was about to "graduate" from her season of therapy. She had worked through her detachment and lack of trust issues, both in our sessions and for a while now with supportive friends, and it had paid off. She was now able to connect without panic and to reach out without withdrawing. She could let herself feel her need for closeness and belonging, and she could openly respond to the safe people in her life.

Val's marriage had deepened and blossomed. She was in a satisfying career and had found a church where she could contribute her musical talents. This was a good time in her life.

In fact, Val and her husband were thinking about having a baby. This would have been unthinkable before, since Val was terrified by the prospect of motherhood. She feared that her attachment problems would hurt the child. "I don't want to bring someone into the world and then not be able to give him what he needs the most," she would say. However, as she began to grow and change, the part of Val that woke up to relationship also woke up to the desire to mother and to comfort as she had been comforted.

In session, I (Dr. Townsend) asked her, "As you look over your time in treatment, what factors were the most significant for you?" Val thought for a moment, then responded, "Three things: relationship, relationship, relationship."

GETTING STARTED

In the last chapter we discussed the problem of the Phantom Mom and the needs that may not have been met by this kind of mother. In this chapter we provide the steps to getting those needs met and repairing what was broken in your own mothering process.

FRUIT PROBLEMS VS. ROOT PROBLEMS

The first step in the process of getting well from mothering problems is to recognize that *the symptom isn't the problem.* The "alarm bells" we described in the last chapter—relational, functional, spiritual, and emotional problems—signal that something is wrong and that life isn't working out for you. You may have discovered, for example, that you are depressed or that you're struggling more than normal in your relationships or work.

You assume that the pain and grief caused by these symptoms is the real problem. And so you address the symptom—you take more vacation time, work out more, change friends, and switch jobs in an attempt to alleviate your suffering. While these changes may be good and help for a time, if you have a real character injury inside, they may also only temporarily anesthetize your pain. For some of us, a good rule of thumb is this: "If a week of R and R fails to solve it, it's more than a 'tired' problem!"

You may also be tempted to get professional counseling for the symptom. You want a therapist to affirm you and help you adjust your perception of life so that you can "feel good again." While a professional counselor's ability to help you evaluate your thinking patterns is an important part of the process, it often addresses the wrong issue. *The problem isn't that we don't feel right. It's that we truly aren't right.* Something is broken or undeveloped inside our heart and soul.

Pain is always the sign of a deeper problem, much like a fever is the sign of an infection. If you identify with the symptoms we listed in chapter 2, you may have some issues with trust and attachment. As you begin to address these character problems, the painful symptoms will gradually diminish over time, just as a fever declines when you treat an infection with antibiotics. The pain has served its purpose: to alert you to a problem. It is the "fruit" of a "root" issue. Jesus taught us that "A good tree cannot bear bad fruit, and a bad tree cannot bear good fruit."[1] Be aware of your pain—it leads to the root of the problem.

It is easy to get stuck in the "symptom solving" routine for a while. People with absent and detached issues shy away from character solutions, often because of the emptiness they know they will need to face at some point. Alex, a friend of mine who had severe detachment issues, explained it this way: "Part of me knew the problem was deeper than negative feelings or taking better care of myself. But every time I thought about myself and my past, I felt I was falling into a black hole of despair, where no one would catch me. It was too terrifying to fall into that pit." Alex had no "good mommy" inside him and could not experience that part of himself alone.

"RELATIONSHIP, RELATIONSHIP, RELATIONSHIP"

After you've determined that the problem goes beyond the immediate pain, you'll need to seek a safe context in which to work on it. As we've discovered, it is in relationships that we can get attachment needs met.

Mothering injuries, at heart, are relational injuries. That is, the deficits were caused by the most significant connection in our lives. And, just as a relationship can break a person, a relationship can also restore a person.

It can be difficult to move from the "symptom" phase to the "relationship" phase, particularly for those with absent and detached mothering issues. If you have experienced absent and detached mothering in the past, you have probably become autonomous and independent. You feel you can depend only on yourself for safety and success. The idea of going to another person for help is not only scary, it would also involve unlearning the very survival techniques you have perfected to help you cope and maintain order in your life.

Val, whom we met earlier, was the self-styled "Queen of Self-Help." An information junkie, she had a huge book and tape library at home on emotions, success, relationships, marriage, and spirituality. But even with all this helpful data at her disposal, things kept breaking down inside. It was when she finally realized that she needed something besides information that she began to seek relational help.

WELCOME TO YOUR NEW HOME

In a very real sense, this chapter is about finding a new home for the lost part of your soul. That part of you that never finished learning to attach, connect, and trust is still alive and waiting to be developed and mothered. It is most likely split off from the rest of your life in a state of suspended animation; it is still in the same young, immature, or injured state it was in when the mothering process broke down. Though this could have happened decades ago, this part continues untouched and unconnected until it is brought back into relationship.

The idea of finding a new home is an old one. We get what we can from the original family, given their limitations as well as ours. Then those days are over, and we grow up and take responsibility for our lives as adults. However, when it's time to get certain needs met, we can't go back to mom and ask her to remother us. Our growth isn't her job anymore, it's ours. And the part of us that is still stuck back there *can* be healed.

Jesus illustrated this idea of home and family when he was told that his mother and brothers were waiting to talk to him. He seized the opportunity to define *true family,* saying, "'Who is my mother, and who are my brothers?' Pointing to his disciples, he said, 'Here are my mother and my brothers. For whoever does the will of my Father in heaven is my brother and sister and mother.'"[2] He wasn't saying Mary was a bad mom—he was *redefining family as having more to do with spiritual and relational ties than blood ties.* In other words, Mary might have been his biological mother, but what made her truly a part of his family was that she shared the desire to love and accept God and others and do whatever else the Father willed for them. That is family.

WHO IS MY FAMILY?

It's common for individuals with absent/detached mother problems to think that because there are warm bodies around them, they have what they need. What type of relationship will heal the Phantom Mom injury? We can easily confuse *proximity with intimacy.* Pam told me, "I thought I was connected. I had lunch three times a week with girlfriends. My husband and I had a full social calendar. I just didn't know you were supposed to talk to people about your insides!" Having social friends is important. But those friends don't necessarily meet our needs for intimate connecting with the unknown part of us.

We must find people who want to connect with us for the purpose of connection itself. These can be from many areas of life: present family, redemptive friends, support groups, church, and therapists. Research indicates that the more healthy relationships we have, the better our prognosis for healing. But the important thing to understand is that you need these people to help you learn how to connect. *Intimacy is not a means to an end—it is an end in itself.* Attachment and dependency are the goal.

Detached individuals often have difficulty understanding this. They see closeness as serving a functional purpose. For example, they'll take tennis lessons or sing in the choir to find intimacy. But closeness is a by-product of these activities, not the goal. When Jesus visited the two sisters, Mary and Martha, at their home, Martha, the "doer," scurried around fixing the place up and preparing food while Mary, the "relater," sat at Jesus' feet and connected to him. Jesus taught "functional" Martha that her "relational" sister Mary was doing the right thing: "But only one thing is needed. Mary has chosen what is better, and it will not be taken away from her."[3]

Support groups, recovery-friendly relationships, therapists who deal with attachment disorders, and healthy churches are often the best sources to fill up this empty part of yourself. That is their specialty. Ask around to find out who has a reputation for helping people with trust issues.[4]

WHAT DO I LOOK FOR?

What do healthy mother-types look like? Supportive people have several characteristics—some of which are universal to all six "mother styles" and some of which are unique to the absent/detached style.

Gender is not usually an issue here. Some counselors would suggest that those with mothering problems should find women to help them, and those with fathering issues should look for men. But this is an oversimplification of the issue. While this may be a good suggestion in some specific cases, most of us simply need to find people who have "good mother" parts in their own character. Men can have mothering (nurturing) parts, and women can have fathering (challenging) parts to them. Just as God the Father is "full of compassion,"[5] some people are well developed in both areas.

Warmth and Empathy

You need to connect with warm, empathic people. Empathic people can "walk in your shoes" and feel your feelings without judgment or advice. An empathic person is *for* you. No matter what you say or reveal about yourself, this person is on your side and wants to help, even if she disagrees with or disapproves of what she hears.

Warmth and empathy provide the basic groundwork of safety and trust that are missing in the adult who had an absent/detached mother. They extend a bridge, making it possible for the broken part of the individual to cross over in his own time.

If you are a detached person, warmth and empathy may be difficult for you to find in others because you look instead for just the opposite. You might find it easier to connect to another distant person, a critical parental figure, or some information-laden type, or you might find a legalistic church to provide you with a sense of structure away from your feelings. This may feel safer and more familiar to you, but it won't solve your problem. In fact, it removes you from the problem.

Nonintrusiveness

While being approachable and warm, your mothering environment also needs to be *nonintrusive.* To intrude is to force oneself on someone without invitation. Intrusive people try to get close prematurely, when they aren't wanted or needed. Those with detachment injuries often have a detached *and* intrusive mother in their background. This kind of mom didn't connect with her children but forced her needs, thoughts, and feelings onto them in the guise of relationship. It was her way of controlling them. The children of this kind of mother generally respond by shutting down and "going away" emotionally. As a friend described it to me, "Mom would talk a mile a minute about I don't know what. I would stand there, but the real me would be far, far away."

Intrusion forces the hurt part deeper inside, away from the control, but also away from attachment. Overzealous, smothering-type people often make the situation worse for attachment-injured people. Feeling overwhelmed and overtaken, the injured ones often simply shut down more.

The nonintrusive helper, however, invites the hurt parts out but doesn't chase them down. Her warmth, interest, and genuineness communicate that the injured person's detached part is welcome, but space is allowed for it to gradually and safely emerge. Nonintrusiveness is a lot like a scarecrow in a cornfield. At first, the crows are frightened by this seeming apparition, but as it stands, arms outstretched, unmoving, they fly closer and closer, until they safely perch on the scarecrow's head. The nonintrusive person allows the other's healing to happen at its own rate and in its own time.

Drawn Toward Dependency

Your new mothering relationships need to be mutually dependent ones. The need for connection, support, comfort, and conversation is a healthy one, and just as a baby reaches out to be held by its mom, these early parts of yourself *need to need*. Your "lost part" needs to know that it's okay to reach out and find someone there in times of loneliness, stress, and conflict.

This is very different from "solution-based" relationships, which tend to avoid dependency and attachment. Often, in these relationships, when the person's dependency needs begin to emerge, their friend will do one of several things:

- withdraw in anxiety: "Maybe this is going too far"
- become critical: "Stop being a baby and grow up"
- give advice: "Here's how to solve all these problems"

Some people understand that *comfort and grace are the fuel of life.* They are the kind of present and supportive people you need in your world.

Honesty

Your mothering people must be scrupulously honest in character. They must be able to tell the truth about themselves and about you. This is true for two reasons. First, if you have attachment problems, you have a highly developed "truth radar"; you could never trust connection, and so you have become hypervigilant. You are suspicious of people and will find all sorts of reasons to write someone off; you'd rather have no connection than another annihilating one. Truthful people aren't perfect, but they generally are who they say they are. Their lives are based on relationship, reality, and responsibility, and they are trustworthy.

Second, honesty is important because you need information and feedback about the process. You may be so disconnected from yourself at times that you are unaware of your needs and desires, your hiding patterns and defenses. Your new mothers need to confront you with these realities and help you see what's going on.

Our original mothering relationship and our new mothering relationships have two things in common: both involve the young, unformed, or injured aspects of our character, and both involve an attempt to get certain needs met in the relationship. The major difference between them, however, is in the *level of responsibility*.

When we were young, we carried little responsibility for our growth and maturity. As we had very little ability, we also had very little "account-ability." Our degree of responsibility increased gradually until we became "our own person" as an adult. This is why we say that our childhood is determined by both mom and our response to mom. It is never just mom's fault.

As adults, the picture shifts even more toward our own responsibility. As grown-ups, when we enter remothering relationships, we don't allow someone else to take over responsibility for our life. That part of the parenting process is truly over and must be grieved and left behind. Our life is our own now, and *we alone are accountable for its outcome*: "For we must all appear before the judgment seat of Christ, that each one may receive what is due him for the things done while in the body, whether good or bad."[6] Thus, your injured parts need the mothering relationship but not the mothering responsibility.

Some counselors blur this important difference in their attempts to "reparent" people. If in doubt, talk to an informed person about the degree of responsibility you as the counselee bear.

YOUR CONNECTION TASKS

While it is important to have the right kind of mothering people around you, this is only part of the healing process. Your part is to respond to their love, truth, and support. Just as infants respond to their biological mother in a mutual give-and-take, you have a role to play in repairing your unbonded parts. Here are some of the tasks.[7]

Make four important commitments.

- Commit yourself and this entire remothering endeavor to God.
- Commit yourself to a serious attempt at the growth process.
- Commit yourself verbally to the people involved in the process.
- Commit yourself to absolute truthfulness in these relationships.

Understand both the value and the limitations of commitment. The word *commit* means to "bring together." You are committed to bringing two things together in the same place: yourself and the growth process. Like a scientist who mixes chemicals to get reactions, you're putting the ingredients of growth in the same room so they can interact.

Commitment—in this sense—doesn't mean you are making a lifetime promise that can't be altered. Nor does it mean that you are promising to be well or perfect overnight. It simply means that you promise to engage in the process, to bring as much of yourself to the table as you can, along with the mothering relationships you've entered.

Be vulnerable. If you did not attach to your mother, you may not be able to even feel needy, dependent emotions. They are hidden in a deep well inside and can't be forced out. They must emerge on their own initiative, encouraged by the safety of the mothering relationships and driven by their own need and hunger. Even if you can't "feel" needs, you can be vulnerable with others about your own emptiness and incompleteness. *These are realities that you can talk about.* And your openness will give you the opportunity to test the genuineness and safety of your mothering people.

Take the initiative. Don't wait for someone to fill up your needy parts. You don't simply receive a quart of caring and then feel full. You have a responsibility. You have to respond to the love you receive. Remember what we discovered in the "Needs" section of the last chapter—the loving feelings we experience don't come from the other person. These feelings are actually our own. We are "filled up" with our own feelings of warmth and gratitude.

Dawn remembers the day she "got it." She had isolated herself from others for a long time and knew she needed to rebuild connections. She found a healthy church, a good support group, and a counselor. But she continued to report that "I can't feel anything. I know people care, but I can't let them inside me." Then one day in a counseling session, she began to remember and talk about the people in her life who had patiently given of themselves to her, who were accepting and warm. She began to feel sad and teary as she recalled all the years of nothingness she'd experienced. And that's when it started coming together for Dawn. She felt grateful for the grace and love she was receiving, and as she let herself respond to it, she began to come alive and feel emotions and needs once again.

Give the process time. Healing from our absent/detached mother issues is not an overnight process. A lot depends on when the injuries occurred and how severe they were, so you'll need to be patient with yourself as you begin to heal. It takes time to begin to make emotional connections. You will need to work through many fears, hurts, and thought distortions with your mothering people even before you can let your needs emerge. Remember that *we can't choose connection. Rather, we can choose a process that results in connection.*

Allow dependent feelings. When you receive the proper amounts and types of mothering, and when you are able to respond, dependency feelings will emerge. This is often a scary time, as you may feel lonely, or you may miss someone who was caring. You may become anxious that you are doing the wrong thing. You might be afraid you're becoming self-centered, or immature. Or you might fear that your mothering people will withdraw in anger or condemnation.

During these times, try to remember that God has built you to depend on him and other people; he wants you connected to him and to the human race. When we fail to express our needs, we remain islands unto ourselves—detached, alone, arrogant, and proud. But when we expose our needs, we are able to receive the supplies and nurture necessary for survival.

Pray and seek God. People who can't or won't get close to others are often doers and achievers. They stay busy and productive, which keeps them from noticing the lack of internal love. They may not seek out the relational world at all. This dynamic often shows up in their relationship with God as well. During this process, be sure to spend time "being" with God and his Word. This is called "abiding," or remaining. It involves simply bringing as much of yourself to him as you have available to you: "Just as the Father has loved me, I have also loved you; abide in My love."[8] Ask God to help you experience his own warmth and empathy for all of you. He is Love itself.[9] His very nature constrains him to want relationship with you.

Be aware of your defenses. If you had a Phantom Mom, you have probably developed ways to hide from your needs. They will emerge, however, when you are at your weakest. Your defenses will then go into play to protect you from the danger of relationship. You can use your mothering relationships to learn about your defenses—why, when, and how they operate. Our defenses are "blind spots"; we need others' feedback so that we can become more aware of how we use them to cut off relationship.[10] Following are a few examples of how this can work.

One common defense against attachment needs is *devaluation.* To devalue a need is to minimize either the need itself or the need-meeting person. We affect a "sour grapes" attitude to protect ourselves from the painful reality of how deeply we do need others. Our mothering connections can make us aware when we are devaluing a relationship.

One of the most helpful things I see in therapy groups is when one member confronts another's devaluation. One person might say something like, "Jerry, when you say you don't think about us or miss us during the week, I feel pushed away." Jerry then has the opportunity to explore whether or not he is devaluing his loving relationships to avoid his need.

Another defense is *omnipotence*. You may have developed a grandiose sense of power and independence to protect yourself against the "needy little child" inside. You could be a high-functioning person—you may do lots of things and solve lots of problems. However, you also have a weak, impotent part that needs to be in relationship with other people. When you can't see this about yourself, your mothering people can. As I heard a husband say to his wife, "Anne, I admire your strengths. But I miss your weaknesses."

A third defense is *avoidance*. The attachment-injured person will simply "go away" when intimacy looms. If this is you, when the opportunity for connection appears, you freeze up, get intellectual, think about something else, or simply shut down. You might try to stay away from emotion-laden situations altogether. You might shift the conversation to a safer topic or simply walk out the door.

These are unconscious actions and you need your remothering people to point out your avoidance. Let them gently tell you that "You've left again. What happened?" They can help you discover which scary emotions or needs surfaced that frightened you and caused you to mentally and emotionally check out. This process of discovery prepares safety to "reenter."

I was recently touched as I watched remothering happen spontaneously. I was speaking at our weekly group meeting in Southern California, and during the question-and-answer period, a woman asked about taking medication for her depression. I affirmed the validity of antidepressants but asked, "Besides medication, have you ever worked on your depression in a caring relationship?"

She said no, and I briefly explained the relational nature of emotional disorders.

When I finished, she asked again, "So what do you think about medication?"

"Whoaaa . . . what were you feeling when I talked about relationship?"

She shook her head sadly. "It won't work." Her despair caused her to totally avoid the relational part of my answer.

However, after the meeting broke up, several people approached her to say they wanted to understand her fears. Right there they were inviting her into relationship. And so, not only did the woman realize her avoidance, but some caring people stepped in to begin the remothering process.

"MOMWORK"

While we are interacting with our remothering friends, we can also do some repair work with our biological mothers. If mom is alive and available, we want as much healing for that relationship as she will allow. Here are a few of the specific tasks:

Forgiveness. Your mother most likely experienced her own mothering injuries. And even if she didn't, you can still release her and cancel her debt to you. Forgiveness means that the innocent party pays: "Forgive us our debts, as we also have forgiven our debtors."[11] We let her off the hook; she must no longer pay for the lost years, the emotional healing, the money spent healing. We assume responsibility because *our attachment issues are our problems now, not mom's.*

Invitation. Mom needs relationship just as we all do. This is true even though relationship is exactly what the absent/detached mom couldn't give. You can't reparent her or take responsibility for her response, but you can move toward her. This might mean vulnerably reaching out to her, saying you'd like a closer friendship in your adult years. You may have to take the first step in confronting some past problems or in sharing present struggles. In doing this, you can bring the love you've received in your remothering relationships to her.

This is a complex decision, however. Some Phantom Moms are so toxic and destructive that any attempts at vulnerability prematurely (or at all, in some cases) can undo a lot of hard work. Let your safe people help you decide if, when, and how to approach your mom.

Setting limits. The Phantom Mom may become critical when feelings are expressed. She may withdraw and pout when people try to get close. Or she may neglect her "grandmotherly duties" and not get involved with your kids. You must decide you will no longer be a party to her destructiveness.

While you can't change your mom if she doesn't want to change, you can certainly set limits on how she affects you. You may need to tell her you'll have to restrict contact with her if she persists in certain hurtful behaviors. Tell her specifically which things hurt you and your family and what you'd like her to do instead. And then give her a chance to change. Setting boundaries with the absent or detached mother may be hard, but it may waken her out of her self-absorption, and she may realize that her behavior has consequences.

Reconciliation. If mom is open to it, attempt reconciliation. To reconcile is to "settle after an estrangement." It involves many aspects:

- confronting and being confronted about attachment hurts and injuries
- apologizing and accepting apologies
- forgiving and asking forgiveness
- repenting and asking for repentance

Like vulnerability, however, reconciliation is a complex task and is dependent on many things, such as how safe mom is and your own fragility at the time. Make sure you are ready before you enter this process. And remember, the goal here is not to repair, take revenge on, or get long overdue mothering from mom. The goal is to establish relationship.

A word about confrontation is important here. The word *confront* means "to face." It is a relational term, and its purpose is to bring reality to a relationship *to foster intimacy*. The goal is not alienation but closeness; not releasing a stockpile of pain but connection. The stockpile belongs to your new mothering relationships.

For example, confrontation may mean bringing up mom's detachment and how it affected you. You might say something like, "I need to explain what your emotional absence was like for me, so we can reconcile it and get on with our present relationship." Once you've explained the hurt and loss, mom can see how she might have injured you. Then it's up to you to forgive and move on. In addition, if mom is interested in more dialogue, you could also talk about her feelings toward you and your responses to her mothering. This would give her the opportunity to forgive you for the times you withdrew from her attempts to move toward you. Even as children we sometimes make destructive choices that hurt our parents. Either way, confrontation's goal is to bring the unredeemed past into relationship, work through it, and finally put it aside.

Acceptance of reality. One of the most important and most difficult jobs of your growth process is to accept the realities of who mom is. If mom isn't interested in a deeper, safer relationship and wants to remain disconnected and shallow, you need to respect her limitations and face reality.

Most people have strong wishes that their own growth will also propel mom into being the person she never was. If this fails to happen, we must grieve our ideal of the mom that never was and probably never will be. However, you can only let go of that wish when you are filled and connected in your remothering relationships. We are only strong enough to grieve what we've lost when we've already replaced it at some level.

THE NEW ME AND THE OLD MOM

If you work at all of the above tasks, what can you hope for in your present relationship with mom? There are two directions it can go, depending on your mother's response.

Mom herself may have grown over the years and wants to make a real and genuine emotional attachment. This can be a time of great satisfaction and fulfillment for both of you. You can establish a mutual friendship in which you can enjoy getting to know one another all over again. It's not a reparenting process; your new mothering relationships have taken that over. But you can have a deep and meaningful connection.

If this connection occurs, it's important that you and your mom keep your own separate "families," in the spiritual and emotional sense. Mom needs a place to grow and repair that is different from yours. Otherwise, you can end up confusing friendship and past mothering issues. Often, the zealous adult child wants to usher mom into repair. You can invite, but you need to keep the "incubators" separate; let mom go to her support groups and counselors, and you go to yours.

I have seen this work. I have observed mothers opening up to their adult child's emotional life and sharing their own. They grow in mutual respect and appreciation for one another. After all, they share years of a common past. When that is reconciled, a rich present becomes available.

But suppose this process isn't mom's priority right now. This generally means more work for the adult child. Patricia, a close friend of mine, had been working on "mom issues" for some time, and then her detached mom became ill with terminal cancer. When she found out about her mother's condition, Patricia wanted to make the best use of whatever time they had left. So she asked Mom if she would go to a Christian therapist friend of hers for a few sessions. Mom agreed, as she also wanted to "wrap things up" in her life. Once there, Mom also gave the therapist permission to talk to Patricia about her, as an aid to resolution.

"How can I get connected to her in the time we have left?" Patricia wanted to know after the therapist had seen her mom.

"Your mom has had a long, hard life," he told her. "She is ready to go, and she really doesn't want to open a can of worms. She told me that her emotions are nobody else's business, and she's right."

Patricia was stunned. "So what can I do?"

The therapist looked at her. "Ask her about the good old days when she supported her husband by working in the factories in World War II. Let her play with the grandkids. Have tea and talk about flowers."

Patricia took her grieving to her support group. Then she did what the therapist said. Later she told me, "It was okay. When Mom died, we were as connected as she was able. I was grateful for that much."

How will you respond to your mom? It's your choice.

Chapter Four

The China Doll Mom

Stephanie couldn't handle her daughter Vicki's infant emotions. It wasn't that Stephanie was cold, distant, or uncaring with her baby. She wasn't. Far from being "not there," she was a warm, attached, and devoted mom. The problem was that she quickly became overwhelmed whenever her little girl expressed herself.

For example, whenever Vicki would wail in her crib, as babies tend to do, her mom would rush to the bed, grab her up, and cry out, "Are you all right, sweetie? Are you breathing? Please, don't let my baby die!"

"Jim!" she would call to her husband. "Vicki is crying and I don't know what's wrong!" Then Vicki's dad would come into the room, pick up his daughter, realize she was wet, and change her.

As a toddler, Vicki would rage about having to take naps or being unable to grasp a toy that was out of reach. Her face would turn red as a beet, she would scream, and her fists would ball up. Stephanie would then become anxious, pull away from Vicki, and say things like, "Please don't yell. That hurts Mommy's ears and makes her sad." Sometimes she would put her hands over her ears to block out her daughter's screams. Vicki was then left to take care of her out-of-control anger all by herself.

As Vicki became a little older, she would go to her mother to be comforted. She would have a scary dream or simply be lonely, and come to Mom to be held and soothed. But before the little girl could even finish telling her what she needed, Stephanie would grab her up, press her daughter's head tightly into her chest, and begin rocking her. "I'm here," she would murmur to her almost-suffocating child. "You can smile now. Stop being sad, honey."

The adult Vicki, now a mother of three herself, came to see me (Dr. Townsend) about her own anxiety disorder. "I didn't get mothered—I got *smothered*," she told me one day in my office.

Smothering, however, didn't describe Stephanie's responses to Vicki's anger at her. Just the opposite would happen. Stephanie would fall apart, seemingly devastated by her child's frustration. Vicki remembers a particular time in grade school when Stephanie wouldn't let her go to a movie with her friends. In normal kid fashion, Vicki tried the "But, why not?" whiny routine for a while. When that failed, the girl simply blew up at her mom.

"You never let me go anywhere!" she hollered. "All my friends will be there, and you don't let me have any fun. I hate you!" Mother and daughter stood in silence for what seemed an eternity. Then, as a building collapses in slow motion in a movie, her mother's face slowly turned ashen, and she seemed to crumble.

"My own daughter!" she sobbed as she collapsed into a kitchen chair. "After all the love I've given you. You'll never know how deeply you've hurt your mother," she said between gasps. Vicki felt like crawling under a rock. She was certain she'd destroyed the person who had sacrificed her own life for her.

Vicki Nowadays

Like her mother, Vicki was a caring and compassionate person. She had good friends and a job she liked. Yet, also like her mother, she avoided strong or negative emotions. Whenever she felt lonely or sad, she would withdraw from others until the feelings went away. When she was hurt or angry, she worked harder in her job. This helped her tolerate her fears of getting "out of control."

At the same time, Vicki was a "problem person magnet." She found it easy to listen to others' pain, soothe it, and bandage their wounds. In fact, that became a problem in itself, as time and time again she found herself on the giving end of the stick. She'd drain herself helping others, then assume that no one was interested in her feelings. Yet at the same time, she didn't want to burden others with her feelings. She was afraid of both overwhelming them and being overwhelmed herself.

Vicki believed that her strong feelings were "bad" and destructive. Actually, over the years she hadn't let herself feel them too often, but in times of loss, pain, or stress, they would surface, and then she would feel she was hurting others, or being selfish or pushing people away from her.

When her anxiety disorder appeared, Vicki knew that this was a feeling she couldn't avoid. That is when she called my office.

WHAT'S THE PROBLEM?

If you identified with the detached mothering issues of the previous section, you might be thinking, "Well, Vicki's situation isn't so bad—at least her mom knows her name." It may be true that this second mothering type doesn't have disconnection problems but Vicki's mother had a different kind of problem, one just as troublesome. She was "fragile." As a china doll is brittle and easily damaged, the China Doll Mom is often unable to deal with unpleasant or stressful situations in life. This mother has difficulty setting limits and controlling herself and her environment. She is unprepared to handle the adult world, especially the mothering part of her life. This translates then to her mothering style; she is as overwhelmed with her child's problems as she is with her own.

This is especially true when the child expresses intense emotions. Though she loves her child, the China Doll Mom becomes quickly overwhelmed with his panic, rage, sadness, and fear. The strength of these feelings frightens her, and she feels at a loss to deal with them. Thus, she handles them in several different ways.

Catastrophizing. The China Doll Mom may *catastrophize* the baby's feelings. Stephanie read more danger into Vicki's tears or yells than was really there, and she overreacted. A wet diaper became a life-threatening emergency.

Withdrawing. When the child is calm and at peace, the China Doll Mom is also calm. But when the child is cranky or scared, this mother will often pull away emotionally. The child must somehow soothe himself before the mother can return to the relationship.

Overidentifying. The China Doll Mom lives in her own painful emotional world, and *reads everything through those lenses*. When her baby is in distress, she feels all of her own fears, confusion, and emotions in the child's feelings. Her own out-of-control self begins to emerge, and this frightens her.

Regressing. Often, the China Doll Mom will, in a sense, become a child herself when her child is unhappy. At the time that she should "be there" for the child, she is falling apart and is looking for support and soothing from the child.

Smothering and hovering. The China Doll Mom overcompensates for the child's feelings and intrudes on her internal world. Or she hovers over her, hoping to protect her from harm. Her attempts to put out a lighted match with a fire extinguisher will often result in the child's withdrawing further and further inside of himself.

Shaming. The China Doll Mom sometimes blames her child for having strong negative feelings. She can't see that the problem isn't her crying daughter but rather her response to and sense of responsibility for her daughter's pain. She may say things such as, "If you love Mom, you'll stop crying."

Reacting in anger. Many China Doll Moms will not hesitate to punish their children for having "wrong" feelings. When a child complains too much, is too difficult, too clingy, or too angry, the China Doll Mom often lashes back at him in an attempt to interrupt the feeling. "Stop crying, or I'll give you something to cry about" is the response of a mom who can't handle her child's feelings.

OUR NEED FOR CONTAINMENT

Our first basic human need is to make an emotional attachment to mother; the second is containment. Containment is the mothering function in which the mom literally *keeps* the child's feelings until he can handle them for himself. Containment can help the child manage and mature his "storm and stress" emotions as well as other immature parts of himself. Let's look at the child's need for containment in both areas.

Emotions. A child's feelings are raw, strong, and unpredictable. A child may be affectionate and close one minute and in tears or defiantly screaming the next. These emotions are rarely expressed moderately. For example, a child

- doesn't become simply anxious, she goes into panic

- doesn't become simply lonely, she clings dependently for dear life
- doesn't become simply irritated, she gets enraged
- doesn't become simply sad, she gets deeply depressed

What are feelings about? God has built emotions into our personalities for a reason: *they are a signal.* Much like a barometer measures atmospheric pressure, emotions work as a gauge to tell us the state of our soul. For example, anger may tell us we're in danger and we need to take action. Anxiety may tell us that the danger is bigger than we are and we need to withdraw. Sadness makes us aware that we've lost something we value and we need to replace something or someone.

Without access to our emotions, we lack vital information and can get in serious trouble. Our "dashboard" is out of whack. Imagine flying in a plane that loses its electrical system. The pilot has no clue about his altitude, speed, direction, or the obstacles that lie ahead. Those who are cut off from their feelings will enter destructive relationships with no intuitive sense that "something's wrong." They wind up getting hurt in love or work because they never saw the problem coming.

God has built feelings into us from birth. Babies enter the world with a wealth of emotions—they yell in terror, in protest, in rage, and when they're in need. These feelings operate more as a signal to the mother than to the child at first. They tell mom that her baby needs food, comfort, or changing.

Just as a baby's body and intellect are undeveloped and immature, so is his emotional nature. He is born with two basic emotional directions: love and hate. He either adores how he's being treated, or he can't stand his situation. A baby has no middle ground and no "gray area."

During the early years, a child's emotions center around one person: Mom. The child's entire world is wrapped up in his mother, as the source of his life, nurture, and safety. A lot is at stake. The child either loves or hates mother with a passion beyond words. And, as the child grows up, he begins to feel strongly about things outside of mother—other people, school failures, conflicts with friends. Mom may not be the object of these feelings, but she is, more than anyone else, the recipient.

This is where containing comes in. These primitive, intense feelings are as frightening to the child as they are to his mom. They are out of control, and they get stronger and stronger to the point that the child fears that either he or his mother will be hurt or destroyed by them. *The child doesn't just have feelings; to a large extent, he is feelings.*

The mothering task here is to help the child mature these emotions by knowing what to do with them. In other words, mother handles what the child is unable to handle. This is what containing is. She takes in and holds on to the feelings that the child can't bear. Then, she gradually feeds them back to the child in a way that he can digest them without being overwhelmed by them. In this way, she then prepares the child for taking responsibility for his feelings when he has matured sufficiently.

Parts of the self. Children have not only immature emotions but also immature parts of their character that need containing. Containing helps these parts to develop and grow so that we can function as adults. Here are some examples:

- Needy parts: the ability to seek out relationship for love and care
- Weak parts: the realities that one is incomplete and can't live life on one's own
- Autonomous parts: the aspect that strives to take initiative and become independent and responsible for oneself

A well-crafted wristwatch has springs, gears, and dials that mesh together smoothly to create a productive and dependable timepiece. In the same way, God made you and all of your parts to work well together as you mature, as you learn to love and to work meaningfully and effectively in life; you are truly fearfully and wonderfully made.

Children have all these parts, but they aren't integrated. They don't "get along with each other." For example, a child may feel dependent on mother's ministrations one minute, but two seconds later want to run a million miles away from her, down the shopping aisle and out of the grocery door. The next minute, it's back to mom in a panic.

That is where mothering comes in. Mom understands these primitive parts and can help the child grow up so that he or she functions together without conflict.

THE SPECIFICS OF CONTAINING

Whether we're talking about emotions or parts of oneself, containing is a mother's task to help her child mature. Below are some of the ways mothers contain their children.

Soothing. Have you ever watched a mom pick up her frightened child and gently rock her back and forth while she murmurs soft words of reassurance? The terrified child gradually cries less and breathes more slowly. The little body relaxes from its agitated state and "folds into" mother's body. The child may then either go to sleep or wriggle out of mom's arms and go off to play again. This is soothing.

Soothing involves an exchange between mother and child. The child is hurt or scared or lonely and full of painful emotion. He also feels very alone with these feelings and that they are "bigger" than him. When mother takes him up and rocks him, she "takes in" her child's scary feelings. The child has a place to put them, with someone who isn't afraid of them. *She exchanges these feelings for calmness, repose, and love.* It's as if the child dumped some toxic wastes into mom and received good food in return.

God is the Great Soother. He longs to comfort our panics and fears: "O Jerusalem, Jerusalem ... how often I have longed to gather your children together, as a hen gathers her chicks under her wings, but you were not willing."[1] Soothing moms are rich in this richest part of the character of God.

Validating. My wife had a bad day recently, full of conflicts and stresses. As she told me about it, I (Dr. Townsend) made suggestions and gave her advice on how to best approach her problems. Finally, exasperated with my cluelessness, she said, "I don't want answers. I want you to hear me." I finally got it, shut up, and listened.

When our emotions are out of control, we need them to be validated; that is, we need someone to experience them with us as real, painful, and scary. This is what empathy is—to walk in someone's emotional moccasins. When we validate, we affirm: "You're not making this up to get attention—these feelings are difficult." If the child thinks no one understands his feelings, then he is left utterly alone with his own worst nightmares. To validate feelings is to normalize them.

It's easy to make the mistake I did and invalidate feelings. We do this in two ways. We minimize them ("You're not really that upset over a little thing like Timmy's hitting you, are you?"), or we deny them ("Just stop thinking about it, and it will be okay"). And the part of the child that needs the most receives the least.

Validation doesn't mean agreeing with the content of the emotions. For example, you don't have to support the child's wish for Timmy to be transported to another planet. You are simply understanding the feelings.

Structuring. Another way that our feelings are contained is by structuring. A mother can help her child put her feelings in perspective. A child's emotions may tell her that the world is caving in on her, and that all is lost. This is what young emotions do in their all-or-nothing way. But the reality might be that the child has lost her favorite Barbie doll. The little girl needs help putting together the "big picture."

A mother can help by talking about feelings *as feelings.* She can help her child see that feelings are something we have, not are. It's immensely helpful when mother can give a child an emotional vocabulary, such as, "It sounds as though you're scared" (or angry or sad). This does several things for the child. She now has words for those deep, mysterious emotions, which, in turn, gives her a little control over them. She can now discuss them.

Not only that, giving the child an emotional vocabulary helps her develop an *observing self;* she can separate herself from her feelings and stand back and look at herself. This provides some distance and safety, which helps calm the emotions down. The child who learns that she's sometimes angry, sometimes sad, and most of the time there's a good reason, feels less chaotic.

How mother deals with her own feelings is vital here. If she is frustrated and "becomes" her frustration, the child learns to stay away, and will tend to "be" her feelings also. If mom fails to take responsibility for her feelings and instead identifies Susie as the problem, Susie will be confused. The mother who can say, "I'm having angry feelings now, Susie, but they are my feelings, and they aren't your fault," is helping her child contain her own feelings.

Structuring also involves *taking action*. The child needs to learn that emotions are only a symptom of a problem; when we concentrate on the problem, the emotion will go away. A mother can teach her child that emotions are not an enemy but a friend by helping the child set limits, confront wrongdoing in others, and know when to get out of danger.

I took my two sons Ricky (then 6) and Benny (then 4) to a kids' adventure movie. Kid-oriented action, fighting, and bad guys loomed on a large movie screen. Ricky was enamored, yelling and laughing and enjoying himself. However, I had misjudged Benny's ability to handle the difference between fact and fiction.

He became quiet in his seat, then turned to me. "Dad, I want to go home," he said. I could see he was scared. We got up to leave, and then I remembered the table of kids' plastic play swords I'd seen for sale in the lobby. As a last recourse, I bought both boys a sword and told them to fight off the bad guys.

I took my sons back to their seats and watched in amazement as Benny came to life in his chair. He swung his sword, yelling and laughing, every time the bad guy appeared on the screen.

"Ready to go home?" I asked, just to check things out.

The boys wailed their protests, and I gratefully sat back and watched the rest of the action.

Benny was able to do something about his fear of the bad guy and didn't feel so vulnerable and helpless. Structuring helps children see that emotions are a sign that some action needs to be taken to fix a situation.

Confronting. Even if a child is well-structured, his emotions can get the best of him, due to his age or perhaps his resistance to some reality he doesn't like. What he needs at these moments is confrontation. Confrontation in this sense helps the child face his out-of-control feelings; it injects reality into his emotions.

For example, suppose little Tucker is walking down the road with Mom. A car drives by and splashes mud all over his new shirt. Tucker cries and screams. He is legitimately shaken, upset, and sad about the mess. Mom picks him up, cleans him off, and soothes him, but Tucker's screams continue. Mom might need to say, "Tucker! Tucker! Stop it, it's okay!" Tucker shakes his head, looks at Mom, and slows down to a snuffle; he's more under control. Confrontation helps integrate emotions and reality and relegates feelings to their proper place—as a symptom of a problem that can be fixed.

Thinking. As we said in an earlier chapter, feelings are a primary process and thinking is a secondary one. As we mature, we need help understanding our feelings and how we should think about them. Thinking about feelings can modulate and calm them.

Children need to know, for example, that feelings won't last forever. A young child's lonely feelings without mom seem to have no end. In the absence of thoughts, emotions are timeless. There is no limit to the sadness and fear. The containing mother helps the child understand the transitory nature of feelings and that, with the proper elements (soothing, time, and problem solving, to name a few), the internal storm will subside.

Another thing mom can help the child understand is that feelings may not mean what he thinks they mean. The child may think that mom is a horrible person because she wouldn't let him have an ice cream bar. Now, if mom had promised the treat and then deliberately withheld it to be mean, maybe she is the monster that he thinks she is. But if mom is simply concerned about spoiling his appetite for dinner, the feelings that led him to think that she is a monster are not accurate. The child needs to learn that he's mad because he's disappointed that he didn't get ice cream when he wanted it. Then, his thinking helps him use his feelings as a signal to explore his situation but not as his Hall of Truth. He can then look at his own disappointments, expectations, and wishes and deal with them.

The China Doll Mom fails in the thinking process. The mother who is paralyzed by her child's emotions is often unable to think about what's really going on. She has no way to look at reality objectively, and she and her child can spiral into an abyss of frightening, never-ending emotionality.

The child needs all kinds of reality input to survive and flourish: mom's feelings and thoughts and his own.

RESULTS OF FRAGILE MOTHERING

If you think you may have had a China Doll Mom, study the following signs and symptoms and see if they fit.

Relational Problems

Those with fragile mothering backgrounds inevitably run into problems in their important relationships. They develop a style of relating that backfires on them: They push away the closeness they need.

Caretaking

Do you jump to rescue and enable friends who are having problems? If so, you are most likely trying to manage your own anxiety and sense of frailty, and this "parenting" of your friends gives you a sense of control over your own unmanageable feelings. This role distracts you from the painfulness of your own strong, scary emotions. Caretaking helps you feel less isolated and that you are at least making a connection with someone. The problem is that caretakers usually end up giving much and receiving little of the love they really need.

Aggressiveness

You may have learned to deal with feelings by condemning the universe of emotions in general. This includes your own and everyone else's. You may be critical of those with feelings, seeing them as weak and irresponsible. When others come to you with a problem, you may be inclined to tell them to "get their act together" and "stop whining." But the reverse is needed, not only for others but also for yourself: "For the despairing man there should be kindness from his friend; lest he forsake the fear of the Almighty."[2]

Withdrawal

As a recipient of fragile mothering, you may simply disconnect when you feel anger, fear, or sadness in yourself or sense these emotions in others. Your emotions may overwhelm you, and, much like a safety switch on a machine, you will pull away, either physically, emotionally, or both. This was Laura's style. Things were fine when there was no conflict between Laura and her husband, Randy. But when she was angry at him or vice versa, she withdrew from him. She feared blowing up at him and losing him. But Randy would feel that he'd lost her already. He wanted a wife who could hang in there with conflict, and he was discouraged when she detached from him.

FUNCTIONAL PROBLEMS

Career Snags

Margaret, an extremely bright and educated woman, has always dreamed of being in high-level corporate work. And while she possesses all the horsepower to run a company, at thirty-five she has never broken through middle management status. "It's the pressure," she says. "When I have to make a large-scale decision, I feel paralyzed inside. I avoid it as long as I can and then end up making an impulsive choice, which is generally the wrong one."

Margaret is terrified of pressure situations at work. She thinks the pressure is the problem, but the problem is actually her reaction to the pressure. Work, by definition, is pressure; it involves our performance, our competency, and our willingness to take risks. If we don't pull off the assignment, a great deal is at stake: promotions, raises, bonuses, and perhaps our livelihood itself. This kind of pressure brings out strong emotions such as anxiety, anger, and sadness with their catastrophic messages. These feelings can overwhelm us unless we can bring soothing and reality to them. Without emotional containing, we can never perform up to our work potential.

Life Problem-Solving

In a similar vein, if you had a China Doll Mom, you may find that you "choke" on basic life decisions: buying a car or house, deciding where to live and where to go to school. You may be afraid of complex problems that involve deliberation; after looking at all the components, you still have no "right" or "wrong" answers. You have little confidence in your decision-making abilities, as your emotions flare up in the place of reason and sound judgment. Often, you may think that you "aren't ready for real life" and so withdraw or let others make decisions for you, as this evokes less anxiety.

Rigid Thinking Styles

You may be one of those with fragile mothering who reacts against all unmanageable emotions and operates solely in the cognitive sphere. You may not trust feelings, seeing that area of life as dangerous, so you live as though life is pure thought. As one man told me, "I took care of my mom's feelings for twenty years. I've been there and done that with feelings."

EMOTIONAL PROBLEMS

Depression

Fragile mothering can cause many kinds of depressions. You may find that you have inherited your mother's inability to handle conflict and strong emotions in yourself or others. As you've encountered the storms of life and love, you've had times of feeling overwhelmed and full of despair, giving up hope that you can function as an adult in the adult world.

Another kind of depression comes from emotionally isolating yourself. You fear that you will never be known for who you really are, strong feelings and all, so you become a person with no one connecting to "all" of you.

Yet another kind of depression results from a "giving out" of resource; you spend all your time being careful not to hurt others with your intense feelings. Eventually, you run out of energy.

Anxiety Problems

Anxiety disorders, such as generalized anxiety, panic attacks, and phobias, are common among people who have had China Doll Moms.

We need some forms of anxiety to signal danger, or to alert us to a possible internal conflict. But clinical anxiety disorders can occur as a result of two problems connected to fragile mothering: (1) a lack of "mother soothing" can render you unable to soothe yourself and manage your anxiety; and (2) for fear of losing love or hurting others, you may try to ignore your scary aggressive parts and angry feelings, and as a result, become anxious instead. Often, the more angry you are (or need to be), the more anxious you become. This can be very confusing to both you and your friends.

Behavioral Problems

Fragile mothering is often the cause of many compulsive and addictive behaviors. Have you ever soothed and modulated intense feelings artificially through drugs, food, or sex? Your "substance of choice" acts as an external anesthetic to calm you down and give you a temporary sense of stability and equilibrium. For example, I was enough of a conduct problem in high school that my Spanish teacher would take a tranquilizer before class. My immaturity was greater than her emotional containing abilities. Swallowing that "soother" was the only way she could tolerate her feelings about having to be in the same room with me!

NOWADAYS WITH MOM

It's difficult to try to relate to a fragile mom who's getting older. Old age brings on its own legitimate frailty. Because of that, many adult kids assume protective and parenting roles with mother. They are unable to separate the fragility of the declining years from mom's character resistance to taking ownership of her life. If this is your situation, you may want to ask your friends who have strong moms of the same age about their own reality. Many older mothers insist on autonomy and pride themselves on not being a burden to their children. They plan for their old age financially, socially, and medically. If you have a China Doll Mom, you may already be worrying that your own older years will be spent with mother in the guest room. You may be concerned that, if push comes to shove, mom's welfare will come before yours.

But the question of taking care of mom in her old age is not all you struggle with. The nature of the entire relationship is an issue here. You may feel obliged to give mom only "good news" about yourself and your family; job struggles and childrearing issues might upset her too much. You avoid talking about yourself. It is easier to talk with her about her problems and fears.

Any attempt to communicate directly with mom about your relationship with her is fraught with dangers. China Doll Moms often insulate themselves from conflictual feelings by getting anxious and upset. You may say something like, "I want to have a real relationship with you, but some things are in the way. . . ." Often before you have completed your sentence, mom is crying, upset, or out of the room.

The adult child feels guilty for "hurting mom," especially if other siblings fuse with mom's self-victimization. The rest of the clan are often unable to understand the control and manipulation behind mom's demeanor. The siblings will then unite against the "black sheep" who is so mean to mother. In this way, they are able to displace their own frustration with mom onto a safe target: the child who tries to reconcile honestly.

There is hope for the adult child of a China Doll Mom. You don't have to constantly walk the tightrope of compliance. You'll learn about the resolution of this issue in the next chapter.

Chapter Five

Getting It Together

Marty felt the rage escalating inside of him. *There she goes again,* he thought, *criticizing me, and then going away and not even talking to me, leaving me with it all.* And his anger grew. Carol sat on the floor crying. She had withdrawn and stopped communicating. Somewhere inside, Marty knew that she felt alone and that she needed him to reach out, but he couldn't get past his anger.

He did not want to yell or hurt her in any way. He loved her dearly. But his frustration was too much for him to contain. It just seemed to grow the more they talked, or didn't talk. Finally, when she had gone to sit on the floor and wasn't saying anything, he went into the garage and started throwing things. The more he threw, the madder he got.

He had fleeting thoughts about her and her pain. He knew she felt misunderstood when they failed to connect. If he could just empathize with her, everything would be all right. But he could not calm down. His anger stayed strong no matter what he tried to do about it. He knew he was in trouble.

Marty felt a hand on his shoulder. He turned around ready to fight some more, but Carol moved toward him just to hold and caress him. As she held him, his rage began to disappear, and soft tender connecting feeling began to emerge.

He reached out to her, too, and the reconnection caused both of them to feel safe with each other again. Marty was his loving self again; Carol's caring had restored him "to his right mind," as he would put it. He knew he had a problem; his rage often grew bigger than a situation called for. He just didn't know what to do about it. And, even though he felt better now, he wondered what he would do the next time he felt it coming.

THE LEARNING CURVE

Marty was at a place where true insight takes place—he had moved past experiencing the problem to "looking at" the problem as a problem. He wasn't just "mad," now—he knew he had a problem with being mad a lot. He saw a pattern and knew that it was time to do something about it. But he did not know what to do.

He had tried calming himself down by saying positive things to himself, memorizing Bible verses, and doing a lot of other things that had failed to help much. They kept him in control somewhat, but they did not make the problem diminish. The rage would still come.

That is the point of this chapter. We must move beyond our symptoms to find the root problem. Marty's symptoms were those feelings he could not contain. He couldn't manage those difficult feelings or other disruptive experiences.

Marty had a China Doll Mom. She had not contained his feelings and overwhelming internal states, and that is what he needed now to move beyond the symptoms and fix the problem.

REMEMBER THE PROBLEMS

As we have said earlier, the real problem is that we need to be restored to mothering. Whatever we failed to receive the first time around, we still need. What do we who have unintegrated feelings, impulses, and parts of ourselves need, and how do we get it? How do we get the mothering we need? And when it becomes available, how do we respond?

And what about our real mother? How do we finish with her? How do we reconcile to her? How do we relate to her now?

In this chapter we will discover what we can do to fix the fragile mother inside.

THE JEWELS

What are the jewels of mothering in this stage? Here are the ones we talked about in the last chapter:

1. Soothing
2. Validating

3. Structuring
4. Thinking
5. Confronting

And now the big question: Where are these jewels? Nicodemus, a member of the Jewish ruling council, came to Jesus one night to see if he was truly a teacher from God. Jesus said something puzzling: "Unless a man is born again, he cannot see the kingdom of God."

Nicodemus replied: "How can a man be born when he is old? Surely he cannot enter a second time into his mother's womb to be born!"[1] Nicodemus realized what we all realize: You can't be born again through your mother. It's too late!

Jesus answered Nicodemus that he had to be born again through the Spirit. We *do* have to start over, but it can't be with mother. We start over when we enter a relationship with God through Jesus and then mature through the spiritual growth process. This is where we are restored to mothering. We find the jewels as we enter into relationship with God and his people. As Peter tells us, "Each one should use whatever gift he has received to serve others, faithfully administering God's grace in its various forms."[2] As others share their gifts with us, we receive the mothering we need. As we connect with God and good people, we internalize this mothering. Let's see how this works.

Soothing

Job once said, "For the despairing man there should be kindness from his friend."[3] If anyone needed soothing, it was Job! He lost his family, his property, and his health. When others understand our pain, when we hear caring voices, we are soothed. Those caring "I knows" that we all hear from time to time have a calming effect on us. As Paul exhorted the Colossians, "Clothe yourselves with compassion, kindness, humility, gentleness and patience."[4] When we interact with people who are "clothed" with these things, we integrate the feelings that we are unable to control. We are soothed.

Sandy discovered how this works when she joined a support group to get help for an addiction. Her pattern was to drink herself into oblivion to escape uncomfortable or overwhelming feelings. But she traded phone numbers with a few people in her group for times of crisis and would call one of them, no matter what time of the day or night. This was their covenant with each other.

After a few months, she noticed that her feeling states would not escalate as much as they once did. When overwhelming feelings did surface, she would find herself thinking, *I can call Suzy.* That simple assurance calmed her down and soothed her anxious and over-whelmed state. Mothering from her support group was working.

Validating

Being validated is being understood and knowing that there is reality to our experience. Research has shown that validation of our emotional states is powerful in its ability to help us contain what's inside of us. In fact, entire successful, proven treatment strategies for out-of-control people have been constructed around this very con-cept. As our feelings are validated, our personality structure comes together, and our overwhelming feelings are less apt to escalate.

When our feelings are understood, clarified, and validated, they are transformed and we are then able to build bridges back to real-ity. A friend's simple listening stance can change everything. "Just hear me," is the cry of our soul.

To do this, we need people to whom we can talk and who will understand without invalidating our feelings by saying the following:

- You shouldn't feel that way.
- It's not that bad.
- You're overreacting.
- Don't be so sensitive.
- Where's your faith?

Instead, they say,

- I understand.
- That really sounds sad.
- What a terrible feeling!
- Oh, I'm sorry you went through that.

While these phrases sound like such simple interventions, they are powerful. They validate us as people, and they show that we have real feelings and that someone understands. They have nothing to do with how true or not true the experience is in reality but how true the feeling and the experience are to us.

Structuring

Structuring our feelings helps add reality to them. In fact, paradoxically, many of the invalidating things that people do are attempts to structure us. But the time for structuring is *after* validation. After our feelings have been validated, we can understand them and put them into perspective.

As we talk things out with someone who cares, we can begin to see the big picture, that we will have other chances, that our feelings will pass, that God is in control, and that this event does not define us. We will remember that we have resources and relationships to bear the event and that we have been able to tolerate things like this before. In short, we are brought back to reality; we realize that, while important, our feelings are just feelings after all.

Also, we can begin to think about what we are going to *do*. When we formulate plans with someone, we begin to regain some sense of mastery and control. We realize that we can change the way we feel and that we can do something about our problem. Developing action plans that others can hold us to gives us the ability to structure things that we are going through.

Another aspect of structuring is time. Jessica had recently separated from her husband, and she had no assurance that they would reconcile. The feelings of potential loss were too much for her to bear. She had crying spells throughout the day and night and was becoming unable to work. The crisis was too much for her to structure.

She joined a support group that met a few times a week for people in crisis. The group got together for an hour and a half and, during that time, people would share. At first, Jessica could not stand the time limits that her support group imposed on individual members. She wanted to talk more. But the members of her group would hold her to the limits. They would say, "That is enough for one day. We'll talk some more next time." And they would end the session by encouraging her to do some of the other activities that she needed to do.

At first, "taking breaks" from processing was difficult for Jessica. But as she kept to the group's structure, her feelings did not take over her head as much, and she developed some places inside to "store" the conflict while she dealt with some other things in life. She was being "contained" by the mothering that the group's structure provided for her.

Confronting

You've seen it in the movies: someone is hysterical and the hero slaps the person into reality. We don't recommend hitting people, but there are times when feeling states escalate to a point of being truly out of touch. At those times we need to hear a "Stop it! You're losing it."

We need honest friends who will confront us when we are not seeing reality. Their confrontation limits our tendency to blow things out of proportion and scare ourselves to death.

Thinking

In a sense, we have dealt with thinking in the structuring and confronting sections. Our feelings and impulses need to be connected to our thinking, but when we have not had containment, we are separate from our thinking. To talk things out with others and begin to think about what we are feeling begins to hook up the two processes.

We need to *think about our thinking.* As we observe our feelings and as we talk them out with a support group, friend, or counselor, then we begin to observe *how* we are thinking in addition to *what* we are thinking. We see themes in our thinking, and examining those themes begins to contain us. We may notice

- negative thinking
- pessimistic thinking
- paranoid thinking
- overly critical thinking toward ourselves or others
- self-centered thinking

Observation of thinking patterns has been shown to calm people down, change their outlook, make them feel better, give them better impulse control, and help out in many other areas of functioning. This is what good mothering does for us: Mothers teach us about reality and where we are out of touch. The feedback of support groups, counselors, and friends helps us to think in more containing ways.

When our mothering people hold us to challenge our negative thinking and other destructive thinking patterns—and teach us how to do it ourselves—they provide a bridge to reality that the containing mother was supposed to provide. They can give us homework assignments to monitor negative thinking, help us replace negative beliefs with positive beliefs, and help us think more realistically. Their support helps us learn to think in more containing ways and is internalized in the way that the containing mother's should have been. Their support says, "It's not so bad. Let's see what we can do to make it better. Come on, you can do it, I'll help you."

OUR RESPONSE TO MOTHERING

As we saw in the first chapter, it is not only how we are mothered that is important, but also how we respond to mothering. If you had difficult mothering, you may have built up defenses such as withdrawal, angry control, and compliance to resist the mothering process in general. Then, when mothering is available, you fail to respond.

This was Diane's problem. Her group would try to "be there for her," as she was for everyone else. But she would always resist their efforts to get her to talk about the feelings she needed to contain. Then she would go home to her lonely life and soothe herself with cookies. They continued to confront her, and she finally began to respond. Until she took responsibility for her response to mothering, she remained stuck with the lack of containment she had had as a child.

If you are serious about responding to the mothering available to you, following are the tasks you'll need to accomplish.

TASKS

1. Find a Safe Place

The first task is to come out of the world of your own head and experience. You must make contact with the outside world of mothering. The Bible says, "What do you have that you did not receive?"[5] Self-soothing is a result of good soothing from the outside.

So, you must find a safe place.[6] This means pursuing one or more of the following:

- a support group
- a professional therapy group
- individual counseling
- a regular meeting with a wise and understanding friend or two
- a Bible study where you can process your feelings and experiences
- an open, relational church that encourages personal growth

2. Risk Intense Emotions

It is not enough to "be there." You need to talk, to open up, to share, and to allow others into the immediate experience of your overwhelming emotional states. Those parts of yourself need to be responded to in the present, with people. Open up and be vulnerable. Take your feelings and confusion to others and be soothed, contained, structured, and the like. Allow the supportive people in your life to enter into your emotional states and learn to depend on them so that you will have the ability to contain those states yourself later. You need to experience mothering to internalize it.

3. Respond to Empathy and Validation

As you open up, you also need to respond to the care you receive. Stop the devaluation of your feelings and accept the validation that others give. Often when someone empathizes with us, we dismiss it by saying something like, "Oh, it's not that bad. I'm just being selfish." Receiving care can be humbling and difficult if you have never had it. Take in the soothing, empathy, validation, thinking, and the other available jewels. Stop resisting love and grace when they show up.

Try to discover the defensive patterns that keep you away from receiving. We all have them, and a lot of love in our life becomes worthless to us if we do not learn how to open up, receive it, and respond to it.

4. Learn to Think About Feelings and Observe Yourself

As people are helping you to think about and observe your feelings and other experiences, work on your own thinking about them as well. You might find journaling helpful; writing helps structure our thoughts and feelings. Find the themes in your negative thinking and challenge those thoughts the way your supportive people do. Join them in thinking differently about you.

I (Dr. Cloud) talked to someone the other day whose negative feelings were escalating. To hear her tell it, there was not one caring person in the whole world, and even if there were, she was so bad that this person couldn't possibly love her.

I stopped her and asked her to look at her thinking. As she began to see how destructive and negative it was, she began to return to the real picture—she was sad over the loss of a friend. She simply needed someone to help structure her thinking that was becoming increasingly negative.

You might find it helpful to keep track of your involuntary negative thoughts during the week and then challenge them. Self-talk is an important form of containment.

5. Develop Action Plans

As you and your support team think about the things that you are dealing with, develop some action steps. These steps might include building more support, reading certain books or articles, doing some homework assignments, studying a portion of the Bible, or confronting someone. Specific plans and accomplishable goals help structure a personality.

6. Give Empathy to and Validate Others

Loving others and helping them with their overwhelming experiences helps us as well. It moves us out of our own self-centeredness and into the larger world. As we validate others, we are validated. We see how others catastrophize and think negatively. And as we listen to their overwhelming experiences, we become less frightened of our own. We are desensitized and can more clearly see reality.

DEALING WITH YOUR CHINA DOLL MOM OF THE PAST

The mothering we receive from the good people in our lives changes our whole direction in life. Receiving what we missed out on the first time around is the bedrock of growth. But there is still a problem in that we *did* receive something the first time around, and if it was hurtful, we need to deal with it. As we saw earlier, you must deal with the mother in your head if you want relationships and realities in the present.

While we do not believe that all personal growth comes from "digging up the past," we do believe that we carry around, in the present, feelings and responses to unresolved relationships in our past. In reality, this is not the past—it is the *present*. But we have present feelings about experiences and people in the past, and they can get in the way of present feelings toward present people.

As the Bible teaches, and research validates, if we want to be finished with the mother of the past, we must go through the process of *forgiveness and reconciliation*. In doing this, we find incredible freedom and love. Let's look at what it takes to forgive the China Doll Mom.

FIND A SAFE ISLAND

Getting finished with mother from yesterday involves letting go of hurts and whatever else may be dragging us down. Those to whom we have had some attachment are still inside our hearts. And all of our internal attachments have an emotional quality to them, either positive or negative.

For example, when you think of someone you love, you feel a positive attachment. Feelings of joy, love, and well-being are the results of positive attachments and add to our emotional, spiritual, and physical well-being. Likewise, negative attachments create feelings of sadness, anger, suspiciousness, and bitterness. These feelings exist inside and are always affecting us to some degree. Our entire personality can be shaped by bitterness if we refuse to let go of those negative attachments.

It is only as we forgive and grieve the problems with mother that we can free up the space and energy for other attachments, or to be able to experience the good aspects of our relationship with her. And we can only do this from a position of strength.

This position of strength can only come from possessing whatever it is that we needed from her. We cannot let go of mother if we are still needing something from her. This is why we emphasize getting the containing that you need from others *first*.

BECOME AWARE

Often, our patterns of relating in the present really belong to our relationship with mother. Dynamics and patterns that were standard procedure in our experience of her as well as the ways that we responded will often still be very much alive when we are adults. Surely you have seen people "withdraw for no reason," or get defensive "for no reason." A reason may not exist in the present, immediate relationship, but it may exist outside of their awareness. Their relationship with mom may be unfinished.

Awareness, in a mothering context, is consciousness of the automatic patterns that belong specifically to our relationship with our mother. As we remember specific interactions, we are able to put them in the past where they belong and stop recreating our relationship with mother in our present relationships. We will begin to relate to people for who they really are and develop true intimacy with them.

If you had a China Doll Mom, look for patterns of relating you may have developed in response to her fragility. Do you withdraw? Do you deny feelings or needs for fear of overwhelming others? Look at some of the signs we have mentioned earlier and become aware of the way that old relationship is still alive. If you work on remembering the patterns and experiences, they will lose some of their power in the present and become less operative. I heard a woman say recently, "I don't want to bother them with my feelings." Then she recognized that it was the "mother in her head" who would be bothered, not her friends in the present.

HOW DO YOU FEEL?

As we become connected and begin to feel safe, and as we look realistically at the way mother really was, we become aware of certain feelings we have about her. Becoming aware of these feelings is the beginning of working through the pain that the fragility caused. Grief work involves the following:

- becoming aware of your feelings
- expressing your feelings
- understanding your feelings
- letting yourself be comforted
- letting go of your feelings

Anger, sadness, or other feelings may still be unresolved in your relationship with your mom. Remember that Jim's feelings of not being trusted and of being thought stupid by his mother were still very much alive and being dumped onto his wife, Debbie. Jim had to get in touch with those feelings before he could go through the grief work of sadness and anger.

A lack of containment creates feelings toward mom that need to be owned and dealt with so they won't get in the way of present relationships. Talk to a safe person about these feelings, and process them so that you are not carrying them around in the present.

FORGIVING

To forgive means to "cancel a debt." This is what it means to forgive mother. We have to come to a place of making peace with her—a place where she no longer "owes" us.

Forgiveness frees us from bitterness, anger, rage, hatred, and many other destructive emotions. Hating someone for what he or she did or did not do in the past keeps the injury very much alive in the present.

This does not mean that we deny what happened. A period of "appropriate blame" is necessary for us to see reality. We must become aware of what happened, gain insight into it, and process the feelings. But eventually, we must let them go.

Let mother off the hook, even if she does not "deserve it." This will free you to find the soothing and containing that you need in the present. It will give others access to the parts of you that need healing. As long as you are still wishing for mother to do it—and holding her accountable for not doing it—you are unavailable to anyone else for soothing. Let your mother off the hook so that you and she will both be free for something better.

DEALING WITH MOTHER TODAY

So what about mom today? What are you going to do with her in the area of containment? Should you try to get her to understand? What's a child to do, especially if that child is over three?

Janet called me very upset. She had just talked to her mother, and was coming apart at the seams. Janet was in a crisis and experiencing some difficult feelings, but when she had called her mom, looking for some emotional understanding, the results were disastrous. Her mother scolded her and told her she "shouldn't feel that way." She came away devastated.

As we talked, she recalled the last few million times this had happened. It was nothing new that her mom couldn't handle difficult emotions. What was new was that Janet could now see the pattern. She would call her mother when she needed soothing and containing, get hurt, forget the pattern, and call again the next time with the same expectations for soothing and containing—and with the same results.

So, she developed a new plan. She made a contract with a few friends—the next time she was upset and needed soothing she would call them instead of her mother. Then, after she was soothed, she would call her mother and talk to her about the things her mother could deal with. Janet's mother was a good source of information and help on a lot of issues, but a "soother and container" she was not. Janet simply had to learn to not take the parts of her that needed soothing and containing to her China Doll Mom. She could take other parts to her, but not those.

The essence of an adult relationship with a fragile mom is this: *If she cannot contain feelings, then relate to her in a way that she can handle. Take your need to be soothed and validated somewhere else.* Do not continue wanting what she can't give. Relate to her in the ways that she can relate. Here are some suggestions.

TALK ABOUT THE ISSUE

We hope that our mothers can be our friends. But if your mother has difficulty relating in a particular area, you'll need to discuss it with her—if you ever want to be able to relate in that area. This does not mean that you *must* discuss it, but if you want to work it out, you must talk about it. There are some mothers who simply do not understand feelings and how to be a friend in times of need. In those situations, relate to her in the degree that she can relate.

You may want to say something like, "You know, Mom, I'd like to tell you how I'm doing, or what I am going through from time to time, but when I've tried that in the past, it hasn't worked really well. In fact, I end up feeling further away from you than before I said anything. I wonder if you could just listen and be there for me when I share what I'm going through. You don't have to feel like a failure, and I don't expect you to fix anything. I just would like to share with you. And I would like for you to do the same with me. But I don't want you to feel threatened or responsible for my feelings. I just want to let you know how I am doing from time to time."

Many moms respond wonderfully to a little coaching. Your mother may not have ever known what it is you've needed or wanted and may be surprised to discover that all you want is a little empathy and not a "fix it" job. She may be relieved to find out that she is not responsible to "do something," but that you would just like her to "be there."

If she understands, you could be on the way to a whole new era with your mother. Most likely, she cannot heal your need for containment now; your support relationships will have to do that. But as the two of you learn new ways to relate, you can have a mutually satisfying relationship.

NOT SO HOPEFUL SITUATIONS

Some moms are either unable or unwilling to respond to your request for a deeper friendship. If this is true of your mother, we suggest the following.

1. Get Safety Somewhere

Make sure that you are getting the containment *somewhere*. Your mom cannot repair what was done the first time around. Let your support system meet this need. And since she cannot understand what you need, do not continue to ask her for what she cannot give! Make sure that you are doing the things we mentioned above to get what you need.

2. Set Some Limits—On Yourself, and with Her

If mom is unable to soothe, understand, empathize, and do all the other aspects of containing, do not expose your fragile parts to her. Set some limits on both yourself and your mother.

Limits on Yourself

If you have a mom who is unable to do anything but hurt you, limit your vulnerability when you're with her. If she is fragile, do not lean on her for the things that you need, for she will only give a fragile response. You will not continue to reexperience the old hurt if you can limit your exposure to her. Also, set limits on your wishes to be understood by her.

Limits with Her

Sometimes, even though you plan to stay away, your mother finds you at a vulnerable moment. Or she may speak out of her fragility even when you did not make yourself vulnerable to her. If you can, simply ignore her. "A man's discretion makes him slow to anger, and it is his glory to overlook a transgression."[7] Try not to get drawn into repeating old patterns. If you are strong enough, let it go and realize, "That's just Mom."

If you are not at the point where mom does not affect you, then you are still too vulnerable and need to be protected. Rather than risk "reinjury," remove yourself from the conversation, by saying something like, "Mom, if you continue to criticize, then I'll have to stop talking. Would you like to talk about something else?"

This is what it means to set a limit with your mother. If you are not strong enough to deal with her, that's okay. Simply end the conversation, and call a supportive friend who can provide what you need. There is no value in your getting injured again and again.

3. Relate Where She Can

My friend Stan was telling me of a recent trip to visit his mother. He went on and on about the wonderful time that he'd had with her. He told me how they toured together, had wonderful talks, and genuinely enjoyed each other. He was overflowing with gratitude.

I wondered if I'd heard right. I had known Stan for quite a while, and I knew his relationship with his mother was anything but friendly. Stan's father had died early in his life, and his mother had gone to work as an attorney. He'd felt abandoned by his mother and angry that she was not more nurturing. When he grew up, he discovered that his father had left them enough money and that his mother hadn't needed to work.

He had had a deep disdain for her for many years, blaming her for all of his difficulties in life. His interactions with her were cold and distant. My curiosity finally got the best of me. "What caused the change?" I asked. "I thought you hated your mother. What happened?"

"A lot of things," he said, "but mostly I guess I just grew up. I have finally started to appreciate her for who she is, not for who I want her to be. I always wanted her to be more 'motherly,' more soft and supportive. What I got was this hard-driving attorney. But now that I have received nurturing from other places, I guess I don't need it from her, and I can just enjoy her for who she is. She is really an incredible person in a lot of ways. Now that I am in the business world and am doing acquisitions, we have so much to talk about. I can't believe how bright she is and what a wealth of experience she has in the legal sides of that world. In fact, I want us to do a deal together."

I was stunned. Here was a thirty-five-year-old man who had missed out on a significant aspect of mothering and had been an emotional cripple much of his life. He had hated his mother, and, as a result, resented all strong woman. But, having gotten his need for containment and empathy met by others, he was free to have an adult relationship with his mother. He no longer asked for what she could not deliver, and he could enjoy what she could give. Indeed, this was the best possible resolution. I have watched them grow in their affection for each other, and they have had some wonderful times together.

4. Love Her in Your Best Way

It is difficult to maintain an intimate relationship with a mother who cannot contain emotions. She is unable to share vulnerably to promote intimacy; she either attacks neediness or is destroyed by it.

But, she still has needs of her own. She yearns to be liked and valued. Find ways to love her. Do the kinds of things that show her you value her. In doing this, you will gain as much relationship as possible, you will ease her pain, and you will decrease the power that she holds over you.

CONCLUSION

If you had a fragile mother in real life, you are still in need of containment. You need soothing, and structuring, and you can get this from other people in your life and from God. They are there to help, but you have to ask.

And you have to learn to receive what is given as well. Do not only place yourselves in good mothering relationships, but make use of them as well. Risk, open up, depend on them, and receive the love and containment that they can bring. If you will respond to mothering in this way, you will find great healing.

Forgive your mom for what she could not do, and then work out the relationship you have with her now. In this kind of love, you both may find something very rewarding. Remember, "Above all, love each other deeply, because love covers over a multitude of sins."[8]

Chapter Six

The Controlling Mom

Ali was an energetic little girl and always into things. When she was three, she decided that the kitchen needed painting. She went into the garage to get some blue paint and then began the remodel.

Ali was Nancy's first child, and Nancy loved having her own little girl. She imagined a wonderful future for Ali; she could envision music lessons, the prom, graduation, college, and a wedding. Nancy was in heaven. She finally had the little companion she had always wanted.

Difficulties become apparent, though, early on. One Easter, Nancy bought Ali a matching white dress and hat. But Ali stomped her foot when Nancy brought the outfit out. "I want to wear my red dress," she screamed. "And no hat!" But Nancy knew what was best for her daughter and insisted on having her way. Ali's father finally intervened and convinced Nancy to let Ali go without the hat this once.

A theme began to develop in their relationship. The two would be close, enjoying being pals, and then Ali would push Nancy away. Nancy would then feel hurt over the break in their closeness and would often pout when it appeared that Ali didn't appreciate or want her mother's help. In Ali's childhood, the conflicts centered around Ali's budding individuality; the conflict over clothes continued, as well as what colors she wanted to paint her room, what games she wanted to play, what playmates she wanted to play with, and when she wanted to play with them. The two had a big conflict if Ali wanted to go to a friend's house on a day that Nancy wanted to be with her.

Since Nancy loved her daughter so much, it was particularly hurtful when Ali rejected her help. Nancy simply knew "what was best" for Ali, and she struggled with her daughter's lack of appreciation for all of the ways she tried to guide her choices. After all, wasn't

89

that what mothers were supposed to do? Nancy knew that if she had had different experiences and opportunities, her own life could have been better. She just wanted those things "for Ali."

Nancy was confused since Ali seemed to want her mother's involvement much of the time. She seemed to enjoy her mother's friendship, but then at other times she strongly rejected her mother's advice and help. Over the years, they developed a "love/hate" relationship.

Then Ali hit adolescence, and her preferences ran countergrain to Nancy's wishes for her. Nancy wanted Ali to be a cheerleader and run for student council. But Ali was more interested in sports and the arts. She wasn't the prom-queen type—she was more into the counter-culture.

Nancy was also upset over Ali's choice of friends and boyfriends. They reminded Nancy of the hippies of her day. She could see no real value in music, art, and social and environmental issues and wanted Ali to press harder in those things that would count later on.

Ali hurt in the same way her mother did. She felt that her mother didn't want her to have a life of her own and that her choices and preferences were never listened to. She longed to get away from her family and have her own space. Somewhere in her heart, she also knew that she had made some of her more negative choices just to push her mother away.

And the story continued, all the way to Ali's choice about college. Ali decided not to go. She wanted to work for a while and figure out what she wanted to do. Nancy felt that she had failed as a mother and that Ali had let her down. In turn, Ali felt lost, estranged from her own mother, and confused about what she wanted to do with the rest of her life.

THE NEED TO BE ONE'S OWN PERSON

In the chapters on the Phantom Mom, we emphasized the absolute importance of a mother's providing a close nurturing relationship for her child. But after connection occurs, we encounter the next big task of mothering: assisting the child in becoming an individual in her own right.

We are designed to be connected to others, to be a "we." But we are also designed to be individuals, to be an "I." We must develop our own identity and own our own lives. Maintaining connection and fostering separateness are the difficult tasks of mothering. To do this, mom needs some important skills. She must

1. Allow and foster independence and assertion of will, intentionality, and separateness.
2. Allow and foster individual identity and differences.
3. Discipline poor choices, behaviors, and attitudes and set limits.
4. Frustrate the child's wish to avoid independence and separateness.

Let's look at each of these mothering tasks.

Allow and Foster Independence and Assertion of Will, Intentionality, and Separateness

In early childhood and then again in adolescence, the child begins to experience something called "will." Some children, who seem to have the assertiveness of three or four people, are labeled "strong-willed." Others are less assertive. But everyone has "will." We all possess the drive to assert ourselves and to be a separate person within our relationships.

This drive forms our ability to be self-directed. When we assert ourselves, we develop *intentionality*, the ability to initiate and follow through on goals and desires. The definition of our ability to intend, according to *Webster*, is "to mean to be." We assert our very being through this drive.

Also inherent in this drive is the child's expression of separateness and independence. He differentiates himself from those he is connected to. He moves away from his mother to be separate—first to experience self, then to go to the playground by himself, later to have a separate life at school and socially, and finally (as we will examine in chapter 10) to leave home.

All along the way, the child is learning to say no: "No, I don't want to be close right now. I want to do it on my own." Or, he is asserting wishes of "I want that. I will do this." He is reaching out to grasp the world *outside of the "we" with mom*. It is not a "we" thing, but an "I" thing.

This drive in a child can be very disconcerting to some mothers, and sometimes a mother may see it as bad. We hear things such as "You must break their will." But, as we will see in a moment, the will must not be broken but disciplined. "The spirit of a man will sustain his infirmity; but a broken spirit who can bear?"[1] The word *spirit* in this proverb means "breath" and "life." We all need a will; to live without a will is not to live at all. The child needs his will to reach his goals and to say no to the evil will of others. If they have no "will to be," they will cease to be a person at all.

If a mother is unable to let her child have a life of his own, separate and distinct from her, moving away and against her, one of two things will happen—the child will be broken, or mother and child will battle until someone wins.

Allow and Foster Individual Identity and Differences

As we establish our identity, we answer the question, "Who am I?" This means that we are someone on our own, and by definition, someone *different* from anyone else, including mother. We saw this dynamic played out in Ali's life. Her desires were different from her mother's. Her mother wanted her to wear a hat, she wanted to go hatless. Her mother wanted her room to be pink; she liked green. A child expresses her differences from others in endless ways. But if the child is not allowed to be different or to make her own choices, then her identity itself is deemed "not okay." Who she is is not okay. And a child will either fight to have her own identity, or give in passively to not having one at all.

Some differences, of course, are not about identity but about the wish to be separate and distinct from things that are good, such as values and morals. As we will see, these need to be disciplined. But expressions of identity need freedom and encouragement. Ali wanted Nancy to appreciate her individual identity and be proud of her uniqueness.

A child needs the freedom, within certain parameters, to make her own choices about things like clothes, friends, and foods. She needs limits to her self-expression, but she needs freedom within those limits. Nakedness is not okay, but the blue or red dress is fine—it is her choice. She can't wear the sweatshirt to her friend's bar mitzvah, but she can select which dress to wear or do her hair the way she likes. Rock music is fine, but offensive lyrics or themes are not.

The trick is to maintain a balance between the boundaries of society, the law, our own culture, safety, morality, and the freedom to be an individual. The mothering task here is so difficult because part of the mother's task is to set boundaries. She enforces limits and allows freedom at the same time. But she must resist enforcing limits only to keep her child from being different from her.

Discipline Poor Choices, Behaviors, and Attitudes and Set Limits

And now we are back to the other side of the coin. Freedom and identity only have meaning within boundaries and limits. A child is an individual, but a child is not God. A child is a person, but other persons in the world deserve respect also. The child is a person in the home, but so are the other members of the family. Sometimes a child's behavior is bad for the rest of the family or for himself. This child needs rules and consequences for bad behavior.

The will should not be broken, but it does need to be disciplined. Discipline is different from punishment, which has more to do with the offended party's anger. To discipline is to teach limits and values and then enforce consequences when the limits and values are transgressed.

When this process is done correctly, the child suffers loss, but he also learns from experience. If he breaks a rule, he loses something. "All discipline for the moment seems not to be joyful, but sorrowful; yet to those who have been trained by it, afterwards it yields the peaceful fruit of righteousness."[2] The purpose of discipline is to teach a child that when he misbehaves or transgresses a value, he will be sorry. If he learns from the sorrow, he will begin to act right and have a more peaceful life.

Some mothers find it difficult to set limits, feeling that they are being mean. Being uncomfortable with being disciplinarians, they may abdicate all discipline to the father. But it is very important for a mother to discipline her child so that he learns relational values as well. If mother can be walked on, the child never learns to respect his love objects. While Nancy was trying to enforce all of her personal wishes on her daughter, she was also allowing Ali to get away with things such as not doing chores and homework.

In short, if a mother can say no to her child, the child learns to say no to herself, and she develops the ability to respect others' limits and boundaries. In this way, the child forms the core of identity called "self-control." She can make choices in line with values and goals, and she will not be thrown off course by impulses she can't control.

The mother who finds it difficult to set boundaries with her child and to allow her to experience the consequences of her own behavior is an "enabler." This mother expects a certain standard of performance, but when this standard is violated, she fails to enforce or allow consequences. She may do her child's homework. She may slide on a deadline for chores to be done and let the child go to the party anyway. She may pay the late fine at the library instead of demanding that the child work it off. Often, this pattern continues long after the child has grown up (as we shall see).

Limits and consequences provide structure to our personality and security in the world around us. The good-enough mother is one who allows freedom, sets limits, and enforces the rules with consequences. If, as children, we have no limits, we learn them painfully as adults—through failure to achieve goals, legal and financial problems, and other forms of lack of self-discipline. Mothers need to

- Set clear age-appropriate boundaries, rules, and expectations that are observable and measurable
- Set, with the child if possible, appropriate rewards and consequences
- Set and then follow through on the consequences for behavior
- Allow the child to experience those consequences
- Offer more freedom as responsibility develops

- Possess clear interpersonal boundaries and self-respect so that the child learns to respect those he loves and will not use or walk over them

If these things are done in a loving way, then children learn an important truth: freedom and responsibility go hand in hand. As they experience the freedom to be themselves, they are held responsible for the exercise of that freedom. They develop a sense of their own property line—and what they are and are not responsible for. They learn the important task of ownership—what it means to own their own feelings, choices, behaviors, and attitudes, and take responsibility for them. In doing so, they learn self-control.

Frustrate the Child's Wish to Avoid Independence and Separateness

"No, I don't want to go to school!" is the oft-heard cry of the young child. The unspoken part is "I want to remain little and have you take care of me." From the door of the nursery, to the door of the classroom on the first day of elementary school, to the doors of junior high school, to that day when the child walks out the door to make it on his own, the wish to avoid growing up can be seen. The child wants independence and fights it all at the same time. "Let me go/please take care of me!" is the dual cry of every child at every developmental step along the way.

Every step of growth comes with anxiety. When the child feels secure with a nurturing mother, the natural drive to separate kicks in. But then, when he begins to take the step of separation, he experiences anxiety and fear, and he resists the step. Clinging behavior can reemerge. Behavior designed to avoid separateness or responsibility, like feigning sickness or dillydallying, can show up. The good mother understands the fear and at the same time says no to the dependency. "I know it's scary, but you have to go to school. When you get home, we'll talk about it." "I know it's scary, but you have to sleep in your room. If you need me, I'll be down the hall."

Some children know how to ward off the increasing responsibility that growing up entails. They seduce mother into cleaning up their room, or they behave in other ways designed to keep them from having to be "big." The good mother does not encourage this regression, but stands in its way. She refuses to tie her children to the nest and instead kicks them out. By "nest" here, we mean dependent behavior past the time when that behavior is appropriate. The good mother then is internalized as a structure within the child against his own regressive wishes to be taken care of when what he needs is to grow up. Then in later life, when the person wants to bail out of adult responsibilities, a voice inside says no.

Problems arise when a Controlling Mom has difficulties saying no to the regressive drive. Sometimes the mother feels it is mean to do so. Sometimes, she simply enjoys the dependency of the child; it counteracts her aloneness. This often happens when mom feels lonely in her marriage. She uses the child to fill in the gap. Sometimes this mother has unmet dependencies in herself, and she projects these onto her child when the child is actually independent and able.

Like the mother bird who says, "Long enough in the nest," the good mother says "long enough" at every stage of development and helps her child move to the next one.

If these aspects of separateness and will are developed through mother's structuring of limits and discipline, children can learn some important realities. They learn that they have a life and that it is their God-given design to express that life assertively. They learn to take a stand for what is good and to stand up to what is evil. They have the ability to "pursue"; they push ahead to their appointed purpose.

They have a strong sense of who they are and everything this means—what they want, don't want, like, dislike, and anything else that makes them different from the ones they love. They learn that these differences are not a threat to others, that they can even enhance relationships. And as they learn these differences, they develop a good sense of identity.

They learn that they are in control of their own lives and that the quality of their life is their responsibility, not somebody else's. Certain choices take them in one direction, and other choices take them in a different direction. We reap what we sow, and that can be either a positive or a negative experience—it depends on our choices.

WHAT GETS IN THE WAY?

Jeri wanted to go on a trip over spring vacation with her youth group. When she asked her mother for permission, she ran into trouble.

"What? And leave the family for the whole time?" her mother gasped. "I thought you cared about me."

"But, Mom, it's only for a week," Jeri pleaded. "I really want to go. All the other kids are going, and I've really been looking forward to it."

"I don't care what the other kids are doing. It's their parents' responsibility if they allow their children to run all over kingdom come. After all I do for you, the least you could do is show a little appreciation by sticking around when we finally have some time to spend together. You're gone all the time as it is. With choir and youth group and sports, I never see you. And now this. It's just too much." Her mother began sobbing and left the room.

Jeri slumped into her pillow and cried. She thought about her mother's words. It just wasn't true that she was "gone all the time." She felt as if she were there all the time, because whenever she wanted to go somewhere with the other kids from school or church, she and her mother had this same conversation. She could only fantasize about the day she would be gone forever.

Jeri's story is not unique. If mom has a problem with her child's budding independence, separating can be a difficult process for both. Mothers can attack their child's independence in many ways. Following are some of the most common:

Guilt

Jeri's mom used guilt to control her. When Jeri would do or plan things that took her away from Mom, the message was clear: "You are destroying me by being independent." A child cannot cope with the fact that she is hurting her mother.

A Controlling Mom can use guilt to attack any of the moves toward ownership that we saw above. It is one of the most powerful attacks on freedom. And guilt remains with the child even after leaving the mother behind. Mothers are supposed to be internalized, but in this case, guilt is internalized every time the adult child begins to take ownership of her life. Indeed, guilt is "the gift that keeps on giving."

Abandonment and Withdrawal of Love

Some children lose their mother's love when they try to separate from her. Instead of guilty messages, silent messages are given. These silent messages actually speak quite loudly. They say, "I don't love you if you separate."

Jason experienced this dynamic in his relationship with his mother. When he became old enough to separate and have a more independent life, he basically lost his mother. The final break came when he decided to go to a college of his choice rather than the one she had picked out for him. She refused to speak to him for a year. She had utilized the silent treatment many times over the years when he would try to differentiate himself from her. When he said no to his mother or when he did not choose what she wanted, she would not talk to him for long periods of time.

Some parents punish by withdrawing financial support, attention, encouragement, and a host of other parental "goodies." The methods can be very different, but the message is clear: "I'll love you when you are an extension of me and my wishes, and I won't when you are not."

Attack and Anger

Susan's teachers noticed her quick tendency to say, "I'm sorry, I'm sorry," in a very repetitive way after every time she expressed some kind of want or dislike of something. For instance, when she would say "I don't want to do that color," she would instantly move into her "I'm sorry" routine.

Her teachers referred her to the school counselor, and the main problem he saw was one of fear. Susan was afraid to assert herself in any way. An examination of the family revealed a mother who would go into a rage whenever Susan would disagree with her or assert herself. Susan's "ownership" was under constant attack.

A child cannot tolerate a mother's anger. She either splits from the relationship, or she becomes terrified. Neither alternative promotes freedom and individuality. Independence, as we mentioned above, needs to be fostered, not attacked by mother. She has the power to send one of two messages: "Your individuality is loved," or "Your individuality is my enemy, and I will destroy it." A child cannot stand up to that kind of attack and develop in the way that she needs to.

Lack of Structure

The last enemy to the separation process is not something active but something more passive: the lack of structure. If a child is to become independent and separate, he needs two things: first, the proper structure and boundaries to internalize, and second, to be related to while he is doing the internalization.

Children with absent or loose parenting do not get the love and structure they need while developing their independence. The love provides the "something to move away from" and the structure becomes the "something to move against." It is only through both love and structure that secure autonomy can be built.

Children need structured environments. When they have predictable times for their activities, somewhat structured days, and rules and schedules, they can begin to develop in the areas we mentioned above.

Our enemies as we discover our true identity are guilt, anger, abandonment, and lack of structure. Our friends are freedom, love, and responsibility.

THE RESULTS OF THE CONTROLLING MOM

In the same way that detached and fragile mothering leaves the child with problems later in life, so does mothering that does not foster ownership, responsibility, and identity. Let's look at some of these problems:

Relational Problems

Inability to Say No

If you had a Controlling Mom, you may have difficulty saying no. Since you experienced conflict when you said no to your mother, you fear negative relational consequences if you say no to anyone you love. Like Susan and Jeri, you experience fear and guilt when you try to exercise freedom in relationships.

Control Issues

If you had a Controlling Mom, you didn't learn freedom in relationships. You learned that relationships are to be controlled. So, like your mother, you may use anger, guilt, manipulation, withdrawal of love, and anger to control other people. As a result, people who love you may grow weary of being controlled and gradually become resentful of the relationship.

Fear of Intimacy and Commitment

Randy was thirty-four, and he wanted to be married. He had fallen "in love" with several wonderful women, but as the relationship would deepen, he would "lose the loving feeling."

His history revealed a Controlling Mom who would not let Randy be himself. He always felt controlled by her. Consequently, as an adult, he was not a separate free person, and, in his relationships with women, he would begin to feel smothered and suffocated, lose the feelings of love, and then break up, leaving the woman wondering what had happened. "Things were going so well," they would inevitably say. When you grow up feeling controlled by your mother, you learn to fear intimacy and commitment.

Codependency

If you had a Controlling Mom, you may be codependent.

Codependency is basically a boundaries problem. If you are codependent, you don't allow the ones you love to be responsible for their own problems. You can't enforce the consequences needed in a relationship. Therefore, you are forever shouldering responsibility for someone else and getting hurt in the process. You are an enabler. Just as your Controlling Mom enabled you to remain in your problems, not giving you the consequences you needed to grow up, so you do the same thing for others in your adult relationships. And you are drawn to irresponsible people.

Mothers who do hold their children responsible for their actions and allow them to experience the consequences are teaching them that "each one should carry his own load."[3] In a healthy relationship, each partner is responsible for his own feelings, attitudes, behaviors, and choices. And each partner holds the other responsible for such things.

The codependent has not had this relational training. Often you were codependent with your mother, or your mother was codependent with you, and neither of you would allow the other to do your own suffering. As an adult, you have repeated the pattern.

Functional Problems

To function in the world of goals and accomplishment, you need to be responsible. You need to take ownership of your own life, tasks, talents, and consequences. As we saw above, you need to be able to focus your attention, pick goals, say no to distractions, and persevere against the problems and hurdles along the way. This all requires autonomy and structure to your personality and character. Unfortunately, this is where the Controlling Mom fails her child. Following are some of the resulting problems:

Disorganization

Take a look at any toddler's playroom and you can see that the ability to organize our surroundings is not something we are born with. Even more than the external world of toys and housekeeping, our personalities need organizing. To be purposeful people who can get things done, we need to be able to organize our desires, goals, time, and efforts. This is an important aspect of functioning.

Mothering is very important here. The structure we talked about above, the containment we saw in earlier chapters, and the consequences and limits of discipline all play an important role in someone being able to organize his or her life and function well. Mothers who do not discipline and invoke structure and consequences produce very disorganized personalities.

Controlling Moms say, "I'll clean up and organize you." If you grew up believing that someone would always be there to organize your life, you may have difficulty now in the areas of goal achievement, identity, direction, and follow-through.

Identity and Talents

The Controlling Mom does not give her child a sense of ownership.

If this is your background, you may not possess a knowledge of what you want to do, what you like and dislike, and what your talents and abilities are. The "can't find my niche" syndrome—the person who goes from one thing to the next—results from a lack of development in this area.

Ownership includes owning one's talents and abilities and knowing what one's passions are and how one feels about certain things. If you have a sense of ownership, you have direction in life; you know what you are called to do. Without ownership, you drift.

Delay of Gratification

To function well in the world of work, we must be able to say no to things we want right now to achieve greater rewards in the future. To achieve a particular goal, we must be able to say no to those things that would distract us or be more gratifying in the moment than the hard work that lies before us.

Children would rather play than finish cleaning their room, or go to the game instead of finishing their chores or homework. Children who learn to work for rewards begin to understand the important task of delay—to put off what feels good until later when what doesn't feel good is finished.

If you had a Controlling Mom who did not discipline your poor choices, behaviors, and attitudes and set limits on them, you may not have learned to delay gratification. You may also not have learned perseverance, which is important in delaying gratification. To persevere means to keep on going even when it does not feel good or when it is going to be a long time before you reach your goal.

Irresponsibility

A Controlling Mom does not give her child structure or enforce consequences for his behavior. Children take ownership to the extent that it will cost them if they don't. If your Controlling Mom bailed you out of your responsibilities, she taught you that those things were really not your responsibilities but hers. You learned that mother will do them "if I don't. I really don't have to worry." You never learned to take responsibility for yourself.

The mother who disciplines and who does not take responsibility for her child teaches him to take ownership and responsibility. Good mothers teach their children to worry in the good way—to worry about reality.

Emotional Problems

Someone with the above relational and functional problems because of a Controlling Mom would not feel so great. There is a lot of pain associated with the above syndromes when life is not working. Let's look at a few of these.

Depression

When you lack structure in your personality, you may struggle with the kind of depression that comes from feeling powerless in relationships, work, and life in general. If you have no sense of ownership in life, you experience perpetual loss—lost dreams, unfulfilled wishes and needs, and a lack of direction in and control over your life. Often, as mentioned above, you struggle with the inability to say no to destructive things in relationships, and you may be hurt at the hands of abusive people.

Feelings of Powerlessness and Hopelessness

A syndrome called "learned helplessness" affects those of you who do not possess a clear sense of ownership. You do not feel that you are in control of your life; life is something that "happens to you." And if you don't ever feel like you are in control of yourself, you have little sense of hope for the future. "Whatever happens to me" becomes the future instead of "whatever I will do." This is the aspect of will that we discussed earlier.

Many people experience feelings of powerlessness and hopelessness when they are caught in destructive patterns in relationships. They feel hopeless and powerless because they lack the interpersonal will that mothers with good boundaries impart to their children. They cannot enforce requirements in their relationships, and they suffer in an ongoing way because they feel powerless to change things.

Addictions and Impulse Problems

Addictions have many components to them, but one common aspect is to feel out of control and unable to say no to the substance or the behavior. Substance abuse, sexual acting out, and over- or undereating reveal a lack of structure in the personality. A good mother can do a lot to ward off her child's tendency to become addicted when she can help the child to learn discipline and the ability to say no to impulses and when she refuses to cover for inappropriate behavior.

The Bible tells us that "self-control" is an important aspect of character. The basic ability to exercise self-control over our impulses would take care of many of the problems we've discussed in this chapter. This process starts early in life when your mother says no to certain behaviors. Then the no of your mother is internalized to be an internal no from yourself.

Isolation

People isolate themselves for many reasons, some of which we have seen in other chapters. But sometimes, it comes from the inability to feel like you have ownership of your life. If you feel controlled by others, isolation becomes a safer option. If you are unable to have intimate relationships without losing your strong sense of "I," you may tend to isolate in order to be secure. But then your isolation can lead to depression and a host of other issues.

Anxiety States and Panic Attacks

Anxiety is often the result when your life is out of control or when you cannot feel a sense of ownership. It's scary when you don't feel in control of your relationships or when you are unable to function in some way. People with a strong sense of ownership face the future and relationships with the confidence that they will be able to solve problems they encounter. They feel secure instead of anxious.

Blaming

Taking ownership and throwing blame are opposites. Whether it's feelings, attitudes, behaviors, or career struggles, ownership says, "It is my problem, and I will take care of it." "It is my life, and I will own it," says the one in control of herself. The one who does not feel a sense of ownership tends to project: "You make me feel . . ." or "I didn't get it done because . . ." or other externalizations of control and responsibility.

A big task of a mother is to set limits on blaming and externalization and to require that the child own whatever is being discussed. She holds firm to "I don't care what Joey did first, your responsibility is to behave no matter what he did." Or, "it doesn't matter if it was raining, you still could have gotten an umbrella and returned your library book like you promised." Ever since Adam and Eve, we have been blamers at heart, but good mothers discipline it out of us instead of joining in the blame. In this way they make sure that the child does not grow up with a victim mentality but becomes a responsible person.

WHAT IT LOOKS LIKE NOW

We have seen how the Controlling Mom affects her child's growing up. The sad reality is that these patterns often continue when the adult child is out on his own. We have seen many people in their twenties through their seventies still struggling to take ownership of their lives, a task that should have finished many years before. Let's look at a few of the ways that adults continue the pattern after they leave home.

She Won't Let Me

I (Dr. Cloud) received a call on my radio program the other day from a forty-one-year-old woman who complained that her mother would not let her choose her own career. When I asked her how that was possible, since she was an adult, she replied, "Well, she just won't. Every time I tell her what I plan to do, she puts all this guilt on me, and I can't do what I want to do."

"So you choose to try to keep her happy instead of choosing what you think is right for you," I said.

"Well, I have to," she said, "or she will get angry at me."

"No you don't 'have to,'" I said. "You choose to because you want her to be happy. Your mother does not control you. Your desire to please her is controlling you. You could do what you want and let her react, but that is not your preference. You want her to be happy, and you want to do what you wish with your career, but you can't have both. Your struggle is not with your mother, but with your own wants. You have two incompatible wants, and that is your problem, not hers."

By the end of our conversation, she finally seemed to get it. Her mother was not controlling her, she was. She was having difficulty separating from and differing with her mother and feeling okay about it. In this woman's case, her mother had never supported the daughter's separate identity, and the daughter was still caught up in trying to get her mother's acceptance of her separateness.

These issues can be lived out over a lifetime when an adult child chooses to remain undifferentiated from mother. We have seen people controlled by phone or letter from 3,000 miles away. They have yet to gain a sense of separateness.

Just a Little to Get Me Through the End of the Month

When Joe was twelve, it was a book report. At nine o'clock, the night before the book report was due, Joe would come to his mother and ask her for "help." Had he read the book? No, but he knew details weren't important, for Mom would help. Together, they would figure it out before morning.

At forty, it was the mortgage. Somehow, his paycheck just didn't make it far enough each month. That's okay, Mom would help. After all, she was the one who had helped him purchase the house to begin with. He still hadn't quite found his "niche," that was all. And his children never went without anything; Grandma was always right there to help. The pattern established early in Joe's life continued: Mom helped Joe do a little better than he could do on his own.

A more severe example of the same pattern is Steve, who got thrown in jail again for drunk driving. Just a little help from Mom would get him out of this mess, and this time he would really "settle down" and clean up his act. His pattern of drug and alcohol abuse had cost him many jobs, run-ins with the law, and two marriages. But Mom was always there to bail him out.

Joe and Steve are examples of the familiar adult pattern of "leaning on mom." This enabling mother cannot allow her child to experience consequences in life. The very consequences that would cause the child to finally grow up and become responsible are blocked by the loving mother who cannot see her child in pain.

———————

We can see how these destructive patterns do not provide a relationship secure in love. Good mothering in this area does provide a relationship secure in love as well as steadfast in the push toward independence and responsibility, which manifests finally in the child's ability to take ownership of his life. This person can become the kind of "I" that does not thwart the experience of the "we." He has a strong identity, but he can relate in a way that is responsible and rewarding to others.

In the next chapter we will see how to repair the problems your Controlling Mom may have caused you and how to deal responsibly with her now that you are an adult.

Chapter Seven

Becoming Your Own Person

You may have bought this book for just this chapter because it provides the steps to repair the breakdown in the very purpose of mothering: *becoming independent from mom.* If you had a Controlling Mom, you've most likely experienced problems in separation, autonomy, and individuation—becoming your own person. If, in the last chapter, you found both yourself and your mom, here you will find the ways to become the you that God intended you to be. We'll go through the necessary steps to repair yourself, but first, let's clarify the real problem.

WHAT AND WHO IS THE PROBLEM AGAIN?

The Controlling Mom may be the hardest mother type to perceive accurately and realistically. The bottom-line issues and dynamics are often difficult to identify. This is because of the following two tendencies:

To see mom as the solution. While the Controlling Mom may be controlling and enmeshing, she can also be loving and supportive. Her care and concern is often genuine. She can be very involved in her child's life in positive ways. Because of this, the symptoms— depression, relational conflicts, and independence failures—don't necessarily lead you to wondering about mom issues. In fact, you may even return to mother over and over again for support in the very problems that began with her.

Amy, for example, was a devoted wife and mother in her early thirties, who loved her mom and stayed in almost daily contact with her. As far as she was concerned, her own mothering was ideal; she wanted her own family's life to be "as good as the one I was raised in."

Amy's husband, Ted, would often argue with and shout angrily at her, and Amy would withdraw in a panic. She lacked the relational skills to confront Ted and set limits on his behavior. She didn't know what to do with her husband's anger.

She would call her mother in tears, and Mom would comfort and console her, then suggest that Amy simply try to be nicer to Ted: "You attract more flies with honey than vinegar," she would counsel. Thus armed, Amy would reenter her conflict with Ted. As best she could, she would apologize, appease, comply, and try to please. That's how she was trained.

Ted would be temporarily mollified but would attack again later. And, though things didn't get better in her marriage, Amy was grateful for her mom's support. She felt that her mother was the only person in the world who understood. "Where would I be in this marriage without Mother?" she would ask herself.

When Amy entered counseling, she asked for my help on her marriage and her depression. Both were real issues. But neither was "the real issue." Amy's undeveloped independence was the real problem.

To see mom as the problem. The second difficulty occurs when you actually know you have "mom problems." You may feel guilty when your mother accuses you of not calling enough. Or you may feel she's controlling and running your life. You may feel smothered by her constant intrusions and overinvolvement. But none of these are the real problem. You don't just have a mom who won't let you go, or a mom who makes you feel guilty. The real issue is that you have a personal character problem: You need to develop your identity and autonomy and learn how to set boundaries.

So pay attention to your relational, functional, emotional, and spiritual symptoms; there may be a connection between your Controlling Mom and your present struggles. Then once you've owned the problem, you are ready to develop your remothering relationships. Certain characteristics are essential in your supportive people.

PEOPLE TO HELP ME BECOME ME

You'll find that it takes a unique sort of person to help you form your separate identity; not everyone is right for this task. So much of your work has to do with "not me" issues; that is, your need to become your own person is tied up in the need to differentiate yourself from others. You need many experiences of saying no, disagreeing with other people's opinions, and confronting others.

Your supportive people need to commit themselves to you in this process. For while many people can connect emotionally to need and weakness, they may have a hard time dealing with an oppositional two-year-old in a thirty-three-year-old's body! So, besides the willingness to commit to you, what other qualities do your remothering people need to have in order to help you? Here are a few.

Intimate

Your supportive people need to be able to be emotionally close. They should be able to relate to and empathize with all parts of you—sad, bad, glad, or mad. They need the relational skills that will enable them to discuss painful issues, talk about their own feelings, and, most important, *stay connected to you even in conflict.* They must understand your need to differentiate, become honest, and define yourself, and they must be willing to move toward rather than away from these dynamics.

Honest

Look for people who can give you truthful feedback, especially about your tendencies to comply or to withdraw from confrontation. Their job is not to help you be more sensitive or a better mind reader of others' needs but rather, to help you develop yourself, your own needs and values, and your own boundaries. In addition, your support network needs to encourage you to take risks in asserting yourself, even if you make mistakes in judgment. Being wrong in an argument is great progress over always avoiding an argument.

Process-Oriented

Finally, you need people who will give you *time to grow.* Becoming a distinct person is hard work and involves a great deal of failure. For example, when you're first learning, you may set a limit with someone, then immediately go back and apologize for being so "selfish and mean." This is part of the differentiating process. As you take risks in honesty and responsibility, you often become panicked by your separateness from others. Like a child who crawls out too far on the limb of a high tree, you fear that you've gone too far and that you will be abandoned or hated for being truthful. So you return to your compliant role.

Your supportive people need to understand that you won't wake up a whole person in a week or two. You need for them to be helpful, not critical, during your struggle to grow up. They should be process-oriented; they expect growth to take time and to involve repeated failures. Those who have experienced failure themselves are the most helpful as they are able to comfort in the same way that they too have been comforted.[1]

THE NEEDS OF BECOMING YOUR OWN PERSON

You need to complete certain basic tasks with the help of your re-mothering people to "grow yourself up." They break down in to several categories:

Develop a Separate Will

In most adult children of Controlling Moms, the will to be self-directed and separate is undeveloped. We all need the ability to decide what we love and don't love, like and don't like, want and don't want. However, the children of Controlling Moms often can't separate their feelings and values from those of the significant people in their lives: mom, spouse, or friends, for example. They aren't able to be distinct in their relationships.

The process begins by first owning a "no muscle." *We can't really know who we are until we know who we aren't.* That's why babies go through the "no" stage first. They must first become aware of their differences from mom before they can explore their own traits and characteristics. In the same way, you and your new mothering people need to permit, encourage, and provoke your distinctness.

This is difficult, as you are probably afraid to disagree or state a different opinion. You will most likely either agree in order to be accepted, or simply withdraw when you have a separate will. But your people need to point out to you that you aren't really "present" when you can't bring your differences to the relationship. This part is what makes you valuable. As the saying goes, "If you and I agree all the time, one of us isn't necessary."

Twenty-eight-year-old Corinne was the ultimate "yes person." She had lots of friends and was a genuinely caring individual. But she was so easy to get along with that her needs often got pushed aside in her relationships. When she joined a support group to deal with issues of character growth, it soon became apparent that Corinne had little will to be different from others. With her permission, her group began helping her with this.

One night, an opportunity arose. Trent, an outspoken member of the group, went too far in disagreeing with Phil, another member, and became hostile and cutting. Corinne was visibly disturbed by Trent's aggression toward her friend. Yet she said nothing. Another member, however, noticed her discomfort. "Corinne," she said, "it looks like you have some feelings about how Trent just talked to Phil. Would you mind sharing them?"

Corinne was stunned. She knew she was angry at Trent, yet she could have never said so. "Well, people have different ways of discussing issues, I guess," she responded, diplomatically.

"Look, I got angry at Trent just now," another person said. "He was out of line and hurtful. I'd really like to hear your thoughts."

Corinne was still doubtful until even Trent joined in. "Corinne, even I know that I blew it. I'd really welcome your feedback." Corinne hesitated, then said, "I guess I didn't like what you said to Phil, Trent. It seemed mean to me."

Her confrontation was greeted with warmth from everyone, including Trent. They were just as happy about her big step as they were concerned for Trent and Phil's situation. Corinne was amazed. She'd confronted someone, and her world hadn't fallen apart. Trent and the others hadn't shamed her or even had their feelings hurt. This was the first step of many for Corinne. She had begun to realize the reality of the proverb: "Better is open rebuke than hidden love."[2]

Create an Identity

You need a sense of "Who am I?" not only as distinct from others, but also as unique to yourself. You need to be able to make your own choices, in order to discover which ones define your unique personality and character. As you make choices, you find out what traits, styles, and aspects of life "fit" you. It's as if you were assembling a jigsaw puzzle; you try on and discard different pieces until the right ones form your real self.

Your new mothering relationships are crucial in developing this need. They will support your search and encourage your freedom to find out what you like and don't like, what you are drawn toward and repelled by. Their attitude is much like the old Marine adage: "A bad decision is better than no decision." They'd rather see you make a wrong choice and learn from it than make no choice at all.

Jeffrey came from an intellectual and somewhat introverted family. His mom had encouraged him to specialize in academic pursuits, and he'd done well. But as an adult, he began feeling he'd missed out on other parts of himself. His wife agreed and supported him as he tried out experiences that would have given Mom a heart attack. They found a church group that encouraged this sort of exploration, and within a year Jeffrey had mountain biked, skydived, and led the youth group on river rafting expeditions! He even shortened his name to Jeff, when he realized he'd never liked the more formal name. Jeff, his wife, and his friends all worked together to develop those parts of him that had lain dormant for so long.

Live Within Limits

Not all choices are good choices, and we need to learn to take responsibility for the consequences of our actions, be they unwise, immoral, or illegal. We must honor life's boundaries and limits.

Your new mothering friends need to follow the path of both freedom and responsibility. They need to support your risk-taking and at the same time, allow you to experience the consequences of poor choices. In this way, they help repair the enabling mother's damage, which protects the child from learning how to control his urges, delay gratification, or think about what he's doing.

Danielle had a problem with tardiness. She believed time was like an accordion; the more events you packed into it, the more it would simply stretch to accommodate the activities. As a result, she always planned too many things for a particular time period, thinking she had time to do them, and then ended up half an hour late for the last one. This not only kept her rushed and unable to relax and enjoy life but also inconvenienced her friends who had set aside time to be with her.

When she joined a support group, she immediately became an active and involved member. She was a caring person and so well liked that when her lateness trait emerged, the group quickly forgave it. In fact, they would wait until she rushed in before they'd start discussing issues. They finally saw that the problem wasn't getting better, so they told her, "Danielle, we care about you, but we're concerned about your tardiness. It's bad for you and for us. So from now on, we're starting on time, whether or not you're here. Not only that, but for the next several meetings, we're assigning the first fifteen minutes of the group as 'Danielle's time.' You can share all your issues during that time, but not after."

Danielle agreed to the plan. The next week she was on time. Then, the next few, she came in late again. She'd have ten, then five, then only two minutes to share. But she managed. Finally, one night she and her teenage daughter had a big fight that upset her a great deal, and she really needed the group's input and support. But she had planned too many things again, and she hurried in, fifteen minutes late. She asked the group for extra time, as it was really important. "We are very interested in hearing about your struggle," they said, "next week."

At first, Danielle was hurt and angry, thinking her friends were too harsh. They held to their boundaries, though, in a loving way. And that week Danielle made a turnaround. She was early for group, and her pattern began to change. When the group congratulated her and asked her how she did it, she replied, "When I got up this morning, the first thing I thought about was how much I missed sharing with you all, and it helped me be realistic about my schedule today." Thanks to her remothering group, Danielle was changing.

Deal with Dependency

We all have a wish and a desire to be taken care of. As we're growing up, our parents bear most of the responsibility for our lives. But when we become adults, we encounter the reality that no one is there to bail us out and solve our problems. Many people have difficulty distinguishing love from caretaking. They believe that "If you care about me, you'll take care of me." Thus, when someone fails to rescue them from their irresponsibility, they feel unloved.

Your supportive network will help you grow through this issue. They are there to frustrate your wish to be parented and to help you learn to say no to that wish within yourself. They'll help you learn how to shoulder your own burdens, "for each one should carry his own load."[3]

When Burt joined the men's Friday breakfast support group, he came with a history of job problems. He wasn't lazy, and he wanted to be successful. Yet his pattern was to want more support from his bosses than they had it in them to give. He wanted them to give him ideas, motivation, and parameters. Then, when the boss required Burt to take some responsibility, he would blame the company and quit. He would hop from position to position, with lots of promise but no results. The group was ideal for Burt, as several of the members were successful businessmen who were interested in personal growth issues.

As the men made themselves vulnerable with Burt, he felt safe opening up to them. They were sympathetic to his career dreams and struggles. But a couple of events challenged his idea of "support." First, as Burt told the group about his career frustrations, the members failed to respond the way Burt expected. While they were supportive, some of the men began to question him and point out his pattern of not following through on work requests. "We can see how your boss might feel you were more interested in your agenda than his," they told him.

Next, when Burt observed the successes in the group, he attempted to capitalize on it. He asked them to help him get a position in their companies. But the group stood firm. "We do support you and we'll help you be the kind of man who can get a job on his own, but it won't be from within our ranks."

Burt was wise enough to value this feedback, and he began developing his own job leads. By the time he landed a job he valued, he was much better at taking responsibility for himself without the wishes for caretaking getting in the way.

SKILLS IN BECOMING YOU

If you're serious about developing the separate identity you were created to be, you must take responsibility for the process. The following steps will help:

Know Your Defining Traits

Part of being a willing, autonomous person is the ability to know who you are—and aren't. Take ownership of this area by becoming aware of your own individual aspects and parts. Awareness will help you develop yourself apart not only from mom, but also from the other important people in your life. Ask yourself the following questions:

- Am I more extroverted or introverted?
- Am I more task-oriented or relationship-oriented?
- Am I more active or passive?
- What aspects of my family background do I agree with?
- What aspects aren't me?
- What do I like in my best friends?
- What do I dislike in my best friends?
- What are my strengths?
- What are my weaknesses?
- What situations make me angry?

Get feedback from your remothering people. Ask them which character traits seem to define you, and which don't. See how this corresponds with your own view of yourself.

Develop Your No Muscle

If you had a Controlling Mom, you'll probably find that your yes muscle is overdeveloped; it works even when you inwardly disagree.

But it's important outwardly to disagree, confront, refuse evil, and stand against wrongdoing. You can learn to change your silent no to an audible one.

We sometimes suggest to people that they grab a friend and go to a used-car lot for practice. If you can hold your own against a salesman who's trained to turn your refusal into agreement, you will have accomplished a great deal. With your friend's support, you can learn how to disagree on models, styles, options, prices, and financing. Just make sure your friend doesn't let you buy a car while you're practicing!

Deal with the Victim Role

Many undefined people feel helpless and powerless in conducting their lives. They feel controlled by the power and threats of others. This is called a victim mentality; these people are resigned to others' taking advantage of them.

True victims are those who have suffered at the hands of others in situations where they had no control. Children, for example, have very little say-so in their lives and are easily victimized. Still, many childhood victims grow out of their helplessness to take control of their lives as adults. *Beware of the tendency to define yourself as a victim, to create an identity out of an event.* You are much more than one event. You are a person with lots of experiences and parts, among which may be a victimizing situation.

Those with victim mentalities see no alternatives to their problems. The reality is that most of the time we do have choices. They are often painful and may involve disappointing or angering others. But they may be the best options for your own welfare and stewardship over your life. Letting people in on your secrets, setting limits with people, and beginning to forgive are choices you can make.

A friend of mine suffered catastrophic abuse as a child. She experienced the kind of horror most people never dream about in a lifetime. As she was hurt by people who controlled her, she could have easily figured that was her role and fate and attached herself to controlling people for the rest of her life. Yet she is an independent person today. When I asked her about her attitude, given her background, she told me, "I can't change my past. It's part of me. But I don't want my past to determine my future. If I do, the people who hurt me are in charge again."

Develop Proactivity

Undefined people are often "reactors." They refrain from making a decision until someone else does, and then they react to that person. But proactive people take the initiative.

Proactivity is especially important when it comes to conflict. You are probably more used to being hypervigilant and anxiously reading the other person's mood before you respond. This prohibits you from taking ownership of the problem. When you see a problem in a relationship, take the first step. This might mean something as simple as saying, "It bothered me when you didn't return my phone call." This isn't an indictment—it's a way to connect with the other person and resolve the problem.

Proactivity also plays a large role in learning to meet your needs. Don't wait for someone to suggest a movie or a restaurant—blurt out something to your safe friends. They'll understand. On a more personal level, take action to get your relational needs met. Many individuals go lonely and isolated for unwarranted lengths of time because they wait for others to notice that they are sad or struggling. Make the struggle your problem, and get in touch with your supportive network.

Set Boundaries

Boundaries are your personal property line. They define where you end and where others begin. Be clear about your limits, then state and keep the consequences if someone continues to transgress your boundaries. Setting limits will help you protect your own character parts and feelings and will ultimately serve as a foundation from which you can love and share with others.

Alicia and her boyfriend, Stuart, were growing closer, and she believed he might even be the one God had intended her to marry. But his sexual aggressiveness influenced her to go further than she believed she should. She said nothing to Stuart, as she didn't want to lose him. But the moral conflict inside caused her a great deal of distress.

Alicia confessed her concern to her supportive friends. They didn't judge her, and they provided a place of warmth, which she internalized, in case Stuart did leave. Then they helped her formulate the words to tell Stuart. Finally, she approached her boyfriend. "I haven't been honest with you about our sexual intimacy. I'm uncomfortable with how far we've let things go, and I want to put on the brakes."

Stuart was surprised and resistant to the change; he didn't want to give up the sex. "If you won't agree with this value," she told him, "I'll have to stop seeing you." Now Stuart realized that Alicia was serious. The fact that she would risk the entire relationship caused him to confront his own moral problem. He apologized to Alicia, asked for her support, and went to his own accountability friends for assistance in the sexual limits. Alicia's friends had not only helped her set limits, but they also helped her establish healthy consequences with her boyfriend.[4]

Respect Others' Boundaries

There's no such thing as a free lunch in personal growth. If we want others to respect our limits, we must respect theirs. The Bible teaches that if we resent and judge others' boundaries, we also judge our own. "For in the same way you judge others, you will be judged."[5] Learn to love and support others' no, even if you are disappointed or saddened by it.

Blair was upset when his best friend Chase canceled a four-day hunting and fishing trip. Blair had been living for this event. Chase had a good reason; he needed to prepare for his first day on a new job. Still, Blair took Chase's decision personally, and told him he wasn't a loyal friend.

Chase's reply was extremely helpful to Blair: "I'm not doing this *against you*," Chase told his friend. "I'm doing it *for me*." Chase's boundary wasn't a transgression to his friend, it was something he needed for himself. Blair began to understand that he had perceived the situation from his viewpoint alone.

RE-RELATING TO MOM

As you become more defined, separate, and independent, you will need to reconfigure your connection with mom. You want, as much as possible, to bring your "me" to the "we" of the relationship. Here are some of the things you can do to move this process along.

Become Aware of Mom's Struggle

While it's easy to resent mother's control, it's more difficult to see her as someone who has also been hurt in the area of boundaries. Most enmeshing moms were abandoned or controlled themselves. Some have had to take the mother role with their parents or siblings. Adopt some understanding and compassion for your mother's journey. You might even ask her about her past in this area. Many mothers are thrilled when their children take an interest in their struggles.

Introduce Mom to the New "You"

If your identity has always been defined by mom, you're a different person now. You are more of your own person with unique traits, characteristics, and distinguishing marks. These can be a valid part of the new connection with her.

Rather than wait for a crisis or an argument, take the initiative to tell mom about yourself. You might say something like, "I'm in a process of personal growth, and I've made some changes. Our relationship is important to me, so I want to share them with you." Then tell her what you've discovered about your character traits, attributes, likes, and dislikes. When you make mom an ally in your growth process, she can feel more a part of your life.

Set Necessary Limits

You may need to establish new ground rules for you and mom. This might mean telling her:

- You'll leave the house if she yells when you disagree with her
- You'll have to hang up the phone if she can't stop nagging because you didn't visit enough last week

- You're the parent of your children, so you want her to operate with the grandkids the way you ask her to
- You want her to try to listen to what you're saying, instead of telling you what you're thinking

But let mom know also that you want her to tell you when you're crossing her boundaries and that you want her to have a part in this mutual process of learning to respect each other.

Confront on matters of principle, and don't worry so much about the details. You don't see mom every day anymore, and you can tolerate the unimportant things. For example, if she goes on and on about the dress her friend wore to the wedding, listen as long as you can, then change the subject to something that interests both of you.

Some moms control by dominating. Others do it by not listening. Still others control by guilt messages or withdrawal. But setting necessary limits is a major issue in dealing with your mother today. In addition, it's also a more sensitive subject, as you are confronting not only mom's hurt, but how she hurts others. Pay attention to your re-mothering friends for tact as well as for determining if you're developmentally ready for this.

You may want to tell her, "I'd like a closer relationship with you, but I know we have problems and conflicts from time to time that can distance us from one another. When this happens with my friends, we talk them out, get them resolved, and become even closer. I'd like to have that kind of connection with you. What do you think?" If mom's agreeable in principle, let her know how difficult it is to disagree with her sometimes and how that distances the relationship. Then ask her if you can both be free to be yourselves, as good friends are.

A great deal depends on mom's willingness to look at herself. If she is able to, you may have gained a friend. If not, she'll react defensively. In any case, you've done your part to improve the relationship, and you may simply have to leave it at that. This doesn't mean you will allow her to control you again. It does mean keeping your limits but not nagging her about the issue.

Help Mom with Her Own Limits

Mom may have difficulty being an individual in her own life. While you aren't her counselor, you can assist her in this area. You can help her see the advantages of being in control of her life and of not having people avoid or resent her because she's a controller.

Many moms have a hard time following through on boundaries and consequences. For example, she may let dad call all the shots with the force of his will or loud tone of voice. Tell her you know this must hurt, and then tell her what you've learned about boundaries. Point her in the directions you went for help: support groups, a good church, therapists, books, and tapes. But resist the temptation to fix her marriage. When children try to parent parents, the lines quickly become confused, and problems ensue.

HOW IT COULD BE

As you continue becoming a separate person in your own relationships, you will also see positive changes in your attachment to mom.

Julia was in her early thirties when she began discussing the ideas of separateness, differences, and boundaries with her mother. It wasn't easy at first: Mom thought Julia was rejecting her as a person. But they both persevered in the relationship. Mom agreed to respond to Julia's truth and try not to hear it as pushing her away.

Julia told her, "Mom, when I tell you I can't bring the kids to visit, instead of withdrawing and being hurt, would you just tell me you're sad about it. And would you try to understand?" Mom learned that Julia's differences were *for* Julia, not *against* Mom. And she began to respect, not resent, her daughter's independence.

In fact, Mom became even more supportive. When Julia came for a visit, her mother surprised her by saying, "Let me take care of the kids while you and Rich leave for a few hours. You two probably don't get enough time together." They gratefully accepted. Then, when the family moved farther from Mother's residence, she accepted it. She told Julia that she had her own life, church, and activities and that she'd miss them but that it sounded like the best thing for them.

Mom was still Mom, however. She still had a hard time discussing differences directly, and she'd still run over Julia's no at times. But Julia had learned to tolerate these weaknesses; she did not need her mother to be perfect. Julia's work on her own character kept her from judging her mother, and Julia's connections with her mothering people kept her from needing Mom to be a parent.

What was most unusual for Julia, however, was the change she felt inside toward Mom. As a little girl, she'd always felt a restless anxiety around her mother, part of her reaction to being smothered. But now that the two women were becoming friends, she actually missed her at times and wanted to spend time with her. For the first time, she and Mom were allowing a good space to exist between them. *When two people create this kind of space, they also create room for loving and intimate feelings.*

Julia's eyes began to open to her mother's good qualities. She noticed and appreciated all of Mom's giving and caring, her helpfulness around the house, and her warmth and acceptance of others. Both women are now enjoying their relationship in a way that neither had dreamed possible. It's not easy, but when mother and adult child can move into appreciation of each other's independence, they can find that closeness they've longed for with one another.

Chapter Eight

The Trophy Mom

As far back as he could remember, Dan had felt that his mother, Liz, was proud of him. When his friends would gripe about their own distant or uncaring moms, Dan could never relate. His mom was always there for him, cheering him on in every endeavor. And she would be just as enthused as he was about his successes. "You're Number One!" she would tell him before his basketball games. And with that kind of support, Dan excelled in everything from athletics to academics to student leadership.

He felt loved and encouraged as he grew up. But then, in his adult years, he recalled other kinds of responses from his mother in which the opposite was true. For example, in second grade, when he lost the lead part in the school play, Dan saw a different side of Mom. Liz was disappointed in him. "You're a Johnson," she told him, "and we Johnsons aren't losers. Don't let me down like this." Then she had gone into action against the school, calling explosive meetings with the teachers to investigate why they hadn't given Dan a fair audition. This was particularly confusing to Dan. Was it his failure or the school's? Liz had seemed to aim her barrels in both directions, hoping to score somewhere.

In addition, Dan felt that Liz had had a vested interest in educating her friends about his latest achievements. He would dread the times she'd host her bridge club in their home. He'd try to sneak past the living room to get outside and ride bikes with his friends, but she was always waiting to pounce on him. "Tell the girls about your science project," she would coo and then stand back and beam as he entertained the club.

Sometimes Dan caught a glimpse of his mom as he talked to the women. She would be so involved in his performance that she would mouth his words along with him as he spoke. *How does she know what I'm going to say next?* he would wonder. It was as if Mom were giving the performance herself.

Liz seemed to vacillate in her need for "specialness." At times she was content to bask in the glow of her son's achievements, knowing that Dan reflected on his mother. At other times, however, she needed the praise directly for herself. She would find an audience, usually Dan and his brother and sister, and regale them with tales of her past and present exploits. Her list of topics was endless: her appearance, activities, friends, spirituality, high school successes, and the men who'd courted her, to name a few. She'd go into great detail about herself with full embellishments and dramatic pauses.

Liz's need for admiration seemed to happen more at dinnertime when she had a captive audience. But since she monopolized the conversation, no one else had a chance to talk about their day. So Dan, his dad, and his siblings developed the "Point Man" strategy.

One person would begin by acting interested in Liz's stories: This was Point Man #1. Liz, flattered, would deal one-on-one with that person. Then, while that individual was occupied with Mom, the other kids and Dad would visit and talk. When Point Man #1 had reached his limit of listening attentively to Mom, he would kick the next person's leg under the table. Point Man #2 would take over, energetically probing Mom to "tell me more about how everyone loved your dress." Liz would automatically turn to Point Man #2, and the retired Point Man #1 would drop eye contact and gratefully enter into the real conversation with the family. Liz never knew about the strategy, as her family loved her and didn't want to hurt her feelings. But they had had to find some way to survive at dinner.

So Dan vacillated in his feelings for Mom. Part of him needed her admiration; it helped him to get through bad times. During his college years, when he'd make a bad grade or lose a girlfriend, he'd call Mom to chat, and she would enter the drama of blaming his professors or that girlfriend who "just didn't understand him." She would assure him that he was the brightest and best-looking kid on campus and that he just needed to find people who could recognize that. As Mom said, "You're on your way to being a star. Make me proud." He'd hold on to that, at least until the next exam or the next girlfriend problem.

OUR NEED FOR ACCEPTANCE

Dan's relationship with Liz illustrates the basic human need to be *accepted in all our parts.* We need all of our "real" traits and characteristics to be connected to the same relational home. We need a person where all these parts can be in one place at one time with one person. We need a place where we can be ourselves, just as we are. Like the theme song from the TV show *Cheers*, where "you want to go where everyone knows your name," you also need a place where someone "knows your parts."

We need this acceptance of our "real selves" for many reasons. When we feel loved for who we are, we are better equipped to deal with the problems of living in a fallen world. Children aren't naturally prepared to deal with the painful realities of sinfulness, failure, loss, weakness, and badness. They are surprised and overwhelmed by both their own and others' failures. They have no tools to handle these issues.

When we are accepted, however, we learn an important reality: *Love is the antidote to badness.* While imperfection will always exist in the world and within our very being, it doesn't remove us from relationship and connectedness. We are "okay" in our badness. We can tolerate and bear the bad things in ourselves and others without fear of the loss of love: "Therefore, there is now no condemnation for those who are in Christ Jesus."[1] When we no longer have to struggle with toxic shame, hiding our true selves, or perfectionism, we can then work on maturing our failing selves. The failing self is no longer starved to death by denial and judgment but receives the grace it needs to grow up.

Good mothering creates an atmosphere of acceptance that prepares us to enter the real world. "Accept one another, then, just as Christ also accepted you, in order to bring praise to God."[2] This is one of the beautiful realities of relationship with Christ; he accepts all of our weaknesses and foibles. We don't have to clean up our act and be perfect for him to love us. In fact, the opposite is true. He first loves and accepts us, and then we are able to change and give up childish ways. After that, we are ready to give that same grace to each other. When we accept each other's failings, we bring praise to the God who loves forgiving.

The word *accept* in the Bible also means *receive*. When a mother accepts her child, she actually receives into herself all of her child's parts. She doesn't deny, withdraw from, or condemn her child's failings. She bears what her child cannot yet bear.

A mother's acceptance also helps her child face reality. Babies are born with godlike perceptions of themselves. As any mother can testify, not only are infants cuddly, affectionate, and lovable, they are also grandiose, self-centered, and omnipotent. They expect a perfectly responsive environment to meet their needs.

Mothers have a difficult task here. They have to meet the child's real needs for safety, love, and structure and, at the same time, gradually humble the child to give up his godlike wishes, grieve his perfectionism, and accept both his and the world's limitations. He may kick and scream, but he finally learns to say, "I did a bad thing."

Acceptance and approval are two different things. To *approve* means "to consider to be good." We aren't to approve of unrighteousness. Mother *accepts* her child's selfishness, demands, and failures; she sees them as realities and interacts with them. However, she may not *approve* of them. To approve would create more confusion in the child about good and bad and right and wrong.

So, acceptance means two things: First, mother connects to the child's real self and gives the child life in his inner parts, both good and bad. Second, she limits the grandiose self and helps the child give up idealistic demands on himself and others. This process prepares the child to enter adult life with sound judgment about what are his actual strengths and weaknesses, positives and negatives, goods and bads. Instead of being stuck in perfectionistic ideals, he is free to deal with the realities about himself and the world.

PARTS THAT NEED ACCEPTANCE

Which parts of the child need acceptance? There are several.

The weak parts. One of the realities about us is that we are "unable" people. Try as we might, we can't always be or do what we'd like. No amount of good intentions, willpower, or discipline can make us people who "have it together." In fact, it is our weaknesses that drive us to supportive relationships. Jesus called this being "poor in spirit."[3] But this poverty is actually a form of wealth. It makes us face ourselves as we really are, give up our pride, and humbly reach out for help. Weakness helps us stay connected to God and others.

In a very real sense, children *are* weakness. They are smaller than adults, don't know how to take care of themselves, and are dependent on others for most of their survival. Children are faced every day with massive problems and needs and must depend on others to get those needs met. The good mother baptizes her children's weakness. She welcomes their needs, has compassion on their frailties, and connects with them emotionally. She makes it okay to be weak. In turn, as children experience that their weakness is good to mother, they are able to respond and mature into strength.

The negative parts. As children grow, they begin making distinctions between the positive and negative aspects of life. They learn to hate things, disagree, and sometimes be oppositional. This is a sign that they are learning to discern, clarify values, and stand against evil and "for" the right things. As they learn, they are often negative about everything in life, from broccoli to going to bed.

The mediocre parts. Many children feel loved only when they are "trophies." That is, mother seems to come alive when they are at their best. Her eyes light up, she becomes more animated, and she seems close and interested. The child feels ecstatically happy. But then, when mediocrity pops up in another situation, it's hard to get mom's attention.

Children need to know that they are special even when they aren't special. All children fail or simply don't excel at lots of things. This can be due to lack of effort, ability, opportunity, or a combination of all three. They need to know that mother is happy for them when they shine, but that her love and pride in them is a constant, whether or not they shine.

The parts mom doesn't like. Believe it or not, kids have aspects that mother simply may not be attracted to! (Just kidding, it's really easy to believe.) Sometimes due to mom's own issues, the child's issues, or mom's particular taste and style, the child may do or be things that mom doesn't like.

For example, a quiet, introspective mother may be raising a naturally aggressive child—the kid would rather play shoot-'em-up than read a book in mom's lap. This is not a good or bad part of the child, it's just "not mom." Mother's task is to accept these parts of her child, to connect as best she can with them, and to love and limit them, rather than withdrawing or condemning them because they're not her style.

The bad parts. **Some of a child's parts aren't just negative but sinful, covetous, and self-centered. These character traits are destructive in the child, and the child needs help dealing with them.**

Just like with any other part, our bad parts need relationship to change. While mother still calls good "good" and bad "bad," she makes it okay to have badness, and she deals with it. While mom doesn't pretend the bad parts aren't there, she doesn't condemn the child. And she helps her child bring the bad parts to her, to safe people, and to the cross of Christ, where they are forgiven.

OUR NEED FOR INTEGRATION

Children need someone who can relate to both their feelings of love and hate about themselves and the world. Since mom's primary job is to love, it's difficult for her to tolerate the intense hatred her child feels for her at times. Yet children desperately need mom to connect to their hatred as well as their loving feelings.

When mom can deal with both kinds of feelings in her child, the two parts begin to *integrate.* The child's love is tempered with reality, and her hatred is tempered with closeness. She develops the ability to be ambivalent—to feel both love and hate in her relationships. This deepens and enriches her capacity for mature love and connections.

But when mother insists that her child always be "positive and loving," love and hate remain split for the child. She can't develop whole relationships with herself or others; people are either good guys or bad guys, with no in-between.

"Stop being negative," my friend Jean chided me. "You need to be more positive."

"Jean, I've had sniffles and body aches for three days," I told her. "While that may be negative, it's also reality. What would you prefer I tell you about a 'true negative' or a 'false positive'?"

Jean thought for a second. "A false positive," she said. "It's less depressing." While Jean may have simply tired of hearing me talk about my cold, she needed to acknowledge the "down" parts of the world as well as the "ups." We stopped talking about my cold, and I tried to sneeze more softly, so as not to disturb her positive thoughts.

OUR NEED FOR FORGIVENESS

Many of a child's parts need a mom's forgiveness. Children lack the ability to deal with their own, or anyone else's, imperfections. Their tendency is to deny imperfection, judge it, or try to earn love back as penance for being bad. Children are unable to understand how they can hurt others and still be connected.

Mother becomes a model for the forgiveness process. She confronts her child on his destructive behaviors, yet stays close. She doesn't make him perform his way back to the attachment. She "cancels the debt," as forgiveness dictates: "Be kind and compassionate to one another, forgiving each other, just as in Christ God forgave you."[4] Jimmy may need to pay for the broken window, but he is still connected to Mom's forgiving love.

In the same way, mom helps her child learn to forgive others for their transgressions. She teaches him to give up his wishes for revenge when friends fail him and helps him learn to deal with them as real and imperfect people.

OUR NEED TO LEARN TO GRIEVE

When we are faced with our own failings, or others' failings toward us, our first tendency is to try to fix things. We get angry, or busy, or demanding. Sometimes things get better, and sometimes they don't. But when things don't get better, we are faced with the reality of *loss*. People leave us, we miss opportunities, and we fail our own ideals of who we thought we were.

In order to deal with and resolve loss, badness, and failure, children need to learn to *grieve*. Grief is the process of letting go of that which we can't keep. It ultimately enables us to receive that which we can't lose—comforting relationships that sustain and support us in our sadness. The good mother helps the child learn to weep, receive comfort, and say good-bye to his losses. She doesn't devalue the losses by saying, "Look on the bright side," or "The election wasn't that important anyway." She weeps with her children when they weep and mourns with them when they mourn. And her child learns to let go and move on in life.

REAL ME AND IDEAL ME

We all have two "me's," or emotional pictures of ourselves, in our heads. One is the *real me*—the self that actually is. This self is composed of our traits, characteristics, strengths, and weaknesses and is who we are in reality. The other is the *ideal me*. This is the person we would like to be. The ideal self involves all of our dreams, aspirations, and goals—who we want to become. This might include character, relationship, and career ideals.

The accepting mother is aware of both of these parts of her child. She loves and nurtures both, and she helps the child live in the "real me," while using the "ideal me" as a goal. That's the purpose of ideals, to give us something good to aspire to. But she lets her child know that she loves the real self more than the ideal self.

When a mother makes the fatal mistake of loving the ideal over the real, of preferring the child who "should be," the child does the same to himself. He tries to be perfect and to "have it together" to keep mom close and involved. Being ideal becomes the "minimum daily requirements" for him—a demand rather than a goal.

BEING "GOOD ENOUGH"

It's not enough for the child to be aware of her real self. We can know about ourselves and yet be in despair about the painful parts of those realities. Our real self needs also to be a *good enough self*. This doesn't mean "good enough" in the sense of performing to be loved. Rather, it means the opposite: as we respond to our mother's acceptance of all our parts, we develop a sense that, because of that love, we feel "good enough." More than that, our mother's love lays to rest the entire "Am I good or bad?" issue. We are not good or bad—we are loved.

GOOD SHAME

We all need a particular sense of shame that makes us aware of our failure to be the kind of person we'd like to be. We call this "good shame." It helps us see where we've fallen short of the mark, and yet it doesn't condemn us. People who are concerned about doing the right thing experience good shame. People who are unconcerned about doing the right thing experience no shame. "Yet the unrighteous know no shame."[5] This kind of shame is different than what is called toxic, or destructive, shame. Toxic shame is the kind we experience when we feel our badness is too bad to be loved. Good shame preserves our loved state, while toxic shame destroys it. With good shame, being loved is not even an issue; it's a given. Good shame is an early warning signal that tells us to look at how we've failed to love or how we've behaved irresponsibly. It alerts us to look at our destructive actions and attitudes and prods us to deal redemptively with them.

The good mother helps her child detoxify the bad shame and shows her how to experience the effects of good shame. She shows the child the "person she can be," the "person she is," and the distance between those two positions. She lets the child experience the shame of that distance without any loss of love. Good shame motivates the child to reach more of her potential.

ADMIRATION VS. LOVE

Children need to learn to distinguish between admiration and love. These may seem the same, but they are quite different. When we admire someone, we are impressed by that person's strengths and good points. Admiration places the other on a pedestal. But, as it does so, it also puts distance between the two people. You can't get close to a person you admire.

When you love someone, however, you love the whole person, good and bad points. Love is a moving toward the entire soul of the loved. *While you can't admire someone's failings, you can love them.*

The accepting mom loves the whole child and admires the admirable qualities. She has a realistic view of his positive and negative traits, and helps him keep his feet planted firmly on the ground about himself. "Think of yourself with sober judgment."[6] She restrains herself from seeing her child as a superstar in everything he does. In this way, she protects him from an addiction to praise and strokes that he often fails to gain in the real world. She motivates him through love and consequences, and he becomes immune to the seductions of flattery.

THE TWO BREAKDOWNS IN ACCEPTANCE

When mom can't accept and deal with the "bad" parts of her child, she tends to use one of two different approaches, both of which break down the child's ability to deal with, forgive, and integrate the good and bad parts together.

Denial. Some mothers have difficulty admitting that these bad parts exist. They would rather pretend that Junior has no problems or negative parts. They may do this actively or passively.

The actively denying mom clearly states, "You're not really sad (or mad or bad)," or "Your bad grades aren't your fault, it's that horrible school." She denies either the negative things or the child's responsibility for the negative things. The passively denying mom minimizes the bad things and diverts attention away from them. She may make statements such as, "This problem will pass if you just ignore it," or "Think about good things." Either way, Junior is forced to deny some realities about himself or take those realities to other people besides mom.

Judgment. The second destructive approach moms bring to bad parts of their children is judgment. Judgment is an attitude of condemnation. It does more than state that something is "bad." That isn't judgment, that's evaluation. Judgment, in the sense that I am using it, withdraws relationship from and adds hate to the condemned part. It says, "This part of you is too bad to be loved. I will not connect this part of you to my love but to my wrath." The child then internalizes this wrath and feels condemned every time this part of him emerges.

This is why so many people feel guilty and hated whenever they disagree, are assertive, or make mistakes. These parts of them have an intensely critical "mom-memory" attached to them. They can't experience these aspects of themselves without self-hatred also emerging.

RESULTS OF "TROPHY" MOTHERING

If you had a Trophy Mom, you may be experiencing some of the following symptoms:

Relational Signs

Performing for Others

Adult children of Trophy Moms are often driven to keep their best foot forward in their relationships. In fact, their best foot is their only foot. They work hard to keep the other person happy and not disappointed with them. They are constantly on the alert against making mistakes in their attachments and exposing their imperfections.

While striving to keep from hurting our friends is a worthy cause, the performing individual isn't as concerned about hurting others as he is about being liked, avoiding others' anger, and being seen as a good person. These people are intensely shame-driven (the toxic kind) and live in fear of others discovering their real self.

Those who hold out the "good self" as the only self usually have a dark side to their relational self. They are "good" with their "good" friends, but they also have a set of "bad" friends with whom they can be imperfect and real. These performers dread the day these two sets of friends meet: "Pastor Smith, I'd like to introduce you to Hell's Angel Jones" is their worst nightmare.

"Appreciate Me Now and Avoid the Rush"

When mother both ignores the bad and fails to limit the grandiose, her child may develop what is called *narcissism.* Narcissists are self-centered and need to be treated as special, rather than simply unique, as God created us. "I am fearfully and wonderfully made"[7] is the psalmist's recognition of how individually and painstakingly God the Master Craftsman has designed each of us. But it doesn't say that we are spared from having to stand in the back of the line at the movie theater.

The narcissistic child is demanding and seeks to be special in all situations and relationships. Being ordinary, mediocre, and average are intolerable for her. She becomes the kind of adult who is addicted to praise and flattery from an audience of thousands.

This dynamic is especially destructive in marriages, as the narcissistic individual expects her spouse to applaud her specialness in the same adoring way that mom did. The spouse will try hard to appreciate the other's achievements and efforts, but it is never enough. The narcissist is insatiable, a "black hole" of needs for affirmation that no amount of validation can slake. It is as if the narcissist needs her spouse to become her mirror, reflecting her glory for all to see.

The narcissist's spouse often seeks therapy before the narcissist does. The spouse burns out in his admiring role and becomes depressed or withdrawn. He gives up, while the narcissist continues to feel entitled to special treatment and is convinced that the problem is that "my spouse just doesn't understand me." The reality is that perhaps the spouse understands only too well and has given up trying to be the new, improved Trophy Mom.

"The Human Mirror"

The children of Trophy Moms not only need constant mirroring *from* others, but they also need constantly to give mothering *to* others. These people are trapped in an ongoing pattern of flattery, praise, and needing to bring out the "good" in others. And they tend to be attracted to the narcissistic types in the previous section.

"What is wrong with being affirming and positive?" you might ask. Absolutely nothing. In fact, we are to think about whatever is praise-worthy.[8] But the Human Mirror does two things: First, she affirms the grandiose self; and, second, she denies the imperfect self. Under the guise of being "encouraging," she actually prevents others from the realities they need to confront in order to change and grow.

The Human Mirror suffers from a disguised form of narcissism. She needs superstars and specialness, but not directly. She gets it in the people she mirrors. Her hope is that their glory will reflect back on her. That's why her friends, coworkers, and relatives are the "best people in the world." She redirects her own entitlement at others without having to own it.

Functional Signs

Perfectionism

Perfectionistic tendencies soon show up in adult kids of Trophy Moms. Because of the internal demand to be good and perfect and the fear of being bad, these people tend to operate with little or no room for mistakes. They will sometimes function at high levels, becoming surgeons, business leaders, or lawyers. At other times, they are so paralyzed by the fear of making a mistake that they are unable to achieve any career goals. The learning curve that comes from taking risks is just too painful to tolerate. The bright, energetic under-achiever who just can't finish creative projects is a good example of what the child of a Trophy Mom looks like.

When Work Is Not a Stage

The adult child of a Trophy Mom will take his expectations of praise and mirroring into the workplace. Because mom has praised and admired all his achievements, real-life work is often a major disappointment.

Dan, in the beginning of the chapter, is an example. His career life didn't pan out as Mom or he had expected. Dan is one of those people who has eight cylinders but only runs on two. Though he was law school material, he never made it past his bachelor's degree. He went to work in sales. He was good with people, but he had experienced serious letdowns at work.

When Dan would close a sale, he would rush to bring the numbers to his boss, expecting a celebration. But his boss would only look at him quizzically, then say, "Good job, I guess. Get back out and do it again." Dan would feel crushed and disappointed. There was no mom to go wild over his touchdown.

Hiding Failure

When Dan would lose an account, a different dynamic would emerge. First, he would attempt to conceal his mistakes. Then, when he was discovered, he would gloss over them, saying, "No problem, it's just a misunderstanding." As things progressed, it would become clear that Dan had indeed failed. When he was confronted, he would blow up, yelling about how the account, his boss, or both didn't understand him and how hard he worked. Dan was unable to confess failure, learn from the consequences, and move on in his career.

Emotional Signs

Depression

It is common for adult children of Trophy Moms to become depressed. As they encounter failures in their personal and work lives, the reality begins to emerge that they won't be living the ideal life they had expected. Unhappy marriages, divorce, problems with children, and career upsets fly in the face of their dreams. They lack the coping skills to deal with failure, and so depression ensues—a symptom of their despair about how they've turned out: "Hope deferred makes the heart sick."[9] Their grandiose hopes have been deferred one too many times, and they are heartsick.

Anxiety, Shame, and Guilt

It is no picnic to bear the Trophy burden. The Trophy Mom's child is constantly anxious that she will fail mom, others, and herself. She feels everyone's expectations are riding on her, and she is laden with shame and guilt as she frantically tries to be perfect. In her heart of hearts she knows that much of her life is fraudulent; no one really knows her buried real self. She is continually tormented with how self-deceptive she has become.

Compulsions and Addictions

As we've mentioned before, compulsive and addictive behaviors can temporarily anesthetize painful realities. The grown Trophy Kid will tend to become dependent on drugs, food, sex, or any number of other substances or activities for two reasons. First, it keeps him from seeing who he really is and all the badness and failure that he can't forgive in himself. Second, problem behaviors serve as the only place he feels he can be "real." Many addicts in treatment report that the only time they feel okay without having to be perfect is in the soothing of a substance. It is as if they are finally receiving the acceptance and forgiveness that mom couldn't give, but in an impersonal form.

Spiritual Signs

The adult child of a Trophy Mom often finds it difficult to feel close and safe with God. For example, she might not be able to imagine a Creator who both knows and loves her. If he loves her, he must not really know how bad she is. And if he knows her, he must hate her.

This person's overwhelming sense of badness keeps her blinded to the light of God's forgiveness and grace. She is forever hiding in shame from his wrath, trying to be good to appease him, or wondering if he's even there. She can't see the One who has loved her "with an everlasting love"[10] and accepts her imperfections without judgment or denial. This kind of love simply takes her badness in its raw and unrefined form and gently lays it at the foot of a bloodstained cross.

Nowadays with Mom

As the child of a Trophy Mother grows up, some things change, but some things don't. Mother may still expect her little one to "make me proud," and, though he is no longer in the school play, her adult child still strives to please her.

These adult children still bring home trophies to mom, even when mom lives thousands of miles away. For example, a husband may receive a job promotion, but he is more eager to share the news with mom than he is with his wife.

Or, during marital conflicts, he runs to mother for affirmation of his goodness: "Sue said that to you? She just doesn't know how special you are!" He thinks he is gaining "support"; he is unaware that he is leaving the person who loves the real him for someone who admires the false him.

Some adult children of Trophy Moms feel betrayed by them. "Make me proud" deteriorates to "I thought I knew you." The adult child's real-life failures and struggles are now apparent, and mom can neither deny nor excuse them. She is, instead, deeply disappointed that her child's life goal of giving her positive self-esteem hasn't been met. Attempts to connect with mom turn into grim reminders of how the divorce, flunking out of the MBA program, or losing that job have wounded her. So the adult child remains the "bad" kid forever, even until late adulthood. It becomes impossible to reconcile who he is with who mom intended him to be.

FOR ALL THE TROPHY KIDS

If you, or someone you love, has had a Trophy Mom, the next chapter will show you the steps to repair the problems, as well as complete what was left unfinished in your own mothering. We all need to mature into real, good and bad, loved and reconciled adults, who then give this reconciliation to others.

Chapter Nine

Getting Real

It was a moment of change for Cliff and one that I (Dr. Cloud), as an onlooker, will never forget. Cliff's gaze was directed at the floor; in his shame, he was unable to look at the group members. As Cliff's therapist, I already knew about his struggle, and I waited now for him to tell the others.

He kept his eyes down, but he finally began to talk. "I don't know how to say this, but there is something I need to confess," he said. "I am addicted to pornography."

I watched the group. They were motionless and quiet.

"I know this is not what you expected of me," he continued, "and I feel awful about it, but I had to tell someone." He began to cry, and he slumped down further in his seat as he continued to tell his story.

I looked around the room at all of the compassionate and caring faces. A few group members even had tears in their eyes. His confession of his longtime struggle, of his inability to break his habit, of the way he felt afterward, was drawing them closer to him, and I could feel a strong sense of empathy in the room.

But Cliff could neither sense their empathy or compassion nor see it, for he was looking down, caught up in his own guilt and shame. I decided that since the group's care was what he needed, I would intervene. "Cliff," I said, "I want you to look up."

"I can't," he said. "I can't." His shame was overwhelming. He strongly resisted looking at the others, but I kept after him, knowing that he would only find compassion if he did. Slowly he raised his head and checked out the group members one by one. His eyes moved from person to person, and I watched a transformation take place inside of him. He became more connected as he could see their compassion and lack of condemnation.

He began to cry, but it was a different kind of cry. He was truly letting go, releasing all of the pain and shame that had been bothering him for so long.

As he slowly stopped weeping, I sensed that he had come out of prison. As a pastor, Cliff's sexual acting out was particularly difficult for him to admit and talk about; he had held it in for a long time. What had happened here was that all of the parts he had felt so bad about were accepted by the others. The power of isolation was broken. And he had discovered something else that was crucial to his future: *He did not have to be perfect to be loved.*

This was a totally new experience for Cliff. All of his life he had worked hard to be perfect in order to gain the love he needed. As we saw in the past chapter, those with Trophy Moms have a split inside their personalities. The "good self" on the outside tries to live up to the requirements of being a "trophy," and the "bad self" on the inside either tries to hide or finds a way to act out.

But by confessing to the group, Cliff was turning all of that around. He was starting to bring his "badness into the light," and the effect would prove to be very powerful in his life. Shortly thereafter, his compulsion began to lose its control over him. He had found something in the group that his mothering had lacked. He had found acceptance for his less than perfect parts, and so now he could begin to be much more accepting of his own inadequacies, while at the same time finding more answers for them. In the process, he was getting better.

In this chapter, we will look at how to repair trophy mothering. And along the way, you will find tremendous growth.

THE DEATH NO ONE WANTS TO EXPERIENCE

"And the LORD God said, 'The man has now become like one of us, knowing good and evil. He must not be allowed to reach out his hand and take also from the tree of life and eat, and live forever.' So the LORD God banished him from the Garden of Eden to work the ground from which he had been taken. After he drove the man out, he placed on the east side of the Garden of Eden cherubim and a flaming sword flashing back and forth to guard the way to the tree of life."[1]

In this story, we find a sad truth: We have lost Paradise, and the door to the garden, where things are perfect, is guarded. We are unable to enter into perfection. We are unable to be perfect, to have perfect people in our lives, and to experience a perfect world. If we try to jump back into Eden, we will encounter cherubim, who will flash the flaming sword to warn us that any attempt to enter will be thwarted.

Oh, but how we try! Makeup, plastic surgery, small white lies, image management, material possessions, achievement, membership in the right groups, clubs, or churches—all of these can be our attempts to be perfect. But in reality, all are doomed to fail. The cherubim will flash the sword. And if we persist, they will break us.

As we all try to get back into Eden, what do the blows of the cherubim look like? What do they feel like? What happens to us as we try to achieve perfection, to be mother's trophy? We will get a severe blow by the sword.

We have seen the blows of the sword in the previous chapter—depression, inability to function under the demands of perfectionism, and relationship problems. Every child of a Trophy Mom in some way encounters the sword and experiences death. But the question that still needs resolution is this: *Have we issued a death certificate?* The question of achieving the ideal me is a dead issue. But the funeral is still up ahead.

I spoke to a group of young professionals this week, and I threw out this question: "What do you find hardest to accept about yourself?" Some opened up about repeated failures, bad tempers, fits of impatience, procrastination, the inability to love others well and to be the person everyone wants them to be. One by one these fifteen men and women became vulnerable. After listening for a while, I asked them to tell me what it was like to answer this question. They told me they felt two emotions: sadness and relief.

The sadness was the funeral. For a brief moment, they had all stopped in their pursuit of glory to acknowledge that their individual attempts at perfection were not working; they faced the reality of who they were. A heaviness permeated the room as individually they confessed what it felt like to acknowledge that reality. One person said it well: "This is really depressing."

The depressing part was acknowledging that they could not be what their ideal self was requiring them to be. They were losing the battle. No matter how hard they tried, they could never be perfect. The room would become silent at times as we sat with that realization.

But one by one they all came to another realization: They were not alone in their struggles. They were relieved to find community in the company of other imperfect people, discovering that everyone has aspects that are not so great. They began to laugh at themselves and one another, that they had thought their failures were of such monumental importance. And they realized that togetherness was more important than perfection, the false images that they had tried to project for one another.

This is what a good funeral is supposed to look like. When someone dies or we lose something, the mourners come together and comfort one another. They find a deeper sense of support in their grief. As Jesus said, "Blessed are those who mourn, for they will be comforted."[2]

This death is the key to overcoming the effects of the Trophy Mom. The first step is to see that our symptoms are caused by trying to live up to the demands of the trophy. At some point, we must do what this group did: Face reality. Own our imperfection, pain, and failure. This common bond will bring us together to find something better than being ideal—being loved as we are. But to get there, we first must acknowledge the death of the ideal, and sign the death certificate.

Once we realize we are not going to make it back to Eden, we must find a safe community who will support us through the funeral. We need the kind of mothering spoken of in the last chapter—people who will *accept* and *correct*. We need people who will accept who we are and love us into who we need to be.

Here we are again saying that we need others to get past the problem of inadequate mothering. This will be true for fixing all the problems that we have with mother. If we did not get good enough mothering from her, we must get it from others.

What do these true friends look like? Look for the following traits in your friends or a support group:

- humility—they have acknowledged their own imperfections and no longer demand perfection from themselves
- absence of condemnation—they are able to avoid making you feel worse or unacceptable for who you are
- absence of denial—they are able to face the reality of your badness, weakness, and imperfection
- ability to confront—they possess the courage to tell you what they see
- acceptance—they embrace and love you where you are

As we choose our support people, we generally make two kinds of mistakes. First, we find people with the same demands for perfection our mother had, and thus repeat the theme of trying to become a trophy. Or second, we find people who are *too* comfortable with their imperfections and who are unable to confront us with the problems we need to look at. A good mother does not demand perfection, but neither does she let faults go unnoticed.

These are generally the kinds of misunderstandings we have about God as well. We either view him as a harsh taskmaster who demands perfection, or we see him as the all-loving grandmother who notices no evil. In reality, God is a God of both grace and truth. He accepts us as we are but wants us to be better. A relationship with God will heal the effects of a Trophy Mom.

Our mothering friends need to have both components as well. They need to accept who we are and, at the same time, confront us with where we need to change. We need mothering friends with grace and truth.

Our Response to Mothering

Cliff's story had a happy ending because he responded well to his support people. Some adult children of Trophy Moms have good mothering available to them, and they continue to thwart it.

Think for a moment of the compassion Cliff's group members showed to him. Or the acceptance of each other I saw in the group of young professionals. Good mothering only "worked" in these groups because Cliff and the others availed themselves of it by opening up and letting others know them. Good mothering will only work for us if we're able to reach and receive it.

OUR PART IN OVERCOMING BEING A TROPHY

1. Join

We must find an individual or a group where the traits of good enough mothering are present. Trophy deaths do not occur in a vacuum.

2. Confess

"Confess your faults one to another, and pray one for another, that ye may be healed."[3] The Greek word that is translated "faults" here in the book of James is one that encompasses both our willful transgressions and our unintentional ones. In other words, "whatever is lacking." We need others to know us. We need acceptance. We need forgiveness. We need love. But these things can only "get in" to our souls if we confess.

Confess what? The Greek word for *confess* means to "agree." We simply need to agree with the reality and the truth of who we really are. As we agree with the truths about ourselves that others bring to us, our demand for perfection goes down. And then healing can begin. Confession is good for the soul. It is God's way of lancing the wounds and infections that we may be carrying around inside us.

3. Process Negative Feelings and Losses

Oftentimes, the Trophy Mom refuses to let her child have negative feelings and admit losses and failures. Guilt, shame, failure, and pain are emotions the "ideal" person is not supposed to feel. The Trophy Mom wants her child to feel good, positive, above it all—free from pain and disappointment.

But if we want to become all that we can be this side of Eden, we must embrace the sadness of the lost ideal, the pain of the hurts we have experienced, and the anger at the demands of the trophy role. In order to bring the real self and the ideal self together, we must process feelings of all kinds.

At some point, you must get in touch with the pain of your lost real self—that part of yourself that has been isolated for so long, with its resulting anger and sadness. As you make available to your support people the entirety of your being, you can embrace and feel these feelings, and when these feelings are felt and loved by others, your real self will be integrated into the whole.

4. Rework the Ideal

Adult children of Trophy Moms have a picture of their ideal self that is not even human. Their ideal self does not feel normal human feelings like weakness, fear, inadequacy, sexuality, or anger. So the problem is not only that they feel unable to live up to their ideal self. It is that their ideal self is wrongly constructed in a number of ways.

In the presence of our safe people, we can discover what real humanity is and construct a realistic ideal. We can even begin to value our weakness and helplessness. We begin to understand that our feelings of powerlessness are part of the normal human condition. We see that it is normal to struggle with temptation, sinfulness, and vulnerability. So we rework our ideal; we integrate our real self into our ideal self to become a person of integrity. We can be who we are, while striving to become a better real person—not that person the Trophy Mom tried to create.

5. Learn to Love Less Than the Ideal

Adult children of Trophy Moms can have a deep disdain for imperfection in others, which they learned from their mother. They may act nice and accommodating on the outside, but their deep contempt for others' imperfections can block true intimacy and community. In the context of real people and good mothering, however, these people can learn to accept others as well as themselves. Growth in the ability to love and accept as they are goes a long way in overturning the internal demands and philosophy of the Trophy Mom. And then the ability to love others translates into the ability to accept oneself.

6. Challenge Distorted Thinking

If you had a Trophy Mom, you may have distortions in your thinking—negative thought patterns, critical evaluation of yourself and others, and pessimism in your outlook on the future, to name a few. Keep track of how you think. Your automatic thought patterns keep you in an internal critical relationship with mom; they need to be challenged and adjusted so that your evaluations are more realistic. The mothering that we receive from others can help in this process.

7. Accept Failure

No one likes failure, but trophy people can't stand it. To overcome the demand of the Trophy Mom and change your attitude toward failure, you must begin to see failure as a normal part of the human experience and accept it when it occurs. In order to cope with failure in the past, you may have employed any number of coping mechanisms—making excuses, blaming others, denial—anything to keep your internal equilibrium intact.

Your mothering people can help you confront your denial and the feelings of rejection that failure brings and thus reduce your fear of it. When you are confronted with your tendencies to make excuses and blame others, you can begin to deal directly with the feelings failure brings up. And you can take in the good mothering until it becomes an aspect of your self.

8. Monitor the Emotional Relationship Between the Real and the Ideal

The emotional tone of the relationship between our ideal self and our real self is internalized from our past mothering. We take our Trophy Mom's anger and condemnation into our real self, and it becomes the way we feel about our real self.

Listen to the emotional tone of your self-evaluations. Is it shaming? Angry? Condemning? Attacking? The process of changing these emotional responses is two-pronged: Check the negative responses and identify with the positive ones you are now receiving from your mothering people. It can't just come from yourself; it must come first from others, and then it becomes a part of yourself. Positive self talk is really "other talk" that becomes ours.

Do not reject this grace. Listen to the way your mothering people relate to your real self and the way that God relates. His attitudes toward you need to become your own:

> The LORD is compassionate and gracious,
>> slow to anger, abounding in love.
> He will not always accuse,
>> nor will he harbor his anger forever;
> he does not treat us as our sins deserve
>> or repay us according to our iniquities.
> For as high as the heavens are above the earth,
>> so great is his love for those who fear him;
> as far as the east is from the west,
>> so far has he removed our transgressions from us.
> As a father has compassion on his children,
>> so the LORD has compassion on those who fear him;
> for he knows how we are formed,
>> he remembers that we are dust.[4]

9. Repent

When those we trust give us negative feedback, we need to take ownership of it. A big part of ridding ourselves of the ideal demand is to take ownership of our real badness.

Our "badness" becomes less powerful when we quit denying it or running from it, and we face it directly. If you are confronted with one of your faults, confess it, but also work on changing it and becoming the best person you can be.

10. Pray

The search for the real self is ultimately a spiritual one. The apostle Paul tells us, "For by the grace given me I say to every one of you:

Do not think of yourself more highly than you ought, but rather think of yourself with sober judgment, in accordance with the measure of faith God has given you."[5] Trophy Moms teach their children to think and demand for themselves much more than God does and more than reality dictates. God tells us to think of ourselves with "sober judgment." This means to be realistic in the way we think of ourselves—neither too high, nor too low.

In prayer, we can ask God to reveal our real selves to us and to give us the courage to embrace who we are and the strength to live out of our real selves. This is a vital part of the art of becoming. "It is He who has made us, and not we ourselves."[6] We need to be in prayer, asking him to show us both our "hurtful ways,"[7] as well as our true giftedness.[8]

11. Respond to Love

We need to take in the love that God and others offer us. Sometimes we devalue the love and good mothering that others show us. Stop the "You're just saying that" response to their love and acceptance, or the "If you really knew me" kinds of remarks. Take the love at face value, and let it penetrate. You will soon experience a deep gratitude for their acceptance of who you really are.

12. Watch for Fears and Resistance

As you are loved and try to respond, you will feel fear and resistance. The real self has been alone and despised for a long time, and it will not come out of hiding without a fight. Remember, it feels the world does not really like it. Become aware of your resistance to grace and acceptance. Then embrace the fear and confess it to God and to others, and allow them to help you over your resistance.

DEALING WITH YOUR REAL MOM OF YESTERDAY

After having responded to some good mothering from those in your community of support, you have to look at the real mom of the past. The process of dealing with the Trophy Mom is similar to the process of dealing with the other moms. It involves awareness, feelings, forgiveness, and reconciliation. (Refer to chapter 5 for a description of the need for forgiveness.)

Be Aware

What kind of interactions did you have with your mother that caused you to feel like a trophy?

Find someone who understands and can give you insight into these patterns. Then learn the patterns of relating that belong to that relationship so that you can leave them behind. Otherwise, they will dominate your present relationships.

I talked to a friend the other day who was in the process of learning about some of his mother's attitudes toward his imperfections. He was new in a professional setting and feared he was not going to be liked. *They'll think I'm stupid for not knowing everything,* he told himself. But then he caught himself. *I think that is just my mother talking to me,* he said to himself. *It's not them.* He had learned to distinguish between the voices in his head and the real world "out there." In the old days he would have just avoided any interactions and kept to himself. But he remembered the real interactions he'd had with his mother and could now look at them objectively. He did not allow them to take up space in present interactions. He was aware.

Process the Hurt Feelings

You have definite feelings about your Trophy Mom and the experiences you had with her. Sometimes you feel great pain and injury because your real self was rejected. You must learn to embrace the pain and sadness and grieve your wish for her to accept you as you really are. You must process the hurt feelings so that you do not experience them in some other way in the present, transferring them onto significant others now, or turning them into clinical problems like depression or anxiety. Feel and grieve your unresolved feelings. Express your anger and sadness to someone who cares, and your brokenheartedness can be healed. Grief is the road to resolution.

Understand Her

Mom was probably not a villain. She most likely did not reject your real self just because she felt like it. She was probably under her own ideal self demands from her own mother or someone else who was significant to her. For whatever reason, she did not or could not work through those issues as you are doing now. She continued those negative patterns in her interactions with you, placing the same demands on you that she labored under herself.

To remember and try to understand mom's frailties and accept them is to begin to love her as she is. This is what you want from others and what you are required to do for your mother as well if you are going to be healed. If you can understand where she came from, what she was struggling with, what kinds of demands were on her, you will find it easier to accept her.

Forgive

An ultimate paradox exists in the forgiveness of the Trophy Mom. Forgiving the Trophy Mom is the same as the cure, and not forgiving her is the same as the sickness.

"I can't forgive her," Regina countered. "Look at what she did to me."

"What did she do?" I asked.

"She never would accept me for who I was. I couldn't be okay with her just for being 'me.'"

"And now what you are saying is that she is not okay with you just for being 'her,'" I returned. "So, you are doing the same thing to her that you will not forgive her for doing to you. Sounds to me like you want to be free from her, but now you have become just like her."

You could have cut the silence with a knife. Being accused of being like the mother she hated was the last thing Regina expected to hear. But it was true. Regina's Trophy Mom could not accept her child's imperfections, and now Regina could not accept her mom's imperfections, specifically the imperfection of being a Trophy Mom. I told her she had become a "trophy daughter," demanding the perfect mother. Seeing this became the key that enabled her to finally let it go and forgive her mother.

Remember that forgiveness is denying neither what happened nor your feelings. To truly forgive, you cannot deny or try to overlook what happened. You must acknowledge the offense in order to be free. And just because you forgive does not mean that the feelings will automatically disappear. When you do your best to forgive, don't be troubled if you still experience anger or sadness when reminded of something. It doesn't mean you haven't truly forgiven.

If you go so far as wanting to punish the offender or make them pay, then maybe you need to examine your level of forgiveness. But staying in touch with the hurt is normal. If you stabbed me with a knife today, I could probably forgive you soon by letting you off the hook, but the cut would still be sore for a while.

So, if you are letting go of past hurts that you feel in relationship to mom and surrounding yourself with strong mothering in the present, you are ready to begin dealing with mom today.

YOUR RELATIONSHIP WITH MOM TODAY

We value lifelong relationship with parents. Multigenerational relationships with extended family are the foundation of culture, morality, and society. Parents, children, and grandchildren are created for relationship with one another. Proverbs 1:22 admonishes us to "Listen to your father who begot you, And do not despise your mother when she is old." There is great wisdom in that. So, with that in mind, how good can a relationship with a Trophy Mom get? What can you hope for?

Stop Wanting Acceptance

You have grieved your longing for her to accept you as you are, good and bad. She will probably never love you unconditionally, and if you are still looking to her for what she is unable to give, then you are still in jail.

She has power over you in the present to the degree to which you still need her acceptance. But when you grieve that wish for her acceptance and get that mothering from your safe people, you can begin to love her better because you do not need anything from her anymore.

Talk It Out

The best option would be for you to talk out the issue with your mom. This approach leads to the greatest intimacy, when you can understand each other at the deepest levels. Ask yourself if this is a possibility with your mother. Some mothers can talk things out, others cannot. Some will refuse to own their side of things, and then the adult children have to relate to them on a more surface level, as we shall see.

If you do choose to approach your mother on a deeper level, you might want to say something like, "Mom, I want to talk about some things I have felt for a long time. I want a good relationship with you, but sometimes my feelings get in the way of feeling close to you." Approach her in a loving way and for the good of the relationship, not to hurt her. Chances are if she is a true Trophy Mom, she will have difficulty hearing any negatives.

Tell her how you feel. Tell her that you are afraid of not being perfect or exactly what she wants. Tell her about the pressure you feel to be "ideal" and that sometimes what she wants for you is not what you want for you, but that you still want her. Go ahead and mention the specific dynamics of perfectionism or ideal demands that hinder your relationship with her.

Tell her that you want to be friends, and so when this dynamic goes into play, you will point it out to her so the two of you can talk about it. Reaffirm your love to her and thank her for listening.

MOTHERS WHO WON'T DEAL WITH THE ISSUE

Set Limits

You have two people to think about as you begin to set limits with your mom—you and her. How much exposure to her trophy demands can you take? In the beginning, you might need to limit your exposure; it is just too painful and injurious.

Only you know how much contact is too much. I have seen adult children in very bad situations who cannot even talk to their mothers at all for a while. Others do not even miss a beat while they are working through these issues. It really depends on two things: how fragile you are feeling and how your mom is relating at the moment. This combination determines what you can and cannot do.

If you are in a fragile place, ask for emotional support in your safe community to help you through the interactions with mom. If you must go into a particularly hurtful situation with her where you feel very vulnerable, make a sandwich of the time. On one side of the interaction, talk or meet with a good friend who can prepare you. After it is over, call your friend or someone else to get put back together.

So first, set limits on yourself; know what you can handle and what you cannot. To some people this may sound very extreme, but some mothers are so hurtful and the adult child so injured that just to make a phone call can cause the adult child to have a suicidal crisis.

Second, set limits with a mom who is continuing to be hurtful. With some mothers who are not going to change in a certain area, you need to just let things slide and say, "That's just Mom." "A man's discretion makes him slow to anger, and it is his glory to overlook a transgression."[9]

If you can't let it go, set some limit on whatever is going on: "Mom, we are not here to evaluate my performance as a mother. I am not asking for your input right now. Let's do something else," or, "Mom, I am not open to criticism from you right now, let's change the subject," or, "Mom, if you don't stop criticizing me for not calling you often enough, then I am going to leave and come back another time."

It's sad to have to enforce limits, but sometimes you have to for the sake of the grandchildren, your marriage, or your sanity. Sometimes setting limits may help your mother see how she is hurting you.

Relate to Her Where She Can

Have fun and enjoy your mom in the ways she can relate. Keep your interactions with your Trophy Mom in safe areas. Talk about subjects that are out of the arena of "looking good" or "being ideal." This can be difficult because some Trophy Moms can turn grocery shopping into a performance. But if she gets off into performance, let that be her thing; you do not have to go there. Do your best to enjoy her where she can be enjoyed.

Love Her Where You Can

Love covers a multitude of sins. Every situation is different and the amount of relationship that you can have with your mom will vary. But you will be able to love her in some way. Love your Trophy Mom as best you can, but not in the ways that the trophy demands—you are finished with that. You are not trying to get something from her anymore. You are getting your acceptance from somewhere else. You are now in the giving and loving mode, not the getting mode. And the giving position is much more powerful.

CONCLUSION

You need good mothering from somewhere to be the person God created you to be. If your past mothering taught you that you could not be who you are and still be loved, then you've adopted some awful hiding and performance dynamics to help you cope. Your task is to overcome the demand to be perfect or ideal, to stop hiding from the parts that are not perfect. If you want to be healed of this dynamic, you must bring these patterns into relationship with God and other people.

Find the mothering you need. Get with people who do not need you to be their trophy. Open up and let them know you, all of you. And in the context of that safety, bring all of your parts together and work on the ones that are not okay. Accept all of yourself, and at the same time, try to get better.

Deal with your mother of the past as well as the person she is today. Grieve, forgive, and let go of the past, and create the best kind of relationship possible with your mother today. In this combination of freedom and love, the trophy can be set aside once and for all.

Chapter Ten

The Still-the-Boss Mom

 B rad and his mother, Sharon, had always been close. Through-out her son's childhood, Sharon was a loving and involved mom. She took her responsibility as a parent seriously, and more than anything, wanted to train up her "child in the way he should go."[1] She worked hard to create an environment at home in which Brad would learn the right values and attitudes and make the right choices. She wanted to impart good, sound principles and ways of thinking to her son. It was a scary world out there, and he needed to be armed and ready for it.

Sharon had definite principles, opinions, and values fixed in her mind. She had a worldview about lots of subjects: school, friendship, career, sexuality, finances, and more. She had read extensively and had reached conclusions on these matters. Sharon was not one of those wishy-washy people who don't know what they believe. She knew, stood firm, and "walked her talk."

Brad was her primary student of the "Sharon School of Thinking." Early in life, for example, she taught him that you could judge people's character by their clothes and musical tastes. The more conservative the style, the better their character. Another principle involved spiritual values: There was a "right" denomination, a "correct" translation of the Bible, and a "true" style of worship.

As long as Brad agreed with Sharon's values, things went well. Once seven-year-old Brad told his mother about his dreams to become a pilot or astronaut. She dismissed him with, "Such nonsense. Your father has a good family business, and you'll be quite success-ful in that when you're grown. You'll see." Apparently, Sharon had missed the real meaning of the above Scripture verse about the "way he should go": It refers to God's path the child should discover for himself, not the parent's preordained plan for his life.

Sharon's views on obedience to authority shaped her childrearing. She believed that life has order and that we all have bosses. The key to success is finding out the rules and then obeying them. She wouldn't stand for Brad's challenging her authority or that of his schoolteachers, coaches, and Sunday school instructors. Sharon's position was, "Obey without question. Authority is there for your good."

During the few times Brad had attempted to challenge school authority, the teachers were actually more supportive than his own mother. They seemed to understand that he was attempting, in his own awkward teenage way, to enter the adult world, and they gave him some latitude. Sharon, however, would quash his "rebellious spirit" in all forms.

Sharon could become critical and unsupportive when her son challenged her opinions. Problems arose between them when he questioned some of his mother's conclusions. One time he had asked his mom, "But what if I disagree with our political party's candidate?"

"What does a twelve-year-old know about politics?" Sharon had responded. "Just listen to me. I've spent a great deal of time researching these complicated issues."

Brad just backed off, muttering, "That's my mom." But not so loudly that she could hear. No sense upsetting her.

As Brad grew older, he went to others with his "taboo" questions. For example, he knew that she believed sex was just a necessary evil: "Men want it more than women, and wives are to endure it as part of their duty to their husbands. Teens and single adults should take cold showers and stay productive to keep from lustful thoughts and feelings." Sharon never understood the big deal about sex. To her, it was simply part of our animalistic nature and not to be succumbed to.

Sharon's answers didn't satisfy Brad, so he talked to his peers and found out more than he really wanted to know. He became sexually active during high school; however, he suffered many internal conflicts over this. He experienced intense guilt feelings over the way he was hurting his mother by his "rebelliousness." He couldn't enjoy sex the way his friends seemed to. "Free sex," for Brad, carried a high price tag.

Sharon was a good person and a well-intentioned mother. But every approach she made to Brad carried one message: "No matter how old you get, I'll always be your mother. And you'll always be my kid." And though Brad was over six feet tall by the time he was sixteen, he felt that his mother and her views were constantly towering over his immature head—that she was still the boss.

PREPARING FOR EQUALITY

A good mother does more than nurture her child. She also looks at her child through the lens of the future. That is, she constantly *sees the potential adult in this child* and behaves in a manner that elicits the grown-up from out of the kid. With mixed emotions, mom watches her sleeping child at night—especially when he is between the ages of five and eleven. She feels the joy of her child's close dependency on her. At the same time, she feels pangs of sadness; if she does her job well, her child will become a grown-up like her and won't need her care and ministrations anymore. She knows that this process, though painful, is right and good, that it is the essence of love.

The emphasis in this chapter is on the mother's responsibility to develop the child's emerging adult functions and abilities that will prepare him for life in the adult world. The good mom wants to see her son or daughter as an equal to her, or any other adult. She wants to help develop a peer and a friend, not a grown child. The Bible tells us to "in all things grow up into him who is the Head, that is, Christ."[2] To grow up means to become a mature person who maturely relates to God, self, and others in all aspects.

These needs are related to, but distinct from, other needs we mentioned in other chapters. For example, the Controlling Mom issues of chapter 6 deal with our need to separate from mom and to establish our own identity. The equality issues in this chapter deal with our introduction to the world as a functioning, mature adult. In other words, the Controlling Mom injures the essence of the personality of the child while the Still-the-Boss Mom injures the child's ability to become an autonomous, functioning adult.

This need also differs from the American Express Mom issues in chapter 12. That topic deals with the actual, physical leaving of the young adult. In our present section, we discuss the child's developmental character issues that lead to this "leaving" later in life. Below are some of the needs of this child.

Authority

Brad's mother, Sharon, was correct in thinking that there is order to life. She just overestimated her role. God has created an authority structure from himself on down. *Authority* means "expertise" or "power." Its purpose is to help govern, manage, and go about the business of living and functioning. From presidents to IRS agents to family doctors and schoolteachers, we all have our authorities in life, as well as our own roles to play. Generally, someone is above us and someone is below us in this hierarchy.

However, children start out with little authority and responsibility and must learn to gradually take on more. They are physically smaller than mom, and she tells them what to do. But she also needs to help them as they move into their place in the world of authority. In this process, the following two tasks are necessary:

Challenge

Mom needs to encourage her child to question her decisions and values. You can only become a peer with other adults if you can learn to challenge the thinking of your authority figures. It is in the process of thinking through, and struggling with, the values of your parents and other authority figures that you come to a place of knowing what your own values are.

When I was a teenager in Sunday school, a friend of mine who was questioning all his beliefs got angry at me because I seemed always to spout the "correct" answer about God and the Bible. "You're a parrot of your parents," he told me. I considered that and had to agree. I had never questioned my parents' spiritual teachings. My friend helped me to begin to challenge what I had been taught and to think through these issues for myself. It made for some interesting dinner table conversations!

Challenging also involves rebelling against improper authorities. For example, the boss at work may be in charge of our work hours, but our morality and ethics aren't under his control. So, if the boss asks us to do something illegal, we need to repudiate his authority and obey a higher law. The good mother isn't threatened by her child's challenges and questions but welcomes them. She knows her child is attempting to work out his readiness for adult life. Mother's constant question should be, *Is this helping my child make decisions when I'm not around?*

Submission

Conversely, we are to move beyond the stage of perpetual challenge and protest to an acceptance of our place in the world of authority. This means giving up the wish to be our own idol and submitting to the appropriate overseers of life. It means realizing, as Bob Dylan's song goes, "You gotta serve somebody." This may mean a governmental agency, a church leader, a supervisor, or the highway patrolman who pulls us over to ticket us for speeding.

Mother teaches her child submission to authority by her own submission to the rules of life. She refuses to constantly gripe about her unfair boss. She pays her taxes and adheres to the structures of the church she has chosen of her own free will. In addition, she also asserts her own authority. She sets house rules and expects them to be obeyed. At the same time, the good mother gradually and progressively allows her child more and more authority and responsibility. "Because I'm the mommy" may work for a two-year-old, but it doesn't help a fourteen-year-old get ready for college dilemmas.

When mom teaches her child to both question and accept authority, she helps him avoid the two destructive extremes: the fearfully compliant people-pleaser who needs constant parental approval and the rebellious protester who can't keep a job that involves working under someone.

Values

Children need to learn good from bad and right from wrong. Teaching core values is a major parental responsibility: "These commandments that I give you today are to be upon your hearts. Impress them on your children. Talk about them when you sit at home and when you walk along the road, when you lie down and when you get up."[3] Children are an "information sponge." They are curious about their world and want to learn about it. They feel secure and in control with the data and look to mom as their central source of knowledge. The observant mother directly teaches her child everything from art to zoology.

Thinking. Mom must teach her child to think for himself. While teaching content is important, it may be more important to teach a child *how* to think. In fact, whenever possible, a mother should frustrate the child's wish for a direct answer to all questions and help him think through, within his ability, how to get information. A nine-year-old who wants to know the difference between spiders and ants can be taught how to look it up.

Additionally, a mother helps her child *think critically.* She encourages inquisitiveness and helps develop the "why" muscle. Mothering can never exhaustively cover all topics of information, values, and growth. Nor should it. The child needs to learn how to observe, check new information against what he already knows, and either reject it or incorporate it. For example, her son may need to learn how to evaluate whether or not his friends are good for him or are mean to him, and how to decide what a friend is. For mom, this means that a "wrong" answer the child has struggled with and owns might be preferable to a "right" answer she fed him via a lecture. In our work with college students, we see over and over which type of answers last into early adulthood.

This is especially true in the spiritual realm. God has no grandchildren. Mom can teach, train, and model her relationship with God, but she can't make her child have a relationship with God. This is between God and the child, as each of us must make our own journey to him. *God will ultimately be the child's only parent.* The mother who can both support the process as well as teach the spiritual issues is preparing her child for that journey. Many destructive teachings in the world today masquerade as spiritual lessons. Children need their own tools to discern the doctrines and ideas that are true and those that aren't.[4]

Talents

To prepare for the adult world, children need to both become aware of and develop their unique gifts, talents, and abilities: "Each one should use whatever gift he has received to serve others, faithfully administering God's grace in its various forms."[5] We all have valuable gifts to offer. When we know what these gifts are, we have a way to give something to the world, and we can then find our place in society.

It's easy to underestimate mother's role in this process. We think that if the parent simply gives the child opportunities at lots of things, he will eventually latch on to what he's good at. For example, give him an art class, get him into sports, and encourage him in the subjects in which he excels. Actually, it is much more complex than that.

When the mother does provide these opportunities, she must also help the child avoid his natural tendency to pursue interests that please or interest her. The child wants to make mom happy. But what he really needs is a mom who is happy that her child is developing talents that he himself values. Mom may prefer her son become an opera singer, but the child is gifted in teaching. The child's talents are the ones to encourage.

A child may resist the discipline a talent requires. As Thomas Edison said, "Genius is 1% inspiration and 99% perspiration." Most five-year-olds would rather draw with watercolors than solve math problems. They may have a talent for math but simply not want to do the work that developing that skill requires. Mothers must draw a fine line here. They are to encourage the child's real, inborn talents, and at the same time not discourage the child by forcing him to give his life to something for which he has not yet developed the gifts. They must help the child structure himself, practice, and work hard at things he both values and excels in. The fruit of this work is an adult who is skilled, disciplined, and grateful for his contributions to the world. This is the key to a work ethic, career aims, and many other job skills.

Gender Roles

Preadolescent children are developing their sex roles. The daughter becomes competitive with her mother, as she tests her own power and control. She will tend to be jealous of mom's closeness with dad and want to be his special girl. Mom needs to gently help her daughter understand that dad and mom belong to each other, but that a world of boys waits somewhere out there for her. The girl learns to win, not by beating mom out for dad, but by identifying with mom's feminine qualities.

The son will, in turn, vie for mom's attention by competing with dad. Now it's dad's responsibility to help his son forfeit this battle and turn his attention to the girls in his peer group. Mom's task here is to resist the temptation to make her son more special than her husband. She can let the boy know that while she loves him, she's in love with dad. In this way, rather than competing with other men, her son learns to identify with masculine roles and qualities.

Mom's responsibility continues as her children continue to develop in their gender roles. Little girls identify with mother as a woman; they want to be nurturing and warm but still strong and definite. The mother can welcome her daughter's desire to be more like her and model healthy femininity. Little boys need to learn that they are different from mom. She can help her son by gently and gradually guiding him into more and deeper contact with dad. Mom also welcomes the "boyishness" that separates the genders.

Friendships

In order to enter the adult world, children must learn to connect to people other than mom. They need to know how to relate to both sexes, people of different ages, and different types of individuals. The reality is that they will spend most of their lives dealing with people their own age. They need to begin taking the emotional investments they have made in their relationship with mom and dad and put them into what will one day be their own family, friends, church relationships, coworkers, and support networks. Mother must actively help her child make these friendships, though they are the same ones he will use to eventually leave her.

This was brought home to me recently when I (Dr. Townsend) was at dinner with my wife and two boys, Ricky, then five, and Benny, then three. As we discussed the boys' day at preschool, Ricky was full of talk about his buddies and their exploits. But when Barbi asked Benny about Steven, a classmate of his, he asked, "Does he talk to me?" Benny didn't even realize that Steven was his friend. At three, Mom was the center of his universe, but it doesn't last much longer than that. Dad, siblings, and friends begin to become important to the child as they form the springboard of relationships that will eventually propel him into the grown-up world.

Adolescence

As late childhood comes to an end, the teen years begin, and the child is caught between two very different islands of life: *childhood,* where the kid feels enormous need for, looks up to, and identifies with mom; and *adulthood,* where the one-time child is now an equal with mom. Adolescence is a transitional period; the child is leaving the first and moving into the second. Since it is by definition transitional, it is also tumultuous and confusing for teen and mom alike.

We will deal with the specific physical tasks of preparing for adulthood in chapter 12, such as the move into the world outside the family, reality limits versus parental limits, and financial issues. For now, however, our focus is on the developmental aspects of leaving childhood. The child is beginning the shift from a one-down relationship to an equal one. The teen is older than a child, as well as larger, more aware, more educated, and more willful. She feels restless; she is about to leave the protective safety of "mom knows best" to go out into the real world.

Since, however, she is neither child nor adult, she struggles with tremendously conflicting feelings. She will be dependent on mom one minute, and the next, see mom as a prison warden. She will be insecure about her readiness to handle boys and work one minute, and abruptly in the next minute, be confident that she knows everything.

She needs these transitional years to gradually work out these feelings and parts of herself, to integrate into both mature dependence and independence, and to prepare herself for adulthood, yet be realistic about her limitations.

This all translates into yet another task for mother: She must change along with her child's needs from parenting by *control* to parenting by *influence*. After age twelve or so, the child isn't helped to become independent through parental control. Mom still needs to set limits and consequences, but they must be much more based in reality. Time-outs no longer work, but receiving an F in math with no parental rescuing might. Because that's how the real world operates. At this stage mom must evaluate everything she does with her teen in the light of *leaving*. This is why mothers who are continually trying to recreate the cozy nest of the six-to-eleven-year-old will have problems. Those days are over, and in only a few short years, the teen will be paying bills, looking for a job, and dealing with spiritual, moral, sexual, and career questions.

The mother of the adolescent needs to accept this challenging, questioning, and pushing against limits as a positive thing and understand that it's better for her child to hash this out now with mom, than later outside the safety of the home. The good mother doesn't have "taboo" subjects; she welcomes and initiates discussion on money, love, spirituality, culture, and work. She knows which battles to fight and which to let go of. The rule of thumb here is that *character takes precedence over style*. The teen can wear baggy pants, but his grades must be acceptable. He can find a church youth group that fits his culture, not yours, just as long as he is in some sort of mutually agreed-on spiritual activity.

Mother needs tremendous inner resources during these years. She must be secure enough in her opinions that disagreement with her child is stimulating, not frightening. She must be able to welcome differences with her child. At the same time, she must keep a firm hold on issues of responsibility and accountability, and stay age-consistent in the boundaries she sets for her child. All the time she is gradually loosening her hold, allowing the child to become more and more responsible.

This is not a time in which motherhood is revered or respected. It is not a time of receiving gratitude from the child. Nor should it be. The chumminess and awe that a child has always felt toward mom's love and wisdom is replaced by distance and competition. The child who yelled in delight, "That's my mom!" when she drove up to pick him up after school, now says in embarrassment, "Can't you pick me up at the corner?"

It is a difficult process. And it is even more difficult because mother bears this process within herself. She is the laboratory for the child to become an adult, and it takes its toll on her. The good mother gets her needs for love, affection, and respect met by God and the safe people in her life. Only in this way can she altruistically and sacrificially do the best thing for the child, who desperately needs safe passage toward adulthood.

RESULTS OF STILL-THE-BOSS MOTHERING

Several signs indicate that the child of a Still-the-Boss Mom has had problems moving into the grown-up years.

Relational Signs

This person has difficulty relating to others as equal adults. The difficulty looks different in different people. A person can have one or more of the following:

One-Down Style

The person with this style persistently feels inferior to others. She feels incapable of making competent, adult decisions in life and consequently defers to others. She may fear creating envy in others by showing that she is even a little talented, intelligent, or strong. She is afraid of losing others' approval, so she complies to gain approval. Often, she will experience a fear of success, though she may have the resources to be successful. She may suffer a string of work and love failures, as well as the inability to reach her potential.

The one-down person doesn't feel like an adult in the adult world. Bosses, spouses, and friends can easily make him feel that they are superior to him and that he needs them to think for him. He is often rule-bound; that is, he only feels secure when he knows the regulations. At work, he is afraid to take creative risks or confront others' ideas. While he may feel competitive with others, he suppresses these feelings and instead complies. He will often follow authoritative "guru" types as a way to avoid thinking for himself, and he will strive to win the leader's approval.

One-Up Style

While the person stuck in one-down relationships is always playing the child, another twist is the one-up relationship. This person has adopted a superior role and aspires to lead and control others. Actually, she also feels one down but compensates with a one-up style of relating. She identifies with the parental role in order to manage her childlike feelings.

The one-up style is impossible to relate to on a peer level. She is critical and condescending with those below her at work and can also be that way in friendship and love. She has to have the last word and is authoritarian on her views. It is her way or the highway. She resents it when others disagree with her and stays away from people who will confront her. Instead, she is a "chief looking for some Indians." Often competent and accomplished, the one-up person still strives to stay ahead of others and is very competitive.

Sometimes these two styles combine at work. With those above her, the one up is subservient and people-pleasing. But with those below, she is demanding and demeaning. Because of this, she often gets high marks from supervisors and low ratings from underlings, who resent her control.

These people tend to parent others in their personal relationships. They are huge advice-givers and suggesters. In the name of caring, they take control of and dominate others, plan everyone's evening, run the household, and hold forth on their views to a captive audience.

Rebellious Style

This third style is also at heart a one-down relationship. However, this individual's resentment of parental authority has emerged and has overcome his fear of disapproval. Developmentally, this can be a sign of progress, as he now has more access to his aggressive energy and can think more independently as he moves into adulthood. Still, he has major relational problems.

The rebellious style resists all types of rules and authorities. He sees bosses, parents, teachers, and other experts as controlling and abusive to his freedom to be himself. He can't work within a hierarchical structure without conflicting with superiors, and so he often migrates from position to position, saying, "The boss had it in for me."

He opines about the lack of respect and freedom he gets, but he doesn't earn those by being responsible. The rebel is in a state of perpetual protest. He knows what he doesn't want, much more than what he does want. In this way, he proves his lack of adulthood. The rebel still defines himself by the parent. He still needs a parent to react to and bounce off of. This is a sign of his immaturity.

Functional Signs

It follows that these "not-quite adults" might also have problems in goals, success, and general functioning. They are, in one form or another, obsessed with the parent. Either they are (1) afraid of disapproval, (2) attempting to be parental, or (3) hating all parents. This gets in the way of life's many tasks.

Most adults set goals in jobs, relationships, and spiritual life, but this person may anxiously worry that he is setting the "right" goals. He is more concerned about what others think of his goals than whether they are really "his" goals—ones he owns for himself. To "seek first his kingdom and his righteousness"[6] is impossible, as he is not free to seek his divine parent.

This "child in an adult's body" often has a problem with follow-through. He may set many good and healthy goals in life, then systematically sabotage them. As he gets closer to his promotion or to getting a certain woman's attention, he becomes anxious and confused and sometimes paralyzed. He is afraid that attaining his goal might mean that he is equal to mom, a position he can't tolerate. To be equal to mother might mean to incurring her competitive envy, disapproval, and withdrawal. It is far safer to stay a little boy, so as not to incur her wrath.

The rebel also tends to have follow-through problems. For him, achieving a meaningful goal means he is identifying too closely with the parent. So the Rhodes Scholar continues to work in a car wash. In his mind, at least he hasn't "sold out." But, in reality, he has sold his birthright for a bowl of stew.

Emotional Signs

Anxiety and depressive problems are common among the "not-quite-adults." These are often indicators of several dynamics, such as

- inability to be an adult in a world with adult demands
- repressed anger and sexual feelings
- guilt over intense emotions and drives
- failures in attempts to please others

In addition, these individuals often suffer from obsessive-compulsive disorders as they attempt to manage the "child" parts raging against the "parental" parts of themselves. Many will have substance problems, sexual addictions, and other compulsive and impulsive behaviors as they try to medicate this conflict. At the same time, they may experience inhibitions, sexual and otherwise. This is a sign that they are unable to integrate sexual and angry feelings, that they are unable to be in the world as adults with these feelings.

Spiritual Signs

Those who had a Still-the-Boss Mom often have a relationship with God, but they experience him in problematic ways. Some see him as a harsh, dictatorial judge. They read the Bible through that particular lens, and so the condemnation passages jump out at them. They are unable to recognize the compassion passages. Their relationship with God is based in fear and is dependent on their performance. They don't believe God could ever love them as they are. Though they desire intimacy with God, they can't feel safe with or approved by him.

Others view God in intellectualized black-and-white or legalistic ways. They learn great amounts of doctrine and theology, hoping to relate to him through their heads, as they are too afraid to relate to him with their hearts. They unceasingly search for answers about God and are unable to accept the mystery of God. The paradoxes and unknowable parts of God cause these people a great deal of anxiety. They need to control their relationships. If they can't put God in a box and keep him appeased, they run the risk of making a mistake and incurring his disapproval and wrath.

NOWADAYS WITH MOM

As she grows up, the "not-quite" adult has several problems relating to mom. For one, when mom says, "No matter how old you are, you'll always be my kid," she means it literally. And so the adult child often finds herself regressing when she visits mom. She won't disagree with her; she'll ask advice only about subjects she knows a lot about, and she'll be afraid of making mistakes. In the car as they back out of mom's driveway, the spouse may say, "You're not yourself when you're around your mother."

Others attempt to make mom recognize that they are okay. They go crazy fixing up the house for her visit, present job promotions to her on a silver platter, and anxiously hope that she approves of their spouse. But it's never good enough, and if mom is critical, they are crushed. For example, a friend of mine, Ashley, actually decorated the guest room for her mom when she came to visit. But when Mom entered the room, all it took was an arched eyebrow and Ashley knew immediately that the room wasn't the right decor. She was crushed for days.

On the other hand, if mother approves, there's still a problem. Part of the adult child is relieved that he or she has passed the test. But another part resents having to answer to mom for everything and hates himself for being so weak. You just can't win when there's a parent in control of an adult.

The rebel type often has a stormy relationship with mother. He attempts to dethrone her by defiance, shock, and oppositionalism.

These two have major conflicts or simply disengage, sometimes not speaking for years. He is unable to take her out of the parent role, and so is she. So they simply reenact the "bad kid/critical mom" drama in a thousand ways. The sad thing is, the angry rebel may miss a loving relationship with mom. He would love to know she was proud of him and cared about him. He just can't get past the authority injuries.

WHERE DOES THE "NOT-QUITE ADULT" GO?

The "permanent child" struggles in many arenas, as we've seen. These painful signs and symptoms are also a wake-up call to repair these undeveloped adult parts of the character. In the next chapter, we'll see how that process occurs.

Chapter Eleven

Rebuilding Your Adulthood

By now you may be confused as you try to distinguish between the Controlling Mom and the Still-the-Boss Mom. And it is confusing because at times these two can sound like the same issue. In a sense they are, but with a little different emphasis.

As an adult, you must become "your own person" and become "an equal with other adults" (the focus of this chapter). Both are aggressive tasks to finding oneself apart from mother. The first task is discovering how you are separate and different from your mother, and the second moves past that to the place of becoming equal with her. You are both adults, and neither has the right to judge the other.

You can be separate from other adults, but still feel "one down" to them. You may know what you feel and think, but you feel inferior or subject to the approval or judgment of others that you are separate from. You may still put other adults on a parental pedestal of knowing what is right just because they are "parent." These relationships have a predictable form—one person is superior, and the other is inferior. As a result, you feel like a child in an adult's world.

In this chapter, we will look at the process of *becoming an equal with the adult mother.* It is time to come out from under the one-down, one-up relationship with mom and other adults. It is time to grow into equality with others.

THE NEW PEER GROUP

The concept of having to grow up after you are grown up may be strange to you. You may be thinking, "But I haven't even lived with my mother for years. How can I still be a child?" A good question, one that can possibly be answered with more questions:

How do you feel when you disagree with other adults?

How do you feel when you have an opinion different from an authority figure? Can you express it?

Are you judgmental of others?

Do you feel inferior or superior to others instead of equal?

Do you feel confident in your own decisions?

Do you feel comfortable with your sexuality?

Do you recognize and pursue your talents?

Can you submit to others in authority without conflict?

Without being judgmental, can you value and love people who are different ?

Even if you have been on your own for some time, you may still struggle with some of these feelings from childhood and need to make some strides toward adulthood. These kinds of symptoms may be related to your inability to gain an equal stance of adulthood with your Still-the-Boss Mom, and if you haven't already, it is time to begin that process.

Samantha, a conscientious mother, labored over which preschool was the best one for her children. One school was known for its early training in skills, the other for its social emphasis. Like Michigan/Notre Dame, it was one of those rivalries that divides a community. Everyone had an opinion. Wanting to do the right thing, Samantha called on a few "knowledgeable" friends for some advice.

The first one went on and on about the importance of skills and preparing children for academics. "Any mother knows how important it is for children to get ahead," she said. "If you don't want your children to become 'average,' then you'd better enroll them this year. If you wait too long, they form bad habits and never get ahead in life." Samantha listened attentively, taking in every word, envisioning her children as society's future dropouts if she didn't get them in the right school today. When she left her friend, she was convinced this was the most important move she could make.

Then she met with her second friend. "There are a million smart, educated people in the world who just can't make it in life because they lack the social skills," her friend pontificated. "All of those academics are important, but truly great people know how to get along with others and interact in a variety of social settings." Samantha was awestruck at the importance of her four-year-old's climbing the ladder of people-interacting skills. How sad it would be if she made the "wrong" decision.

She felt totally confused as she left her second friend. In Samantha's mind, these two people were always right, and now they disagreed. Whom should she listen to? If she made a decision, one of her friends wouldn't be pleased. Could she bear to face her? She decided to call her husband. She would let him make the decision, and then she would be off the hook.

Perhaps you have experienced similar dilemmas. You look up to certain people and find it difficult to disagree with them. They play the role of the Still-the-Boss Mom in your life. You would like to be able to listen to the advice of wise people, weigh it for yourself, and make your own decision. But how do you get there if you have had a Still-the-Boss Mom and always turn others into parents? Let's look and see.

Step One: Get Sick and Tired Enough to Make a Change

Remember the bumper sticker, "I'm mad as hell, and I'm not taking it anymore!"? No one knew what the driver was mad about, but we all identified with the feeling. The truth is, "You don't have to take it anymore." You don't have to let other adults parent you. But that requires the first step: *Get sick and tired of being sick and tired.* I have a friend who, whenever she encounters the parental type of person, says, "She makes me tired." If you are living under the demands and expectations of all the "mothers" in the world, feeling judged every time you don't do what they think you should, you are probably sick and tired.

But are you sick and tired enough to do something about it? This is the point of change—when you realize you have been trying to please parent figures long enough and want to be your own adult. When you get to this point, the time has come for a revolution. It is time to revolt against the Still-the-Boss Mom inside and establish your own government inside. Use your anger and tiredness to fuel the revolution.

Step Two: Find Your True Peer Group

To become an equal with mother, you must join the adult world as a peer. Because of your past with your Still-the-Boss Mom, you see other adults in the one-up position, and you in the child position. You have never really joined other adults as peers. *You treat them as parents.* You may tend to gravitate toward those who treat you like a child, which continues the pattern. In order to break the pattern, then, you must find those people who will not play the one-up game, but support your attempts to become equal with them.

Be careful of the mentor who always wants to be on top and looked up to, and who discourages your efforts to challenge or disagree with his ideas. What you need from a new peer group is adults who are not afraid of your being an equal with them. Choose the kind of support people who respect your freedom and ability to think for yourself and have your own opinions.

You need safe people who can provide the mothering you did not get and who will validate your adulthood. Find friends who will support your ability to question, have opinions, take risks, and be your own person. From this "safe haven of peers" you can begin the process.

The New Tasks with Other Adults

You left some tasks undone in your growing-up years. Let's look at what you must do to complete them now.

1. Reevaluate Beliefs

We all think we know what we believe. But, in reality, some people just believe what they were taught to believe as children and have not established their own beliefs. Their beliefs and values are the ones that they inherited from mom. However, to be a true adult, equal to mom, your beliefs must be your own. What do you think about

- church
- religion
- politics
- finances
- childrearing

- minorities
- career

Beliefs about these issues are often inherited from parents and then never questioned. Use your new support people to help you work out your own beliefs and values. Make sure they are yours, even if they turn out to be the same as mom's.

2. Disagree with Authority Figures

Roger sat in a management meeting, knowing his supervisor's idea was faulty. He had information that would shed light on the new acquisition, but he was afraid to speak up. He didn't want to rock the boat.

Do you still feel like a child around parental figures? You fear disapproval, so you don't voice your thoughts or opinions. This state of mind is left over from childhood. If you had a Still-the-Boss Mom, you may have to push yourself to voice your opinions when you're around authority figures. Good leaders want to hear their people's opinions, even when those opinions are different from their own.

3. Make Your Own Decisions

Like Samantha, who couldn't decide on the best preschool, those stuck in the Still-the-Boss Mom syndrome fear displeasing their mother figures and are always deferring to what they think. Indecisive husbands who had Still-the-Boss Moms are often afraid to make their own decisions; they drive their wives crazy. As we become true adults, however, we gather information from knowledgeable people, sort through it, and then make our own decisions. We take the responsibility and heat for the decisions because they are ours. With the support of your new mothering friends, you can step out to make decisions on your own.

4. Deal with Your Sexuality

Rose loved her husband very much but was unable to respond to him sexually. When she came in for help, we discovered that she had a lot of guilt over her mom's puritanical views regarding sex. She had inherited her mother's "hush, hush" feeling toward sex and had never given herself permission to be sexual.

When she had worked on her "one down to mom" feelings, and when she could stop feeling judged for having sexual feelings, she began to own her sexuality as part of her value system, and she soon became very sexual with her husband.

Children are repressed sexually, adults are not. If you are still in the child position with mom, then you are probably suffering sexual consequences of some type. Get together with your peers and talk about your sexuality. Explore your values, feelings, thoughts, and opinions about sex. When you are able to do that, your sexual functioning will be under your domain and not mom's, whatever her views were.

5. *Give Yourself Permission to Be Equal with Your Parents*

Sounds simple, but many people feel guilty for assuming an adult position with their Still-the-Boss Moms. Think about your feelings. Is it okay to be equal with mom? Does it feel bad to have just as many rights and privileges? Do you still feel that you must obey all of her wishes? You have the same rights to your life as she does to hers. Ask your friends to hold you accountable in this area.

6. *Recognize and Pursue Your Talents and Dreams*

Children dream of what they will one day do. Adults go and do it. Children dream of careers; adults go and study, practice, risk, and build one. If you have undeveloped talents and unfulfilled dreams, adulthood is the time to do something about them. Challenge the negative thinking that is keeping you from trying to discover what you are good at, and go for it. Get feedback and teaching from coaches and others who know you. Discover your own talents, no matter what your mother figures think. If you are still under mom's thumb, fear of disapproval or failure may be hindering you from developing talents and giftedness. Adults take responsibility for their gifts, develop them, and serve humanity with them.

7. *Practice*

No one ever gets it right the first time. It takes practice. But many who are still under mom's authority as adults are so afraid of failure that they won't go out and practice. They see practice and failure as the same thing. They labor always under the critical mom's judgment. They fear not doing it right the first time and so are not free to try new things and grow in their careers, hobbies, life view, and so on.

As you begin to feel like a true adult, you can let go of your fear of doing it wrong and start to practice. You will see practice as an opportunity to learn. A good support group will give you a place to fail, and get up and try again. Risking, failing, and trying can be an exhilarating process, but those under an internal critical mom's judgment never know that joy. You can confess your fear of failure to your support group and let them know that you need their acceptance. Then begin to take small steps toward your goal. Go back and get feedback, and try again. This is the way learning takes place. Risk, fail, get feedback, and try again. This is practice.

8. Gain Authority Over Acting Out

Rebellion is for teens. Adults discover value in exerting self-control in their lives. Addiction to things like drugs and alcohol, substances, sex, food, spending, anger, or other behavioral problems often indicates that someone still feels in the "one-down" child position. When we feel like we are under the parent, we rebel against rules, even the ones we set for ourselves.

The way out of impulse problems caused by adolescent rebellion in adults is not to try harder, but to get out of the one-down position to the parent. As long as your mom or anyone else is in the parent position, you will rebel and not have adult self-control. If you can get out from under the "should" of the parental command, you can independently choose your own values. If you are trying to lose weight to meet mom's or someone else's expectation, you will always rebel. But if you are doing it for your adult self, your chances for success are much higher.

As long as you continue in an immature behavior, you will perpetuate the immature child in your life and will not reach the true adult maturity you desire. An accountability support system can help you to stop acting out and gain control of your out-of-control areas.

9. Submit Out of Freedom

True adults can submit to authority structures without a fight. Haven't we all known those who put up a big fight any time their boss or other authority tells them what to do? When people do not feel like equal adults with the ones in authority, they will rebel against the office to win the battle with the person.

As you learn to see yourself as equal to those in authority, you can submit to their authority without its meaning that you are less of a person than they are. All it means is that they are your boss. You can stop using so much energy to rebel against bosses, the IRS, and other structures that you find yourself under. This is not childlike compliance; it is a validation of your adult choice to work for that company or live in this country.

10. Do Good Works

A hallmark of true adult identity is the moment when you are ready to embrace your gifts and talents and begin to give back to the world. When you feel like a child, you are often unable to serve; you feel that you are doing chores for mom. You never feel the freedom to give in a "giving back" sort of way. When you feel free from having to give, you can give because you want to, and you are then validated as an adult and free forever from the Still-the-Boss Mom.

11. Love People Who Are Different

Teens are a cliquey group; they look at others as "in" or "out." If you still are in the one-down position to your Still-the-Boss Mom, you may be holding petty sorts of prejudices toward those who are different from you in some way. If you can learn to appreciate people who are different and love them for who they are, you will take great strides in getting out from under the Still-the-Boss Mom and on the road toward adulthood.

DEALING WITH MOTHER OF THE PAST

By now you have seen the pattern of dealing with the past mom of various types in your head. The process for dealing with the Still-the-Boss Mom is the same:

- Find a safe place with people who support your growing up and becoming an adult.
- Gain awareness of the particular patterns of the Still-the-Boss Mom that are yours. Awareness of the patterns helps you to get them out of your head so that you will stop repeating them with others. What were the main ones you saw about yourself from the previous chapter? How did you deal with them? What relational patterns do you need to change?
- Process the feelings involved—resentment, sadness, anger, grief, or whatever it is you are carrying around. Get rid of those feelings so that you do not displace them onto others and so that they do not continue to interfere in your life. We find good advice in the book of Ephesians: "Get rid of all bitterness, rage and anger, brawling and slander, along with every form of malice."[1] These feelings will hinder your relationship with mom and others. But you cannot get rid of them by denying them. You must acknowledge them and work them through with your safe people. Grieving truly does resolve painful feelings.
- Challenge the messages. If you had a Still-the-Boss Mom, she gave you various messages, which you have internalized and which are now your own critical or limiting voices inside. "Don't think like that, or you'll upset someone." "Don't disagree, or they won't like you anymore." "Don't feel sexual; it's not nice." "Don't pursue that career; Mom will think you're wasting your time." Become aware of the messages that encourage you to remain a child. When you are able to challenge them, you can break the Still-the-Boss Mom's control over your head. These messages will then become "automatic thoughts." They will show up, but they won't severely limit your functioning and development. Keep track of the way you talk to yourself and always challenge the automatic beliefs and thoughts that keep you in the child position. Learn to replace them with positive messages. Listen to your support of people, and internalize their "you can" messages.

- Forgive. We continue to talk about the power of forgiveness, so we won't belabor it here. Let mom off the hook, and then both of you can be free of the past that haunts you and keeps you down. (See more on forgiveness in chapter 5.) Forgiveness will free up the energy and space inside of you that you need for more positive things than holding on to grudges.

DEALING WITH RESISTANCE

It's strange how we resist the very thing we need and have been longing for. We are like the codependent who is finally offered care and responds, "That's okay. I don't need anything." Or the proverbial prisoner who upon release from jail commits another crime because of his fear of freedom. Humans have been known for many years to work hard to "escape freedom," as Rollo May entitled his book.

Watch out for your tendencies to resist adulthood and freedom, to escape equality, and to return to the child position with your mother figures. Ask your support people to call you on your attempts to avoid the adulthood you are longing for. Tell them to watch for the following attempts to

- Blame your inactivity on others
- Excuse your lack of performance on external factors
- Complain about your mother as if she is the one keeping you from doing what you want to be doing
- Gripe about authority figures as if they have control of you
- Get down on yourself for failure and resist the practice cycle
- Whine about your lack of talents and abilities instead of pursuing them
- Bow down to figures you have placed on pedestals
- Repress your own opinions
- Seek approval or try to avoid disapproval from equal adults
- Settle into a "taking" position to avoid service
- Dream instead of "doing"

These are all attempts to remain in the child position. Even once you have the ability and the opportunity to become an adult, you will find yourself returning to these patterns. So when you are confronted by your new support/accountability partners, receive it as a gift. Resistance is from the one-down child position. Receiving confrontation as a gift is a sign of wisdom. "He who listens to a life-giving rebuke will be at home among the wise."[2]

Remember, if you had a Still-the-Boss Mom, part of you does not want to take instruction from anyone; you are still fighting to be an adult. The important difference here is that this is feedback that you asked for *as an adult;* it is not being forced on you like it was when you were a child. So, do not resist truth; it may save your life.

NEW RELATIONSHIP WITH MOM

Still-the-Boss Moms rarely get the message that their children have become adults and are in control of their own lives. They don't usually approach the child and say, "Here is the baton. I am passing it to you and trusting that you will become an adult and begin running your own life. Good luck." It just doesn't happen that way.

But whether or not your Still-the-Boss Mom recognizes it, you are the one in control of your own life now. She may, however, not know quite what to do with the new you. You could enter into some conflict as you work out of your new relationship.

The Ideal

The ideal scenario is for you and your Still-the-Boss Mom to talk out your problems and to work through them. You do not need to engage in a battle, but you do need the opportunity to tell her that you want to be more in charge of your own life. Talk to her about the issues; you want to make your own decisions, be treated as an adult, be free from worry that she might be upset or judgmental if you decide something different from what she would have decided, and anything else that will help you feel more like an adult in the relationship.

The following tips may help as you approach her with your needs:

- Affirm her and the parenting job she did. Thank her for everything she has done in the past, and tell her you appreciate her.

Still-the-Boss Moms often do a great job; they just do it too long.

- Do not sound "blamey" and like a victim. Remember, you are an adult and the one who has allowed her to be in charge. To blame is to remain a child.
- Focus on the fact that you want to be friends and that you want to relate as friends. You appreciate her input, but you also need her respect as an equal adult. Tell her that friends give each other advice and input, but they also respect each other's freedom to choose whether or not to heed it.
- Let her know that you need her help. Ask her to confront you at those times you revert back to being a child with her instead of an adult so that you can change.
- Ask her what she wants you to do if she starts to mother you in a way you do not want. How would she like for you to tell her? What is the best way for you to let her know so that you can remain friends?
- Discuss your individual roles and expectations in the relationship to come. What do you expect from each other in the way of calls, visits, advice, and ways of relating? All of the aspects of your relationship may need to be clarified with the goal of becoming better friends.
- Ask her where you have hurt her and if you need to apologize for anything. The child of the Still-the-Boss Mom may need to own and apologize for some unattractive ways of rebelling. Have you done or said anything in anger that you are sorry for now? Tell her and ask for her forgiveness.
- Explore with her some new things that the two of you can do together as friends. Sometimes those caught up in the Still-the-Boss dynamic get stuck in some rigid roles and activities. Consider doing something together you have never done before. Go to the theater instead of shopping, for example.

All of these strategies are ones that value her and the relationship, and that is the twofold goal: *to preserve both your adulthood and your friendship with mom.* If it goes well, then each of you has gained a new friend and will have a lot of fun together over the years to come. And it will alleviate future problems for your children, for they will not be caught in the middle of the parent/child battle. They will be free simply to enjoy their grandma and vice versa, instead of being pawns in a larger game.

Not-So-Good Situations

The above scenario is usually a normal step as we work out the shift in power that happens in our growing-up years. It just happens a little later for some than for others. The above process, in order to work, takes two pretty honest and responsible people. We hope this is your experience.

Unfortunately there are many situations that do not work out so well. Some Still-the-Boss Moms just refuse to respect their adult children as equals and want to continue to dominate and rule them to varying degrees. If you have tried the above process and did not get anywhere, then you have to take a different route. The goal in the above scenario was to preserve your adulthood and to preserve the friendship. In the not-so-good scenario, the goal is to preserve your adulthood and act responsibly to mom. If she is interested only in managing your life and not in being your friend, then obviously you must forfeit the equal relationship you desire. But you can still be responsible toward her and avoid getting into the child role again.

The following tips may help:

1. If it is apparent that mom is not interested in seeing you as an equal, deal with that wish inside of you before approaching her. Talk it out with your supportive peers. Grieve it. Give it up. If she is refusing to let go of her Still-the-Boss Mom role, you must let go of your desire for her to change. To hold on to your wish for her to treat you like an adult will keep you in the child position forever and always frustrated as well. Let her be who she is: someone who wants something she cannot have. She wants to still mother you, and she can't, so allow her to be frustrated. Do not allow her to gain control by your intense wish for her to be different. If you

do that, she wins, for then she has control of you. The only way to win is to refuse to play the game. And the way to refuse to play the game is to deal with your internal longing for her to be different.

2. Do not respond in anger. When mom does her thing—orders you around or criticizes you—do not get angry back. Her ability to make you angry means she still has control—you are still feeling like a child with her. Deal with the problem inside of you, not with her. Yes, she wants to remain "parent," but deal with what you can change, and that is you. Proverbs 25:28 lends insight to this: "Like a city whose walls are broken down is a man who lacks self-control."[3] If she can still get to you, you need to work on your "walls." You need stronger internal boundaries. *This is not her problem anymore; it is yours.* Don't act out your anger. Simply understand that it is a sign that you still feel one down.

3. Do not respond out of guilt, either. Just as anger is a sign that you still feel one down, so is guilt. If you begin to cave in and respond out of guilt, go talk to your support peers. You cannot be objective when you are acting out of guilt. Guilt is the other side of anger. They are both indicators that you do not feel equal to mom and others.

4. Feel free to disagree. When she says you ought to do *a*, *b*, or *c*, avoid the "Stop controlling me" stuff. You know she does not want to stop, so stop requesting it. Just say, "No, I don't think that is what I want to do." Be direct and assertive, and when she shows her disapproval, empathize with her. "It seems like it disappointed you that I am not going to do that." This response makes it her problem; you are caring about it, but you are not *obeying* it. "Aw, Mom, I'm sorry that when I do what I need to do, it's so hard for you." Empathy diffuses many situations.

5. Set limits on yourself. You might still be too injured to interact in these ways just yet. You might have to set some limits on your interactions with mom right now or on the particu-

lar kinds of interactions you have with her. You might need more space for a while to recover and get through whatever it is that you are dealing with. You might need to tell her that you don't want to talk about certain things. You will have to be the judge of what you can tolerate and what you cannot. We have seen some situations that have been so bad that deep depression or even psychosis comes out of just having one more horrible interaction. Know your limits, and let your supportive people help you to find them.

6. Set limits with mom. Sometimes relationships get so abusive and hurtful that no one is helped by ongoing interaction. This is true especially where your health or your children's welfare is concerned. If someone is so hurtful or abusive that current harm is being done, you need to set some limits. Tell her that if she continues to do *a, b,* or *c,* that you will have to do *d, e,* or *f.* If she continues to yell or criticize, for example, hang up and call her another time when she will not do that.

7. Use your support system. If this is all new to you, you cannot do it alone. Lean on your support system. Call them before and after an interaction that frazzles you. Make a Still-the-Boss Mom sandwich—support, interaction, support. Put her in the middle, and the support on either end. That way you will be prepared for your interaction with her and will get put back together afterward by those who are *for* your adulthood.

8. Relate to mom's strengths. Maybe she cannot be a friend. But there may be times and ways where her need to parent can be okay with you. You may need some information or some "how to's" from time to time. She loves to be in that role. Or there may be other times when she just doesn't bother you, and you can love her where she is and ignore all the parental stuff. "That's just Mom" is a good line for you to learn and remember as you relate to her.

9. Above all, love your mom. The adult position is one of love. Your goal is to achieve adulthood and to love her as you do

so. Remember, love does not mean "obey." Sometimes it means "confront." But it does mean to not return evil for evil; it means to treat her always with respect and care. She can bother you the least when you are loving her. Honor her as mom, love her as you do yourself, and be in charge of your own life.

Chapter Twelve

The American Express Mom

We have all heard the commercial's familiar words, "American Express. Don't leave home without it." Great advice for a credit card, not so great for a mother. As adult children, our task is to do just that—leave our mothers. They give us life, and then we take that life away from them and move on. That is the eternal dance, to cleave and to leave. For many, leaving mother is a task riddled with difficulty. And as with a credit card, there is always an outstanding balance.

This is how it was for Catherine; her leaving process was full of conflict. Like all leaving-home processes, it started in her mid-teens when her activities began to take her outside the home more and more. That, in and of itself, was not a real problem, for her mother, Joyce, prided herself on the independence and feistiness of her first-born daughter. She even bragged to her friends about Catherine's independent and adventurous spirit.

The conflicts arose when Catherine made choices that took her outside the actual definition of the family. For instance, she decided that she'd go to a certain parachurch youth ministry instead of the Sunday school program at the family's church. Joyce saw this as rebellious. She did not listen to Catherine's explanation—her friends were all there, and it met her spiritual needs better. In Joyce's mind, Catherine was a heretic. Most mothers would rejoice at their daughter's interest in spiritual things, but that was not enough for Joyce. It had to be her way, within her narrow guidelines.

They fought and fought, and Joyce would win by playing on Catherine's guilt. "What kind of Christian would disobey her mother and leave the family?" she would say. "Doesn't the Bible preach love and obedience?" Catherine always gave in, but more and more she looked forward to the day she could get out of the house.

Another battle surfaced over Catherine's choice of college. They lived in a small southern town, and Catherine had her eyes on the big city. The two colleges that appealed to her were a great distance from home, and this displeased her mother greatly. Joyce was connected socially to two of the nearby state schools. She had graduated from one herself and wanted her daughter to continue in her footsteps.

"Absolutely not!" was Joyce's reaction when Catherine tried to share her thoughts on her college plans. "You can't go traipsing three thousand miles away for school. Why, we'll never see you!"

I know. That's the whole idea, Catherine thought.

The battle waged on with threats to withdraw financial support and to make Catherine an outcast from the family, until finally Catherine succumbed. She decided to attend a school nearby, and her mother was happy. Happy, that is, until the next time Catherine wanted to do something that would take her away from the family.

"What do you mean you're not coming home for Christmas?" her mother cried. "Of course you are!"

"But Mom, it will be so much fun. My friend's parents have a place in Colorado, and we're going skiing. A lot of my friends will be there, and we'll have a blast. Please let me go."

"No, Catherine. I won't hear of it. Christmas is family time, and I want you here with us. We have a special time planned to all be together, and you cannot miss it. I don't want to discuss this any further."

Catherine came home for Christmas. But in her heart she was with her friends, thinking of all the fun they were having. She felt like a child, who still had to obey her parents at every turn.

The theme continued throughout her college years—summer vacations and weekends spent somewhere other than at home, friends who lived farther and farther away. And a slow but sure change of values that reflected Catherine's attempts to be different from her mother.

And then Catherine's big break came. At graduation, she announced she was moving to San Francisco to take a job with an accounting firm. Her mother was mortified. She threw out the same arguments she had used in the college battle, but this time to no avail. Catherine knew she just had to get away.

GUARDIANS AND MANAGERS

The Bible draws a picture for us of the child's position. "Now I say, as long as the heir is a child, he does not differ at all from a slave although he is owner of everything, but he is under guardians and managers until the date set by the father."[1] What an accurate picture of what it's like to be a child, especially an adolescent. All the equipment is there, but no permission to use it! Every adolescent could say: "I am able, and I don't have permission from my guardians and managers."

This is a good way to think about the growing-up-and-leaving-mother process. Children must leave their parents in the *governmental* sense in order to be full-fledged adults. This is truly what "leaving home" is all about—taking over the governmental aspects of their lives. The good guardian and manager gradually delegates this freedom. This is not to be confused with geography or other symbols of space; an adult child can live a thousand miles from mother and not have emotionally left home, and another adult child can live in the same town and be totally in charge of himself.

To leave mom means that we leave a role behind. We move out from "under her guardianship and management." We establish our adulthood apart from her psychological domain.

As previous chapters, this one deals with the same issue of becoming a separate and free person from mother. But it deals with a particular time of separating—being separate and independent while still "under" mom and then moving out from under that role into adulthood. Let's see what this process looks like and what is involved to make it happen.

Adolescence: The Beginning of Leaving

We looked at some developmental aspects of adolescence in chapter 11. In this chapter, we'll see the aspects of adolescence that specifically affect the child's ability to leave mother when the time comes. Let's look at what has to happen in that relationship during those critical years for the move away to occur like it is supposed to. What are the important aspects of adolescence that prepare someone to leave home?

Experience of the Larger World

One important aspect of adolescence that prepares one to leave home is the move into the larger world, or the "real world," as it is sometimes called. The early adolescent's life revolves around the home, while the later adolescent's life begins to revolve more and more around the outside world. The act of getting a driver's license, for example, is a big move toward independence, as the adolescent can now travel without mother.

The adolescent's world no longer revolves around his parents, as school, friends, and extracurricular activities become more and more important. He truly has a culture that is more and more his own. Concerts, sports events, service clubs, trips with friends, hobbies, intellectual and artistic interests, and the world of dating pull him more and more into a life apart from his family. Discovery of the outside world does two very important things for the middle and later adolescent. First, it lets him know that the world has more to offer than what his parents have shown him. Second, he learns that he can negotiate the world without holding onto his parents' hand. These two discoveries prepare him to eventually leave home.

Increasing Power of the Peer Group

While the preadolescent is still playing with her friends, the later adolescent is becoming increasingly dependent on her peer group for emotional and social support as well as a powerful influence of values and norms. Her sense of where she belongs is slowly being enlarged to include not just her family but also her peers.

As this shift happens, the adolescent is learning a powerful lesson that will serve her for the rest of her life: "There are more people 'out there' than just Mom and Dad. And they have opinions and abilities to love too. I can depend on them for information and support." In order for any of us to become fully functioning members of society, we must learn an interdependent dance with the community in which we live. We need each other. We need our friends. We need teaching and information from sources other than our parents. When we learn to use the community to meet our needs for relationship and truth, we can then be grounded wherever we find ourselves in life.

However, if mom gives her child the message that she is the only source of love and truth, the child never learns to move past her. This then sets up a developmental issue—the child clings to others in a childlike dependent fashion instead of relating to them from a place of healthy adult interdependency. When we are able to move away from maternal dependency, we can develop the ability to lean on others in a more responsible way. We begin to realize that we are responsible to get our needs met instead of waiting for our mother to anticipate and take care of them. We are responsible for getting our own help, as well as for how we respond to the help offered to us. We move from needing mom to needing others.

Increasing Experience of the Limits of the Outside World

I (Dr. Cloud) was at a friend's house for dinner recently, when out of the blue the adolescent son turned to his parents and said, "Oh, yeah, I didn't tell you. I got suspended from work for a week."

"What happened?" his dad asked quickly, exhibiting everyone's anxiety, for we all knew how difficult this job had been to secure in the first place.

"I was late twice."

"That's too bad," his mother wisely said. "You needed the money." She continued eating, and we chatted for a minute more before the subject turned to something else.

I was so proud of his mother I wanted to scream, "Way to go!" She didn't get hooked into taking care of him or hooked by her own anxiety into lecturing, trying to ensure that he would never be late again so he wouldn't lose his job. She just empathized and listened, allowing him to shoulder the problem. She also did not offer money, talk about how unfair "they" were to do such a thing, or enter into any other codependent behavior. Her son was learning that the real world has limits for his behavior. Fortunately, his mother refused to shield him from that lesson.

If mom can stay out of the way of the outside world's limits, the child learns an important reality: *Parents are not the only ones with rules.* This realization helps the child see rules not as parental but as part of the real world. If allowed to suffer, he learns that the world has requirements from which mother cannot shield him. This realization does wonders to stop his regressive slide back to mother's protection; the child learns to deal with the consequences of reality in a way other than just the parents' discipline.

Unfortunately, some mothers cannot let their children suffer. When junior runs into trouble with school, or the law, or on the job, she will do something to bail him out. When she runs to his aid, she often attacks or undermines the limit he should have experienced at the hands of the outside world. She storms the principal's office, for example, protesting a grade or lack of promotion or recognition. Certainly it can't be her child's fault; it must be the teacher or the school. And if someone doesn't do something, there will be hell to pay, or some other version of parental threat. This type of mother just cannot accept the fact that her child is not making it and needs to suffer the consequences.

Sometimes a mother will not interfere so blatantly as storming the principal's office. She may just join her child in blaming the limit setter. "Well, you know how those teachers are," she might say. "They don't know anything about the real world, they just teach. Wait until you get to the university where they know what they are talking about." This reaction undermines the effect of what could have served as a wake-up call that the child needed to help him grow up.

The chief mothering task in this area is to not get in the way. The mother's job is to resist not only undermining but also joining the limits her child experiences in the real world—using them to say, "I told you so." Using the outside limit to her advantage diminishes its power. She might say something like, "I told you if you didn't start to be more responsible that this would happen. Now look at the mess you've made." This kind of reaction nullifies any positive effect the outside limits might have had on the child; the outside limits and mom's nagging become the same in the mind of the child who is trying to separate from mother. What started as an outside limit has now become mother's, and the child must separate from her and thus, from the limit. As a life lesson, it is canceled out, as if it never happened. This does not negate valid coaching and interaction but only joining.

Mother would do best to just step out of the way and allow her child to have his own experience and relationship with the outside world. Like my friend's remark: "Sounds tough. What are you going to do now? Pass the tuna."

Toward Financial Independence

The more the teen enters the world, the more money is required. It costs money to drive a car—the initial cost of the car, as well as the expenses to run it. Then there are movies, sports events, hobbies, dating, camps, school-related activities, clothes, and everything else teens love to do that cost money. A small child's financial ability is limited, especially her earning power. But teenagers are able to earn more money for a number of reasons: They are more mobile, more able and competent, and more marketable. This is good timing, for at the same time, their need for money is growing.

Mother's role is to allow and encourage the teen's separateness and independence while at the same time setting limits on her child's regressive wish to be taken care of.

Problems arise when mom thwarts the independence of the teen by either sabotaging his separateness or giving him too much so that he doesn't have to learn the work ethic. It's sad to see adults who have to learn, for the first time, the value of work to meet their needs; they should have learned it as teens.

This is a tricky balance, for teens still need parental support. They need both support *and* increasing responsibility for financial management and earning. We have seen mistakes at both ends of the spectrum; the parents abandon all support as the teen begins to earn, or they offer too much support that keeps the teen from having to earn any money at all.

LATE ADOLESCENCE AND EARLY ADULTHOOD

As the child moves through the years of adolescence and begins to look at adulthood, the reality of leaving home unfolds. The late adolescent grows in independence during college, and then after college a child should be able to manage her own life. The parent gradually turns over the management of the child to the child. The parental role disappears. The axiom is this: *To the extent that a person is being parented, to that extent this person is still a child.* The person who is an adult, yet acts like a child, will encounter problems when jobs and relationships require adult behavior.

Both parents should be guiding their child to that moment when she sets up her own life apart from the family—somewhere to live, somewhere to work, her own friends and support network, her own spiritual life. And she should be paying for it all.

The Mother's Wound

This all sounds so harsh from mom's perspective. Will her children ever return, once they're out? Of course, if this process goes well. In the meantime though, the essential reality is that mom gets *abandoned*.

As the book of Genesis puts it, a man shall *leave* his mother. The Hebrew word for *leave* means "abandon, refuse, loose, forsake, neglect, set free," among others. This passage is speaking specifically about marriage, as the next significant word concerning a man's action is to *cleave* to his wife.[2] This process of leaving mother emotionally is the final developmental step for the child, enabling him to make a full commitment to adulthood.

The first separation from mother, a physical one, is called *weaning* in the Bible. The Hebrew word translated *wean* is a positive word that sometimes means "brought up" and "to deal bountifully, to reward, or to ripen." The child is taken off the breast when he has had enough of the good stuff of early dependency and is *ripe* for the next step.

The second separation—leaving home—has been described as the wounding of mother, which every child eventually does. They abandon her, in the sense that they grow up and no longer *depend* on her as *mother.* This does not mean that they no longer love, adore, relate to, give to, or receive from mother. *The relationship is not over, but it is changing.* Mother is no longer *the* source.

A mother takes great satisfaction in being her child's source. She is his first source of life and nurturance. And then his source of wisdom, discipline, friendship, teaching, values, and many other virtues. It is a very satisfying and rewarding role for mom. This entire book up until now is about how impossible it is to overestimate the role that a mother plays.

The sad news for her is that the role is designed to end. She gives life, prepares her child for life, and then lets go of the life she has created.

The "letting go," as we've seen, is the hard part for the mom. The child's task is to inflict the wound of leaving—to "take" his life and run with it. The mother's role is to "take" the wound and contain it. She sheds the bittersweet tears of letting go and mourning the empty nest. She watches as an independent person emerges—the fruit of her nurture, discipline, and love. Joy and sadness are the combined themes of this wound. It is at once a happy and painful tearing away.

To the extent that a mother is able to allow this step to take place peacefully, things go well. She has to reclaim the values of separateness, difference, limits, and assume a stance against regression that we mentioned in chapter 6. She should relish in this sad step, and that is a difficult thing to do. But as she does it, she can see the independence of her child not as a threat but actually as a symbol of her good work: He is now on his own. She is not being a credit card company, and she is not trying to collect on a debt. She sees her giving as a gift, and the only return she wants is the enjoyment of seeing the good life of her child.

RESULTS OF AMERICAN EXPRESS MOTHERING

As we have seen in the steps above, certain signs and symptoms indicate if things are not going well in this separating process. Take a look.

Relational Signs

Unhealthy dependency creeps into the significant relationships of the "supposed to be adult" who has had an American Express Mom. Relationships may begin on mutual ground but are quickly jockeyed into some sort of dependency/independency battle.

Mother Me, Please—How Dare You Mother Me?

This dynamic crops up often in dating relationships and in many marriages. One person, often the man, is to some degree irresponsible; he depends on others to do things he should be doing for himself. He may neglect personal issues like finances, laundry, cooking, clothes, the car, insurance, taxes, and so on.

He finds someone who is codependent to take care of him, and then he fights the person for nagging and trying to "control me." He likes the caretaking but resents the control. The helper "nags" because she soon discovers that she has a child on her hands and grows more and more dissatisfied. The "child" resents being "mothered": "Don't tell me what to do," "Get off my back," "You are such a nag." And he goes back to his hobbies or fun, avoiding adulthood, but resenting the parent.

Abandoning the Partner

Those who have not separated from mother will turn significant others into mothers. They will be close to their loved one for a while and then in some way abandon her. It may be to break up a serious dating relationship, or it may be to separate from a spouse. But the natural order sets in: *We are made to leave mother. If we relate to someone as a mother, we will abandon that person.* People who turn their wives, husbands, boyfriends, or girlfriends into mothers end up abandoning them in some way.

Abandoning may not result in divorce or breakup but in an emotional departure instead. Adult children of American Express Moms may detach, withdraw, find outside interests, or spend their time with friends or hobbies. They avoid intimacy with their significant others. They are separating from mother, but the problem is that mother, in reality, is now wife.

Avoidance

Some people, in order to separate from mother, do not enter into the world of relationships at all. They work hard to avoid the intimacy of an adult connection. Some are happy with this, some are not. Some love their tightly held independence so much that they loathe the thought of an attachment and the responsibility it entails. Others are depressed about being alone and desire a relationship. In either case, they are not moving to the adult stage of good relational connections.

Idealizing

Some children of the American Express Mom are still so fused with her that no one can measure up to the ideal person who provides everything they need. They devalue everyone who comes along, remaining safely tied to mom. The main function of this defense is to preserve the fusion with the ideal fantasy of mom and avoid the potentially disappointing relationship with a real person.

Caretaking

The person who has not emotionally left home sometimes identifies with the mothering function that they have not separated from and becomes the mother to others. This is a well-known codependent pattern.

Functional Signs

The functional signs in this section are similar to the ones in chapter 6: disorganization, developmental problems in the areas of identity and talent, problems delaying gratification, and other signs of irresponsibility. The world of adult functioning requires us to act as independent adults. Show up, do your job, don't make excuses, take responsibility for results, pay your bills, clean up after yourself, relate to others as peers, and don't make trouble for anyone else. Functional symptoms are seen primarily in work or parenting roles.

Emotional Signs

Like the functional symptoms, the emotional ones mirror those in chapter 6 as well. Depression that comes from not owning one's life is usually somewhere in the picture. Feelings of powerlessness and helplessness are common. Addictions come into play with mother bailing her child out of the consequences. Those who have not cut the cord often suffer isolation, anxiety, and panic attacks. They tend to be "blamers," feeling that someone else is responsible for them: "If it weren't for her, I'd be a good person."

Spiritual Signs

The spiritual life is one of direct relationship with God and being responsible for that reality and relationship. Since the one who has not left home is still a child inside, her relationship with God is more like that of a grandchild than a child. She depends on others either to motivate her in her spiritual development, or to structure that aspect of her life "for her."

To be spiritually mature is to achieve true adulthood—true existential responsibility before God as his child, image-bearer, and steward. When we are still tied to mom's apron strings, we answer primarily to her, rather than to God. In a sense, she buffers the demands of his reality. It has been said that true maturity is when we stop asking life to meet our demands and begin to meet the demands of life. A mother who is either the holder of the demands or the one who meets them for her adult child actually hinders the child's growth in maturity.

WHAT IT LOOKS LIKE NOW

If you are still connected to your mother in an unhealthy way, you are avoiding the separation and independence of being an adult. If you've had an American Express Mom, you may have current problems in one or more of the following:

- Finances
- Daily functioning. It may be difficult for you to take hold of the kinds of adult responsibilities that mother would be doing for you if you physically still lived at home: laundry, insurance policies, and career opportunities.
- Establishing a "home base" of your own

- Building an emotional support system away from the family
- Relating to in-laws. Problems arise where allegiance or control is in some way divided between spouse and mother.
- Breaking away from pleasing mother
- Avoiding an adult relationship with mother. If you do not have a good friendship with your mother, provide help to your elderly parents, have multigenerational ties with her, visit home, write, or call, you may have a problem in this area. Abandonment of mother should never include abandonment of the person, just her role as mother.
- Argumentative relationships with mother
- Codependent ties with mother. Both you and your mother have to take responsibility for your own lives.
- Tendency to live out mother's dreams for your life and career instead of pursuing your own
- Struggles to achieve mature sexual identity and functioning

SIGN OF MATURITY NOW WITH MOM

It is a sign of health when you can have a good relationship with your mother. In fact, it is essential to the survival of society, values, culture, and growth for multigenerational ties to exist. We should always honor our parents, as the Bible tells us to. It actually goes further and says that we need to make a "return" to our parents, giving back to them for what they gave to us as we were growing up. They need us more as they get older.[3] And our children need their grandparents as well.

It is rewarding for parents and grown children to enjoy a friendship after a child has reached adulthood. That friendship includes holiday celebrations, the giving and taking of sage advice, mutual support, sharing fun times with the grandchildren, vacations, and other fun times. These are all the fruits of growing up and establishing a healthy adult relationship with parents.

To truly enjoy mother in our adult years, we must emotionally leave home first. We must do the tasks we have been talking about in this chapter. If you've had an American Express Mom, you need to cancel the account. In the next chapter, you'll learn how to do that.

Chapter Thirteen

Leaving Home the Right Way

Mark and Shannon were stuck on the horns of a dilemma. They had a good marriage and loved their two kids. Yet Mark was on the verge of, as Shannon phrased it, "blowing a good thing." This was the couple's first large crisis.

The problem revolved around Mark's conflict with his mother, Jo. A widow for several years, Jo was left a wealthy woman by Mark's father, who had been a successful businessman. She was kind and devoted to her children and grandchildren.

One of the ways Jo expressed her love was through expensive gifts and financial support. She was generous and somewhat lavish; at different times she had bought Mark and his family beautiful pieces of traditional furniture, travel vacations, and had even paid to remodel her son's home. Mark and Shannon both worked in middle management positions and were grateful for Jo's support. There was no way in the world they could afford the lifestyle extras that Mark's mom provided.

They felt a little awkward sometimes with their neighbors and friends. They lived in a middle-class neighborhood, and their companions observed the discrepancy between them and Mark and Shannon. They would get comments such as, "Did you guys win the lottery?" or "Your company must have a great incentive package." They saw sidelong glances and knew some of their neighbors were envious. But the couple wrote it off as their friends' problem and ignored it.

Then the real problem arose. Mark had begun to change his attitude toward his mom. He felt smothered, and he began to resent her involvement in their family life. "I want to be my own man," he told

Shannon, "not a kid with my hand out to Mom." He became argumentative with Jo and provoked fights with her.

Jo was surprised and hurt by her son's change. It seemed out of the blue and uncalled for. Suddenly Mark seemed ungrateful for her love and support. She really didn't know what she was doing wrong, since Mark never directly told her. After a few painful arguments, Jo began to withdraw from the family. Her calls, visits, and gifts began to diminish.

Shannon was undone with this. She had appreciated Jo's help. Shannon knew that they needed it in order to live in the manner to which they'd grown accustomed. She feared that the cushion Jo provided was about to be destroyed by Mark's foolishness. Shannon saw no reason on earth for Mark to kill the goose that was laying the golden eggs. "There's nothing wrong with your mom giving to us," she would remonstrate her husband. "It's out of love. She enjoys it, and so do we. Why can't you see that you can be grown-up and still get a little help from time to time? Do you want to have to move to a smaller home on our income?"

"You just don't understand," Mark would tell her.

Actually, neither one understood. They were both right and both wrong. When they came to see me (Dr. Townsend) about the crisis, both Mark and Shannon were distorting the picture. Mark was right in wanting to become more functionally independent, but wrong in attacking his mother for being generous. Shannon was right in seeing Jo's motives as loving, not controlling. But she didn't understand Mark's need to truly leave home.

And that's the subject of this chapter. As we saw in chapter 12, we need to leave mother in real, practical, day-to-day ways. We are created to "abandon" her and set up our own home and support system. Here, we'll provide a structure for this last task: the real-life decisional part of leaving the child's role and coming into your own as a grown-up in a grown-up's world.

THE LONGEST YARD

The task of leaving mom in your everyday life is the longest yard of growth, as it involves making painful adjustments to long-standing patterns with mother and others. This is the time we truly begin to walk our talk—we begin to live on our own in all areas of life.

This can be a difficult step because we often can't see the benefits of leaving. In this chapter, we'll be dealing with issues like financial responsibility and the dependence on mom for her emotional support and for the extras in life. These are areas in which mom can really come through for her kids. She likes it, and they like it. And, like Shannon, many adults don't see a downside to mom's remaining in this role.

Yet, there truly is a downside, and it applies no matter how many miles apart and years distant you are from home. If you are still going to mom for things you should be providing for yourself, *you will always be a prisoner to your relationship with her*—and that's not mom's fault. Like Mark, you might fight her "control." Or, like Shannon, you might try not to upset her. Neither are adult ways of relating. You will be constantly reacting to your dependency on her, rather than living life deliberately, autonomously, and according to your own values and directions.

Let's look at several of the important tasks you can undertake to begin this longest yard.

TASKS

Develop Your New "Home" Before You Leave

No matter how motivated, miserable, or mad you are at your situation with mom, don't even think about leaving your American Express connection until you have created, developed, and stabilized your own emotional home base. In other words, cement your re-mothering relationships—spouses, friends, support groups, churches, and therapists. Make sure you are deeply rooted and grounded within these connections.

Remember that *we can't separate from anyone in a vacuum.* If mom is still the only one residing within your heart of hearts—the one you still truly depend on—you won't be able to tolerate the tearing and isolation that will occur when you attempt to leave. Some people, when this happens, simply return to their American Express

Mom or find someone much like mom onto whom they transfer the dynamics. It works much like the rebound syndrome in romantic relationships: The new choice isn't a more mature attachment; it's the same one with a different name.

You may think that because you have an active social life, you've got your home base set up. But if you haven't truly left home, you probably have a built-in limit as to how much intimacy you will allow in your relationships. You may have difficulty experiencing painful feelings, being dependent, and revealing your "bad self" around others. At some level, you reserve these parts for mother. You stay on the surface with the rest of your relationships.

I have a forty-year-old friend who lives in a metropolitan city with her husband and children but has no really close friends. Yet she's on the phone, long distance to mom, twice a week. This is her lifeline and support system. She has left, but she hasn't left.

It's often helpful to get feedback about this from people you trust. You may be surprised at the answers you get when you poll your friends about how intimate they think you are with them. As one person told a friend of mine who tried this, "Jeannine, we spend a lot of time with you at church and with the kids, but we don't really know you." Jeannine was taken aback, but got the message and began to let her safe friends know the real her.

Answer to Your Support Relationships

While it's important to develop close relationships as we create our own home, it's not enough. We need to take the counsel of our friends seriously. Friends have a dual function: They attach to us, and they tell us the truth. The attachment provides fuel and a place where we can be accepted. The truth brings the light of reality to those parts of us that are hidden, injured, distorted, or destructive. In other words, love makes it safe enough for us to tolerate the truth about ourselves.

Becoming answerable to your support relationships is key to creating your own home. When you answer to your support relationships, you are telling others that they matter enough to meddle in your life. You are opening yourself up to their perspective and opinions on many areas of your life such as

- how you handle your relationships
- how responsible you are
- your conduct and character
- how you deal with your marriage
- your parenting style
- your physical condition and habits
- your spiritual life
- your finances
- your work habits and directions
- how you maintain the house

This isn't easy! It's much more palatable to look to others only for things like comfort and companionship. Yet we need those who will help us with our blind spots, weaknesses, and failings. And we need to listen to them without defensiveness or a "you don't understand me" attitude.

This is a major key as you prepare to let go of your American Express Mom. When we keep good friends politely at arm's length, we are actually protecting our enabling relationship with mom. *Mom would never confront me on how I treat my spouse; she'd understand me.* Yet, when we listen to our friends' loving truth, we deepen and cement our new home: "Wounds from a friend can be trusted."[1]

Move beyond the social and conversational in your safe relationships. Ask them, "How am I doing on the leaving home end of things? Do you see any problems in my cutting the cord?" And listen to their realities.

Take Ownership

Next, begin to develop a sense of "no excuses ownership" over your successes and failures. Children of American Express Moms are often blamers and rationalizers. Every time there's a problem, mom's there to send them a check or stand up for them, right or wrong. If this is happening, you will never learn to resolve your own issues.

Start evaluating every failure and problem in your life this way: *character before circumstances.* Don't look first at your environment, your friends, your enemies, or God. Look first at your issues through the lens of your character.

For example, if you don't get the work promotion, don't go looking for a friend who will listen as you gripe about the boss. Instead ask, "How did I contribute to not getting the promotion?" If a relationship falls apart, ask, "What did I do to destroy this?" If you're chronically late, don't blame the freeway; traffic jams have been around for years, long before you even started driving. Ask, "Did I plan too much again?" or "Did I leave late again?" Ask your friends to hold you accountable in this area.

Cherish Your Spouse

Children of the American Express Mom often wreak havoc in their marriages. They're either (a) comparing their spouse unfavorably to mom; (b) wanting to overinvolve him with her life; or (c) trying to get the spouse to take sides in some argument with mom. If this sounds like you, take steps to cherish your spouse over mom. Marriage vows often include the phrase, "forsaking all others." This means more than leaving other potential mates. It also means separating from the child-mother role.

This move doesn't mean you abandon mom as a person. It simply defines the roles: You've made your spouse's welfare a higher priority than your mom's. Tell your spouse this often and ask for help maintaining this important value. By doing this, you will be bringing the most important person in your life into the deepest part of yourself. You will be truly cherishing your loved one.

Bring Mom In on the Process

As we've said in other places in this book, many moms aren't in denial about these issues; they simply were raised a certain way and didn't know any alternative ways to rear their children. You may find mom a welcome ally in your process of leaving her. She may be fully supportive of your being on your own. That's why it might be helpful to let her in on your process. If she is a safe person, bring her in. Leslie, a friend of mine, once told her mom, "You're too easy, and I need your help. I have a key to your house, you have a key to mine. We drop over to each other's houses without calling first. I can talk to you anytime. There's always food in the kitchen. You're so accessible that I end up seeing you more than I see my husband or friends. I don't have to plan, cook, or anything." They returned their keys to one another, and Leslie started having to call first. The discipline helped, and Leslie developed more ability to take responsibility for her friendships. And Leslie's mom actually felt proud that she'd contributed to the process.

Then again, mom may feel hurt when you ask her to help you abandon her. If so, don't press the issue. Let your support people help you.

Manage Your Money

Chuck Swindoll used to say, "If you want to know about someone's spirituality, look at his checkbook." The same applies here. Finances are probably the single most measurable, quantifiable, and observable gauge about how you're doing in leaving your American Express Mom. If you haven't yet become autonomous, there's probably a money symptom somewhere: help during tax time, luxury expenses, emergencies, privileges the kids couldn't have otherwise, and others.

Take hold of your finances and learn to live within your means. You may have to lower your standard of living, learn to budget and save, delay gratification, and somehow make do with what you have. It is never easy to reverse dependent spending. No one likes to have to think, *Can I afford this?* It's much easier to ask, *Do I need this?* Get budgeting help from a finance expert, or a wise friend. Get on a program and anticipate the day you can live without the checks from home. There's nothing intrinsically wrong with money from mom, as long as it's not in the budget. When you can enjoy it, but don't need it, it's in the right place.

Should you borrow money from mom? This is a complex question, but generally, it's probably best to save up your own money to buy something. If you do find it necessary to borrow from her, treat her as you would a bank, with all the protection and benefits due the lender. Draw up a legal contract, pay her a competitive interest rate, and enforce penalties if you get behind. Don't enter into the scenario where mom lends you thousands, and then, when you can't pay it back, she has no recourse. Few moms are willing to see their grandkids on the street. In the end, mom loses out.

Be Responsible for Functional Tasks

Too many people stay dependent on mom for things they should be doing for themselves. In this way, they never have to grow up and find ways to shoulder their own load. Take responsibility in your own life for the following:

- Do your own laundry; don't take it to mom's.
- Buy your own furniture. Let mom contribute pieces, not the entire set.
- Have your own insurance policies.
- Find a number of babysitters you can depend on besides mom.
- Plan your entertainment around what you can afford, not what she can afford.
- Do your own errands: pick the kids up from school, buy groceries, clean the house. Let mom help, but as an occasional favor.
- Take vacations you can afford; accept only an occasional one from mom.
- Make your own decisions. Listen to her, but you decide.

Parent Your Kids

Adults who haven't left home often want to be their own children's "best friend." They fear the authority and the distance the adult role necessarily brings with children. They also fear the distance the adult role creates with mom. So they play, trade secrets, have fun, and goof off with their kids. But they have a hard time being in charge, confronting, setting limits, and handling the child's rage.

Go ahead and be your child's parent. Not only is this good for your child, it's good for you. When you assume the role of parent, you truly begin to grow up and leave mom's home for your own home.

Take Charge of Your Own Self-Development

This task has a little more gratification to it than some of the others, as there are benefits when you take charge of developing the adult parts of your character. *In other words, not only does great privilege confer great responsibility—in the same way, great responsibility confers great privilege.* You can enjoy the benefits of being a responsible, grown, independent adult, in three important dimensions.

Talents. First, develop your own unique strengths, gifts, and talents. You are a craftsperson at something, be it artistic, financial, spiritual, athletic, or professional. Your talent may be in how you make your living, or it may be a hobby. Either way, it's a mark of maturity.

Sexuality. Another benefit of leaving home is that you get to develop your own sexuality. This may mean growing into your gender role as a man or woman, or it may mean growing in tenderness and passion with your spouse. It's often the case that as people leave home, their sexual responsiveness begins to flower.

Taking risks. When you no longer have to answer to mom, you can pay for your own risks. This means you can dream, explore, and find challenges and opportunities she may never have imagined for you. Consider issues like career changes, travel, appropriate lifestyle changes, and cultural exploration. Deal with these dreams in the context of your safe network. Be prepared to take full responsibility for the risks you take. This is all part of God's command to us to "fill the earth and subdue it."[2]

REVAMPING YOURSELF WITH MOM

Leaving your American Express Mom means leaving the role and the dynamic, not the person. You can keep a good connection with mother, but it will change, as you change. Here are the tasks you need to perform.

Establish a Friendship

Begin the shift to friendship with mom. Friendship is a mutual connection between two equal adults. This is in contrast to the child-parent role, in which the child depends on mom emotionally or functionally. This friendship with mom is not a survival relationship; rather, it's an enjoyment of one another's company. You enjoy mom, but you no longer need her to survive.

Your friendship may include doing mutually enjoyable activities together. This might mean going to her glee club performances or seeing a show with her. True friendship always involves a certain amount of self-sacrifice. You may need to do things on occasion that you aren't drawn to simply for her sake. Attending her garden party or church reunion may be boring, but friends do that for each other. Adults have the ability to give wholeheartedly to one another without resentment. Friends receive joy from seeing their friends receive joy.

Receive Favors, Not Needs

As we mentioned in the last section, there's nothing wrong with receiving favors from mom, be they cash, products, or services. She may want to give out of her abundance. If so, receive and bless the giver. However, mom's favors should always be "extras," not something you need, plan for, depend on, or budget for. Avoid the trap of not being in control of your own life. Gratefully receive the favors, but set limits with yourself and mom here.

Decide How to Help

How can you make a return to mom? As she ages and slows down, she will need emotional and functional assistance. This may include time, money, decision making, errands, and home repairs. It is your responsibility to give back to her for what she has given. Jesus said that those who hold back from helping parents in need are acting against him: "Thus you nullify the word of God by your tradition."[3]

By making a return to mom, you are taking your place in the seat of the adult and letting her move on to her golden years of less demands and responsibility. You are behaving according to the principles God has set up for us. In his structure, the very young and the very old are protected and assisted, and those in between carry the largest amount of responsibility for themselves, the family, and the culture. You are assuming your proper place in that hierarchy when you assist mom.

The complex task is to figure out the extent of your return. Will you visit her once a year, or will you move her into the guest bedroom? Discuss this with your support people. Here are some questions to ask yourself:

- Is mom's need small or severe?
- What kinds of resources does she have to provide for her own needs (friends, church, finances, and so forth)?
- What is your level of responsibility? How much of a relationship was there and is there?
- What are your own resources and responsibilities? Your present family must come first. Will helping mom compromise their needs, or can you provide adequately for both?

Decide If or How You Will Parent Mom

Sometimes "giving a return" can get out of hand. On a plane recently, as I worked on this book, the two female therapists sitting beside me asked what I was writing. They seemed very interested in the "mom" subject, and so I asked them what was important in the mothering areas for them and their clients. One of them replied, "I want you to answer one question: I'm forty-five years old now, and Mom's seventy-two. What do I do with Mom's newfound dependency on me? I feel like I'm the parent, and she's the child."

This therapist was describing a major problem with adult children of American Express Moms. As she gets older, mother seems to regress, needing more support than usual from her children. She calls more, has more needs, and can even be demanding or manipulative if her children aren't there the way she thinks they should be. This issue is different from the more functionally based one of the previous section, though the two interact. There we dealt with responsibility, money, and assistance. Here we deal with relationship, support, and time.

This is a common issue. Many adults feel obligated to be the total support system for mom in her failing years. They feel they should be her confidant, best friend, and advice giver on all her medical, emotional, and social issues. Mom sometimes wants to take her child through every detail of her day. One person told me, "It's as if I'm the mom baking in the kitchen, and she's the eight-year-old coming home from school. She wants to sit at the table and tell me all the stories, interesting things, and problems of her day while drinking a glass of milk and eating chocolate chip cookies."

These adult children alternate between feelings of obligation, guilt, and resentment. They argue with their spouses who say, "I didn't marry her, I married you." They can't please everyone, and they feel they aren't doing anything right.

Even if you and mom have a healthy relationship, you probably feel some responsibility to be one of the members of her support system. The key here is to remember that you are only *one* of the members. It is not your responsibility to become her parent or best friend; you support her without feeling that you have to be or do everything.

Life's ideal is that we end it up with deep roots. That is, we are designed to relate better and deeper as time goes by. As good relationships flourish, they become more satisfying over the years. Men have best friends with whom they affectionately exchange insults for forty years. Women have close alliances with whom they know every nuance, joy, and pain.

The problem with the American Express Mom is that, while she may have social relationships, her dependencies often lie with her children. She may see her kids as her emotional retirement fund. Then when her kids form their own lives and interests, she feels let down, and they feel guilty.

If this is your situation, decide what you can give emotionally as a friend to your mother. Think about your available time and your responsibilities to self, God, family, work, and friends. Give what you can. And help mom find friendships. Perhaps she needs to deepen the ones she already has. Or maybe she needs to find new ones. Help her explore the neighborhood, nearby churches, social clubs, and activity groups. Let her know that the time you do spend with her is given wholeheartedly, but that there's only so much of you to go around. I have several friends whose moms lived in another state and who called several times a week, using my friends as a personal support system. The result was doubly horrible: The children felt crazy, and mom always felt neglected and lonely and as if she never got enough. She was right. Phone calls aren't enough. Like everyone else, mom needs flesh-and-blood relationships.

Learn from Your Anger

Children of the American Express Mom often struggle with anger and resentment. But they don't feel they can or should express it to her. Anger signals a problem. We need to first figure out what our anger is about, then use it in our relationship with mom.

You may experience two types of anger at the American Express Mom: *intrusion anger* and *wish disappointment.* Use your supportive remothering relationships to separate the two. They may feel the same, but they're very different. The first anger is useful for you and mom, and the second is reserved for you alone.

Intrusion anger is the irritation you may feel at mom's violation of your space: complaining about your not being with her enough and insisting on more time than you have. This anger is most likely based in reality and involves tendencies on mom's part to ignore your limits and adult life needs. You'll need to confront mother, explain the problem, and help her adjust to your limits. This anger is useful, as it helps you mark your territory yet continue to love her.

Wish disappointment occurs when we hold on to old desires for mom to be someone she never was, or someone she used to be. When mom isn't the mom we'd like, our younger parts become angry and hurt. For example, you might want her to be more sensitive to your needs to be on your own. Or you may wish for her to respect your adult decisions. This type of anger isn't the kind to share with mom. It's based on early needs and hurts that now belong to your support group. Allow your network to comfort and care for you, then grieve your sense of loss and move on. Grieving will free you up to accept mom for who she is, rather than to blame her for who she isn't. It can bring you closer to the real person in the friendship you are now developing.

The Mother-in-Law

Finally, a word about mothers-in-law. When we were in the early stages of writing this book, we canvassed many friends and colleagues about the subject of mom. Invariably, we heard one of three emphatic responses: "I need this to deal with my mother!" or "My spouse needs this to deal with her mother!" or "I need this to deal with my spouse's mother!" Mother problems are often mother-in-law problems.

Problems arise if your spouse still hasn't left his own American Express Mom. You may get pulled into the arguments or get ganged up on by your spouse and his mother. This can be as uncomfortable and crazymaking as your own mother problems.

Two pieces of advice may help here. First, whatever the problem with your mother-in-law, it is really an issue between you and your spouse. Instead of trying to convince your spouse to separate more from his mom, help him see that he isn't functioning as a spouse with you—no matter what the reason. You might say something like this:

- I feel alone when you spend so much time away from me.
- I can't support your financial irresponsibility and will have to take some action to protect myself.
- When we disagree and you withdraw from me and call your mom, it distances me more. I don't feel cherished by you, and I don't feel as if I am a priority with you.
- When you continually bring your conflicts with your mother to me, I feel she's sitting here at dinner with us every night. I'd like to have just me and you in the room; would you take your problems with her to your support group?

Secondly, work out your own relationship with your mother-in-law. If she is critical of you, don't ask your spouse for protection; call her and work it out. Or if she wants to talk to you about that son of hers, politely direct her to him and bow out. Keep the lines clean, and avoid the triangulations that occur. You'll save yourself years of trouble and perhaps come out with an amicable relationship with your mother-in-law.

WHAT IT CAN BE LIKE

Here are two examples of what can happen as you leave the American Express Mom relationship and begin to shoulder your own adult load.

In the first, mom doesn't respond well. In the second, she embraces the changes.

#1. Megan, a woman in her twenties, worked hard with her supportive friends to cut her mom ties. She had been living at home with her mother, and now realized that she would prefer her own apartment. She got a decent job, saved her money, and within a couple of years had her own place. Megan found she really enjoyed the peer friendships, dating relationships, and new experiences that the real world offered. Her twenties were becoming the exciting, growth-producing time they were meant to be.

Mom had a difficult go of it. She couldn't understand why Megan would ever leave, as she told Megan, "until you've got a marriage to go to." She felt that her daughter's moving out was a betrayal of their friendship and told her so. She tried to entice Megan back with promises of financial help and support: "If you'll move back in, you can have all the freedom you want, and no more worrying about where the money will come from." But when Megan would decline the offer, Mom would withdraw and pout.

It was tempting at times, as Megan did go through tough periods. She ate a lot of peanut butter sandwiches and spent evenings with videos and popcorn instead of in nice restaurants and at shows. But all in all, life on her own was worth it. She missed Mom's support, and her rejection was hurtful to Megan, yet she could honestly say, "Mom made it an issue of *her or me.* I wanted both of us, but she couldn't see it. So I had to choose me." It is to be hoped that one day Mom will reconnect. But Megan can't make it happen. In the meantime, she has a life to live.

#2. Brendan had a different situation. With his American Express Mom, he was the grown-up, and she was the child. He was faced with the problem when he married Gina and they had kids. Mom would call several times a week to ask why they weren't visiting more.

With the support of his wife and friends, Brendan sat down with Mom and explained how he wanted a friendship with her, yet some things would have to change. Mom needed to find other friends, and

Brendan and Gina would help in any way they could. It was hard to say, as Brendan thought Mom's feelings would be hurt.

Mom was saddened by the news. However, she was basically an honest person, and she understood the issue. She took Brendan up on his offer, and they began to investigate her neighborhood and city for social and supportive services. Mom was surprised and happy to find a good church and volunteer group at the hospital. She began to volunteer twice a week.

Brendan and his family called Mom and visited regularly. Their times together were fun and had a different quality than previous visits. Before, Mom had spent most of her time talking about her loneliness. Now she had stories to tell about her church and volunteer work, and she expressed more interest in their lives. The kids loved to bring their school drawings and crafts to Grandma. The change made Brendan want to visit more often, as he no longer felt under the weight of being Mom's life preserver.

As Mom grew older, she seemed to reverse the aging process. She began traveling, tried new hobbies, and kept making new friends. In this vein, she became a more interesting person to Brendan. He didn't realize they had so much in common. These growing up years, for both of them, were good ones.

CONCLUSION

Now we've worked through the six mothering types and the attendant problems and solutions. We hope that if you've seen yourself in at least one of these types, you are now able to follow the tasks involved in developing what you didn't get the first time around. In the next section, we will look at the special problems men and then women face in their mother issues.

Chapter Fourteen

For Women Only

Robin and her boyfriend Toby were at it again: Interminable Argument #25. It was like a finely scripted play in which both actors know their lines, the movement of the acts, and especially how the play will end. Argument #25 was always about Robin's mom, and both she and Toby always said the same things to each other. They were deeply in love and moving toward marriage, but this one argument always tended to muddy the waters for a few days.

Robin just couldn't say no to her mom, and Toby couldn't understand her difficulty. She would always plan their dates around Mother's schedule and cancel planned events if Mom wanted Robin around. Toby would say, "I know your parents' living room better than I do yours. Why can't you just get a life with me and without her? She'll be okay." The conflict tore Robin up, as she knew, on one level, that Toby was right. But another part of her would think, *He doesn't understand. How could he? He's a guy, and he can't feel what mothers feel. If he could only know how much Mom needs me and how hard it is for both of us.*

Robin was right about one thing: Women have unique struggles in their lives with their mothers. That is why this chapter is dedicated to those special problems only women face with mom.

Women and men are different in several ways: From womb to tomb, the sexes have anatomical, neurological, hormonal, and emotional dissimilarities. This makes for an interesting world, and it also creates the foundation for the differing ways the sexes relate to mom. They bond with her, grow up with her, and leave her in their own unique ways.

However, while men and women are different, they are still more alike than not. A great deal has been written that's quite helpful about the differences between the sexes, but much of it stereotypes the sexes in ways that are inaccurate. Women have assertive parts, and men have nurturant parts. The difference tends to be more a matter of degree and strength, rather than some huge dividing line between the two. There is a great deal of overlap between men's and women's issues.

But something is far more crucial than our sexual differences, and that is our character issues. So bear this caveat in mind as you read this chapter and the next.

LIKE LEAVING LIKE

Little girls are more like mom than they are like dad. They share biologies, emotions, and cultural mores with mother in ways that they don't with father. So, one of a father's tasks is to help coax his daughters out of the "mom orbit" into the larger world, beginning with himself.

Father functions as a sort of wedge between the early ultra-closeness between child and mom when the child is ready to separate more. With mom's support, the child is entranced by this second figure in her life with the deep voice and hairy chest. She begins to enter other relationships, starting with siblings, and moving on to neighborhood pals, school peers, career buddies, and finally to a marriage partner. Ideally, the child begins her leaving-home process in the early years of life, as she gradually works on both connecting with and disengaging from mom.

Girls have a disadvantage here as they learn to separate and develop their own identity. Boys are moving from someone unlike them toward someone very much like them. Thus, there is a biological reinforcement as little boys are drawn toward father. Girls, however, are moving from someone feminine and warm to someone a little scary and intimidating. The problem is a little like a rocket leaving Earth's orbit. The little girl has more "g's" keeping her close to Mother Earth. She must work harder than her brother at leaving that orbit in order to move into the outer world.

Because of this, many women find it particularly difficult to become independent and leave mom's nest. They feel the regressive tug back to mother more exquisitely than men; they miss her comfort or feel unprepared for the outside world.

As you become aware of this dynamic, surround yourself with supportive people who understand and who can be emotional anchors for you as you leave home. Toby couldn't "get it" with Robin; maybe he was too personally involved with the problem. But others, both male and female, can "get it" and help you with your own struggle to separate and become an individual. These safe people need to function like the "father wedge" and help you keep moving out, but without shaming or being critical of you. Your own task will be to accept that unique reality of "like leaving like" without either denying it or giving in to it.

WOMEN AS CONNECTORS

Women are more connectors at heart than men. They have more constitutional strengths in bonding, just as men do in aggressiveness. But being a "lover, not a fighter" brings its own special problem.

If you are a loving person, you have a well-developed ability to empathize. You feel the pain of others. You sense the depth of others' struggles, and you know what they need. It is a primary prerequisite for any meaningful relationship. Women have wonderful abilities to be empathic.

Yet empathy is a double-edged sword. If you have trouble separating from people, empathy can be a hindrance to you. The pain of the other person becomes your only reality. You get hung up here with mom as you sense her loneliness, fragility, or abandoned parts. You empathically "dive into mom" without even realizing it and give yourself over to comforting and protecting her. And you find yourself doing the same in your close relationships.

If you're the empathic type, realize you have a gift from God, one of his own deep character traits: "As a father has compassion on his children, so the LORD has compassion on those who fear him; for he knows how we are formed, he remembers that we are dust."[1] At the same time, add to your strengths in empathy such things as reality, truthfulness, and responsibility. Ask your friends to help you be a loving and honest person with mom and with them.

AGGRESSIVE CONFLICTS

Women tend to have more problems in the aggressive arena than men; this can lead to problems with both mom and life in general. They may have more struggles with the following "aggressive conflicts":

- assertiveness
- taking initiative
- confrontation
- experiencing and connecting with anger
- problem solving
- identity formation
- setting and keeping boundaries

Reasons for this are complex and involve the above constitutional problems, as well as emotional and cultural factors. But the real problem is that aggression is one of your two primary tools for leaving and cleaving. The other is love and support from others. So if you're struggling with mom, one reason may be that you have one leg tied behind you.

You can grow in healthy aggression. Find a supportive framework of people who want to help you take more ownership of yourself. Explore why you can't say no, or why you let people run all over you, or why you are passively compliant. Work on the tasks we mentioned in chapter 7. Start to repair and develop your abilities to be righteous, holy, and honest. You will begin noticing progress in all arenas of life: mom, love, and work.

MOTHER ISSUES DISGUISED AS FATHER ISSUES

We hear much today about dysfunctional father problems. Many women note their poor choices in boyfriends and husbands, or they may develop depression anxiety or compulsive disorders and make the connection that they had a problem father. They recall absent, distant, critical, abusive, weak, or scary dads. They are relieved that their present struggles have a past pattern that now makes sense to them, and they begin working on "father issues."

It has helped women to realize the reasons for and roots of their problems and that much of their current pain has to do with a past relationship. In addition, we have made a lot of progress in unearthing the father issues for people, looking at all the damage dads can do and discovering how to recover from those injuries.

However, some of this thinking oversimplifies and confuses important issues. For example, picking bad men isn't always due to having a bad dad, and having a distant father doesn't always create depression. We must investigate more deeply than this. Many women who grew up with absent fathers also had mothers who were both nurturing and assertive. Mom took responsibility for both mothering and fathering needs and made sure her daughter grew up in relationship with several safe men who could help in her character growth. These women may have grown up technically fatherless, but they still received all the "good stuff" they needed.

Some believe that all attachment problems are mom problems and that all aggression problems are dad problems. So the logic goes, if a woman has a hard time setting limits and being her own person, it's because of fathering issues. This is true, but incompletely so. Moms also have a lot to do with childhood assertiveness, and dads are able to teach tenderness. In fact, much of the material in this book has to do with how children are to learn their first no, their first independent steps, and their first identity moves with none other than mom. Mother issues of assertiveness occur years earlier than dad issues, which are a secondary process.

Kristin, for example, knew she was picking the wrong men. She found herself in her mid-thirties, leaving a second marriage, and then quickly getting involved with yet another man. The men she chose all tended to be strong, self-assured, and in control. Yet when she committed to them, their self-control would quickly turn into Kristin-control. They'd become dominating, critical, and perfectionistic with her.

When she talked to a friend about her destructive pattern, he said, "You had a distant dad, and you're looking for his strength and protection in the arms of a husband." That sounded logical. Kristin's mother had been quiet and nurturing, so as far as she could tell, Mom wasn't the issue. Kristin began working on the loss of her father. Yet after all her work, Kristin still found herself attracted to controlling men. It was only when she began seeing a therapist who recognized the deeper "mom" issue, that Kristin could truly begin to change.

The reality of Kristin's background was worse than she'd thought: Mom's quiet nurture disguised a passivity and lack of identity in Mom herself. So Mother failed to lead her daughter through the separating, individuating, and assertion training that Kristin needed. She taught Kristin to be sweet, passive, and dependent, but not to strike out on her own. As little girls do, Kristin then reached out for Dad, to repair what Mom couldn't. But he wasn't there either. Thus began the eternal search for the Knight in Shining Armor. The truth was, underneath the armored helmet was the face of a structure-building, assertive mother. Kristin had unknowingly disguised mother issues as father ones.

Like Kristin, you may think that your "man" problems are "dad" problems. They may be, but keep in mind the possibility that two dynamics are in play here: the mother who couldn't let go and the father who couldn't make his little girl feel special. They tend to occur simultaneously.

MOMS AND THEIR LITTLE GIRLS

Moms often hold on tighter to their daughters than they do their sons. There are certainly exceptions to this, as we've seen in this book. But mom usually exerts more regressive gravity force upon her daughter than her son. Everyone knows you have to let go of sons sooner or later.

A friend of mine once told me, "Mom always said, 'Boys grow up and go away; girls grow up and take care of Mama.'" And that had been my friend's game plan until she became depressed and began looking at the issues. This is an especially common dynamic among women who have problems with the Controlling Mom of chapters 6 and 7. Mom has her own separation problems, which she then places on her daughter. The little girl then grows up into a woman who feels guilty for leaving her "best friend" behind as she moves out into new relationships.

You might have experienced more of mom's clinginess because of your gender. You might even see this dynamic emerge: Your mother views you as her "soul sister." She may say things like, "We know what each other is thinking without saying it" and "We women need to stick together." Help mom understand that you want to stay close to her, but that you also have other friends now, and you want her to have her own. Watch out for her attempts to make you an ally in any conflict with dad, siblings, or friends, and disqualify yourself from these predicaments.

ONLY WOMEN CAN BE MOTHERS

This sounds self-evident, but the reality has a great deal of impact upon how you go about working on your mom issues. Whether you're a mother already, a potential mother, or childless by choice or circumstance, you still possess strong mothering parts created in you to nurture and protect. This makes a difference in how you move through your own growth process. Following are some of the factors:

Deal with Guilt and Anxiety

Many women are reading this book with fear and trembling. They are looking at the issues through two lenses: the lens of their own relationship with mom and the lens of their relationship with their kids. This second lens can cause a great deal of guilt and anxiety as you consider how you're impacting your children. One mom who was going over the material with me told me, "I wanted to read it for myself, but my own mothering issues kept getting in the way. I'd think, 'Am I too detached, or fragile, or controlling?'"

This is a real concern. Mothering is the most important relationship we have, and, if you are a mother, you have a tremendous responsibility. You're in the process of creating and developing life in another person in God's image. It's good for you to see the weight of your mothering for what it is and treat it as a serious task.

However, you can easily become paralyzed with guilt and anxiety, fearing that your character deficits will ruin your child. Some mothers become unreal or false, perfectionistic, or withdrawn from their child over these fears. This creates even more problems for the child. Not only does he have a mom who is imperfect, but now he also has one who's acting strange and worried about it.

If this is a concern of yours, here are two things that might help.

Good Moms Get Good Mothering

Being a good mom is a high calling and a wonderful goal. The best moms are people who have reached out and gotten remothering for themselves. It's like a law of physics: *You can't give what you have never received.* But you can give liberally when you've humbly internalized love and structure from God and his people: "We love because he first loved us."[2]

It's not selfish, then, to work on your own character issues. Rather, it's your responsibility, and it's good stewardship. It prepares you to take your place in the world as someone who has been offered to and now has something valuable to offer. Otherwise, you are giving from an empty cup. As you get involved in repairing your own issues of trust and identity in the context of helpful relationships, you will be surprised at how much more you have to give to your children. You will become less reactive to kid follies, and you can see better what your child really needs, whether it be love, limits, or education. You can look into the heart of the child, as your heart has been entered and loved.

Good Enough vs. Perfect

Give up the Supermom model of motherhood. It never worked anyway. Perfectionistic mothers tend to either go crazy or make their spouse, their kids, or their kids' spouses crazy. Stop trying to be the perfect mom, and be content with being a "good-enough" mom.

"Good enough" means adequate but fallible and still growing. It means you are working on the six dimensions of motherhood we've been discussing. You want to be

- emotionally present instead of absent/detached
- containing instead of fragile
- supporting of separateness instead of resisting it

- accepting of badness instead of demanding a Trophy Child
- promoting of adulthood instead of keeping her a kid
- helping him leave instead of being an American Express Mom

Don't let this list intimidate you as you look at it from your own "I'm a mother" lens; it is only meant to give you *direction*. Good-enough moms are aware of their weaknesses and tendencies. They are working on doing the right thing for themselves and their child. They are getting help in their mothering weaknesses from safe people.

Good-enough moms assume they will make mistakes with their child, and they factor that in to their mothering. They know they won't always be there as they should. They aren't surprised by their failures; they are prepared to correct them, learn from them, and move on. As my (Dr. Townsend's) son Ricky, at five years old, said when he dropped the ball as we were playing catch, "Oops, learned again!"

Stay in the Light of Relationship

It is not enough simply to prepare for being a fallible, real mom—you need to provide solutions. This might mean making yourself vulnerable and accountable to others who can help you see blind spots in your mothering and support you as you change hurtful ways. You'll need to stay exposed to the light of your safe relationships: "But whoever lives by the truth comes into the light, so that it may be seen plainly that what he has done has been done through God."[3]

Resist the tendency to hide your weaknesses because of shame or guilt and to try to work them out all alone. Stay in the light of loving and safe others, who know your foibles, will accept you where you are, and help you get better. Every isolated Supermom has some weak or condemned part of herself that she is concealing inside.

I've seen miracles happen to those in groups who "stay in the light." One single mother was having a horrible time with her fifteen-year-old. She was trying to make him "want" good grades, "not want" bad friends, and "want" to spend Saturdays with her. Her life had turned upside down as he continually stymied her with his counter-moves. Finally, another mother in the group said, "Toni, he has three more years with you. He's almost grown. Give up the Beaver Cleaver

image, tell him the rules and consequences, and let him decide." Toni
heeded the counsel. The next time her son got into trouble, she
refused to rescue him. And, as she told it, "Two weeks in Juvie Hall
brought more reality to him than all my nagging and pleading ever
did." Better for him, less trouble for her.

Admit Your Mistakes to Your Child

Moms would like to protect their child from the knowledge that
they are imperfect sinners. Some mothers hide their failings to protect their own sense of entitlement, specialness, and self-esteem. But
most hide because they fear the information will injure the child at
some level. They are concerned that the child will be unable to trust
mother, as she has proven herself to be unsafe.

But, children are smart. When mom fails, they wait to see what
mom does with failure. When she comes to the child, admits failure,
asks forgiveness, and changes her own behavior, she has truly mothered her child well. Here are some of the dynamics that occur when
you admit failure to your child:

You take responsibility for your own badness. Children, by definition, are porous and spongelike in their developing character. They
aren't solidly defined in their identity apart from mom, nor are they
solidly defined as to what is their badness and what is mom's. In
abused children, for example, we often see a grandiose sense of
responsibility for mom's maltreatment of them; the child actually
believes that mother's abuse is his fault. He thinks, *If I hadn't been
bad, she wouldn't have hurt me.* Taking on mom's badness causes all
sorts of character and emotional problems in later years for children,
such as isolation, guilt, masochism, and seeking out destructive relationships.

But when you confess your mistakes to your child, a wonderful
transformation occurs. *The burden of your badness is lifted from your
child's shoulders and put back where it belongs—onto yours.* It
becomes your problem, one for which you can take responsibility. The
child no longer has to deal with your mistakes, but only her own. This
models for her such good things as clear boundaries, the ability to sort

out fault and responsibility in conflicts, and the ability to reject guilt-producing messages from others.

You provide the opportunity for reconciliation. Your child needs to know that conflicts with you can be resolved. The distance a problem creates can be overcome with your ability to reconcile. Children need this knowledge to be able to deal with disagreements, arguments, and value conflicts in adult relationships. They need the ability to have distance without fear that conflict will remove them from attachment and love.

For example, when Geena yelled in a burst of anger at her seven-year-old daughter Courtney, the little girl withdrew and became silent. The safety of the loving mother inside of her was suddenly disrupted by this yelling, angry mom. Geena, aware of what had happened, went to her side and said, "Honey, I'm sorry. I yelled at you, and you probably don't feel close to me right now. It wasn't your fault, it was mine. Please forgive me, and I'll work on changing my temper." Courtney began to feel her loving mom inside of her again, as her real mom came to her in reconciliation. She hugged Mother and went off to play, reconciled inside in the same way that Mom had reconciled outside.

You model ownership and forgiveness. Your child also gains the advantage of seeing how a grown-up takes responsibility for her problems and asks forgiveness from those they've hurt. They are quite interested in this process and aware of what's going on. They want to learn how to deal with these issues in a way that's "caught," rather than "taught." My wife, Barbi, and I have watched this process many times in our own children. As we give up our "good self" to admit our faults, they begin taking on these qualities in their relationships. It makes everything worthwhile to walk around the corner and see a six-year-old taking initiative to apologize to his younger brother for hitting him.

Children have a remarkable ability to forgive if you present the problem to them in a way they can understand. They want to be loved and close, and they don't hang on to resentment and bitterness in the same way we do. If their needs are met and their feelings are not minimized by a defensive mom, they don't take long to grieve the pain she causes them and move on to more growth. Much better for them

230 • THE MOM FACTOR

to forgive you now, than thirty years and a couple of marriages later in a therapist's office.

You take up the slack. Admitting weaknesses to your child also "covers a multitude of other things." In other words, children of confessing moms are able to bear and tolerate many other weaknesses in her. They can encounter attachment or boundary problems in mom and recover from them much more quickly. Without the emotional confusion of taking responsibility for mom's mistakes, they can accept the reality of her failing them, and still flourish.

We have noted this principle time and time again: *People who come from high-functioning but in-denial parents tend to function worse than those who had more dysfunctional but confessing parents.* If a child knows that mom is weak but growing, she won't take her mother's problems as her own, but she'll get help from others to shore up her own weaknesses. From an honest mom she learns that even painful truths are better than secrets and hiding in her own life. She'll learn that reality is her friend.

Give the Kid Some Credit

Finally, moms, you might as well admit your weaknesses because, much of the time, children are aware of our foibles anyway. They may be young, but they haven't yet figured out how to deceive themselves in quite the sophisticated fashion we grown-ups have. So you're often-times simply affirming verbally what they already know deep inside. Validation of reality can bring enormous structural growth to a child.

I was working with my son Ricky once on his tendency to dart away from me in parking lots. Fearing that he might get hit by a car that was backing up, I told him, "I'm going to have to give you a consequence the next time you dart from me." Ricky's response surprised me. "You give me too many chances," he said. "You should put me in time-out for this one." I wouldn't have told my parents that when I was six!

Ricky was telling me two things. First, he wanted more structure from me; he needed me to pull the reins in a little so that he could feel safe within his own structure. Second, he was telling me he knew where I wasn't parenting him correctly. Why should I hide it? Let your child know that you see his or her unspoken reality and that you take responsibility for it.

Remember this rule of thumb: *People who are looking at their own issues are always better parents than those who are looking else-where.* When you own your mistakes, you don't displace, deny, or blame—all of which put the problems somewhere where they cannot be resolved. Whatever mistakes you make, if you own them, you are in control. You can do something about them and get help and support.

We hope you are encouraged about working out your mothering issues as a woman. Remember, you are a part of the legacy of Eve, who is the grounding and source of nurturance for all of us. You have a critical and special place in the survival of the family, our religion, the culture, and humanity itself.

As you become the woman God intended you to be, you redeem the mothering you received, and you redemptively pour out your own love onto the world. By so doing, you make it possible for the growth process to continue in future generations. These words of Mary's cousin Elizabeth, then, also apply to you: "Blessed is she who has believed that what the Lord has said to her will be accomplished!"[4]

Chapter Fifteen

For Men Only

Bill walked into his supervisor's office for the weekly management meeting. He did not expect anything out of the ordinary, but he had only been on the job a few weeks and had not had much experience with his new boss, Peggy. She seemed nice, and he enjoyed her personality; however, most of their interactions so far had been somewhat surface, as he was in an orientation period. Still, he had no reason to expect any trouble.

"Bill," she began, "I want to talk to you about this Westward account. Something here doesn't look right. Can you explain these bids you put together?"

"Sure," he replied. "I put together a pricing plan that would fit with all of their consulting needs for the duration of the project. Is there a problem?"

"There most certainly is," Peggy continued. "I think you need to recommend an entire line of risk coverage that you have totally omitted. Why did you do that?"

"Well, on review of their present coverage, I think it would be overselling them. They just don't need it." Bill felt good about trying to save the customer money.

"Well, you're wrong," she replied. "Go back and redo the whole thing and include a bid for the extra line. They are clearly exposed in that area, and I want to make sure you sell them all that they need, or we will find ourselves with one dissatisfied customer later on."

"I disagree," he continued. "I have been selling that product for years, and they just don't need it." Bill felt himself becoming tight around the collar. He was getting angry.

"Well, I really think you are wrong, so I want you to redo it and get it to me by Friday. We really need to write this business," Peggy said. "That will be all."

Bill felt himself losing it. "Look, lady," he said. "I don't know who you think you are, but I have been doing this a lot longer than you have ever thought of. And I know what I am talking about, and these people do not need that product, and I am not going to sell it to them. So, if that is a problem for you, then you can take this job and do whatever you want with it." And with that, he left.

As Bill walked out, he felt an initial burst of freedom. It was exhilarating. He walked out the front door, got into his car, and began to drive home. And then it hit him. "What in the world have I done?" he wondered aloud. "There was no reason for that. She was just doing her job. What's my problem?"

He began to reflect on other times when he had reacted in similar ways. Have a disagreement, get mad and harsh, walk out instead of "lose." The problem was that he had "lost" a lot in the process: customers, relationships, and promotions. Chances were that he had lost a lot in his relationship with Peggy, if not his job.

But nowhere did the problem bother him as much as in his relationships with women he cared about. He just couldn't seem to make a long-term, romantic relationship work. Thirty-five, successful, and still single, he was discouraged about this pattern. At times like this, he wished he were in a serious relationship so he could go home and share all of this with someone. But just the previous week, he had had an argument with his girlfriend and broken up. His aloneness was particularly poignant as he thought of the similarities between that breakup and what happened this morning. What was his problem?

Many men have similar patterns. They are "good guys," charming, socially adept, talented, and generally do well in the world of people . . . until. Until they find themselves in a situation in which they feel threatened by a woman, or more accurately, feel threatened "with" a woman. For in reality, it is not the woman who is threatening, but their own internal stance toward women in general. The pattern goes something like this:

1. Have an initial or sustained good connection, with mutual enjoyment of the relationship.

2. Deepen the relationship based on things going well, and some sort of appreciation of who they are, either in love or work.
3. Have an interaction or two where the woman becomes assertive in some way.
4. React to her assertiveness with either anger, control, or avoidance of the relationship.
5. She returns to her previous stance and things go on okay, or she remains assertive and the relationship comes to an end.

Every day, and in a variety of contexts, men have problems with women, problems that are mostly of their own making. Their internal stance and the pattern of their relationships with women are set up in such a way that the cycle repeats itself and leads to one broken relationship after another. Or the two parties do a stilted dance in a long-standing relationship that is unsatisfactory to both partners.

In Bill's case, a woman's assertiveness led to the conflict. Sometimes it will be a woman's connecting parts that bring about the exit.

David was a charmer. A successful businessman and an active social person, he was attractive to everyone who knew him. Especially women. Something about his boyish charm and personality drew women to him like a magnet. He always had "several going at once," as all of his friends put it. But, they would all seem to fall by the wayside after a few months.

David would initially meet a woman, charm her, be very interested in her, and have all of his friends thinking that this time he had found "the one." There would be a whirlwind romance, lots of fun and travel, and the woman would be hopelessly in love. And then, predictably after about three months of dating, David would just fall out of sight. The woman would call his friends, searching for answers. "What happened? Things were going so well." To which his friends could only reply, "That was probably the problem."

For it was when things were going well that David would begin his exit. He would call less often. He needed more time with his buddies. His business all of a sudden needed more from him. His withdrawal could always be explained and seemed legitimate. But eventually the picture would become clear. He was out of there. As soon as love entered the picture, David was out, and another heart was broken.

So, in David's case, it was not a woman's assertiveness that ended the relationship. It was a woman's desire for the relationship to become "something more." It was when her attachment to him increased and she asked more from him in the area of commitment. For Bill, when it got equal and direct, he was gone. For David, it was when it got deep that he heard the train whistle blow.

Both of these men were single. But the pattern is just as common with married men. They may not leave the relationship as in divorce or separation. But they do leave the relationship emotionally when they encounter assertiveness or attachment from their wives. What causes men to do this? In this chapter we will look at several reasons why men struggle in their relationships, especially with women, and what that has to do with the mothering process.

LOVE HER, LEAVE HER, RETURN TO HER

To understand what is going on with men in their relational world, we must first look at some developmental pattern in their childhood.

In the beginning, the young male is connected to mom. If things go well with the attaching mom who we described earlier, he learns to feel comfortable with his dependency on her. Bonding, needing, and connecting are comfortable for him, and he enjoys being close. He is one with mom.

He begins to separate from her in the second year or so of life and moves out of "oneness" into a separate identity. It is important that he not only become a separate person, but that he become secure in his gender identity. As he moves away from mom and toward dad for identification with a male identity, he accomplishes two things. One, he becomes a separate person, attaching to his father and gaining more autonomy from the oneness with mom. Two, in his attachment to his father and identification with him as male, he gains gender identity. From this strong base he becomes someone who is comfortable with connection and dependence on someone, but separate enough to be autonomous and an individual away from his object of dependency. He also becomes secure in his male identity. In short, he can love mom, be independent from her, feel like a man with her, and never fear loss of his masculinity.

As he continues to grow, he continues to find out more and more about who he is as a person. Mom disciplines him and does not allow him to rule her. She teaches him to respect her limits and boundaries. Then as he experiences himself in many arenas, he learns that he does some things well and some other things not so well. He learns that he is not ideal, but real. He has good parts and bad parts. And if mom has no agenda for him to be perfect or ideal, they can both become comfortable in the reality of his "good-enough" imperfection.

Then, a bit later, he begins to identify more with his father's male role. He notices the sexual differences between himself and women, and he finds himself attracted to them and wants to gain their attraction as well. In childhood, his need is for affirmation and love, and later, during puberty, it becomes more sexual, although the sexual underpinnings are there from childhood. He figures out the attraction thing with mom; if he likes her and she likes him, he is set up to find "one just like the one that married dear old dad," as the old folk song goes.

In adolescence, he moves farther and farther away from his childhood dependency on mom, and into the world of male competition and female pursuit. If mom is able to encourage him to be strong as he enters the world, to find women of his choice, to rough and tumble in his favorite competitive arenas, and to remain respectful of her in his budding aggression, he continues the path. Eventually he leaves her altogether, and then, in one sense, he returns.

He finds a woman to whom he can have a significant attachment, and he marries. With all of that secure identity, he depends on his new love, is strong and separate with her when it comes to boundaries and limits, stays free of her control, is comfortable with both his and her imperfections, and sees her as a sexual object of desire while feeling secure in his attractiveness to her. In this way, he has "returned to woman." As Genesis puts it, "a man shall leave his father and mother and cling to his wife, and the two shall become one." He leaves mom and finds another woman, and the two live happily ever after.

That's a nice story, and it happens every day. But not always. If men do not do well with mom, they often are not going to do well with the woman they return to—unless the conflicts and stances with mom are worked out first. God has designed us to return and to cling. To be "one with" again. But the second time is from a place of adult maturity instead of a dependent and "trying to find oneself" stance like one was with mother. If things go wrong, the "return" will not be to intimacy, freedom, enjoyment, respect, and fulfillment but to the old conflicts and their oft-practiced solutions. When men have not gotten what they needed in the mothering process, or they have not used it, or if they have rejected it in some way, they go into their present relationships from either an unfinished or otherwise conflictual stance. Let's look at how unfinished business with mom specifically affects men.

LOOKING FOR OR AVOIDING NURTURE

Remember the "Connecting Mom" of chapters 2 and 3? We talked about our need for learning how to connect and depend on another person relationally. Getting close, trusting, feeling our needs, and all of the other basic aspects of being a connecting person begin with mom or the one doing the mothering. What do men do when they can't connect? Usually, they either avoid intimacy, or they fight against it.

Do you remember David's story? He was fine until a woman wanted to connect more deeply with him, and then he would slip away. What was really confusing is that often after he had created enough distance, he might return. He would reignite the relationship, and the woman would get her hopes up thinking he was now ready. They would date, get back into the swing of things, and then he would leave again. He got scared when the connection deepened.

David may have been abandoned as a child, or had a detached mom, or was one of those children who just could not be comforted. Whatever the reason, the fear and the conflict over dependency is still there. When he gets close to a woman and starts to depend on her, then he gets afraid. So the woman *is not getting someone who has loved mom, left her, and returned to love a woman.* She is getting someone who may be looking for mothering but is so afraid of it that he runs or fights.

Aggression and fighting are another way that men avoid their dependent longings. To avoid the closeness, couples will often begin a fight just as things are beginning to go well. Often, this is because of men's fears of connection and dependency. In reality, the man is a fussy child in a two-hundred-pound body—it looks frightening, and it can be, but underneath it is really weakness.

Addictions can be an attempt to finish those dependent longings. Men will replace their need for connection with just about anything other than connection: work, sex, drugs and alcohol, sex, hobbies, sex, food, and a host of other substitutes. Anything but intimacy. The problem is that the need for intimacy still remains. As God said of Adam, "It is not good for man to be alone."[1]

LOOKING FOR CONTAINMENT

If the containing mother failed or was not utilized, men will do the same thing with this function as with their need to connect: look for it and avoid it at the same time. This is the story of men who cannot allow their significant other to get close when they are upset. Many women say of their husbands, "It seems like when he most needs me, he goes away or pushes me away." And that is accurate. If a man is not used to having his feelings contained, he will try to contain them himself and fear someone else getting close to the chaos.

He may demand containment aggressively. Some men won't allow their significant others to leave their side. They won't allow them to have feelings or chaos of their own. They just demand that the woman be a "soother." She has to remain calm, soothing, present, and "be there for him," in a way that only a mother can. When she fails, there is conflict.

DON'T TELL ME WHO TO BE

Unless men have good boundaries from their mothering, they will not have a chance with women. They either control, intrude on, and damage women, or they feel controlled and smothered by them.

Kevin loved his wife. He adored her. But he was not strong enough in his own boundaries to say no to her. The chief area that he experienced this in was his own need for time with a hobby or with friends. When he wanted space in which to pursue a hobby or be with his friends, she wanted him home, and he just could not stand up for his own separateness. He would comply and then resent her, and then his loving feelings would begin to disappear. This pattern continued until finally his resentment built up to the point that he left her. He complained that he "felt smothered and controlled." What he could not see was that this was his own fault. Boundary issues are always our responsibility, not the "controlling" person's.

Kevin had never established boundaries with his own mom. A strong-willed woman, she was content to be in control of him, and he had never left her. So, instead of leaving Mom and cleaving to his wife, he turned his wife into Mom and left her instead. This is one of the most common divorce scenarios. The problem is that sometimes these men never resolve the issue, and then they repeat the pattern.

Men cannot stand for women to control them; it feels too regressive to lose their independence, separateness, and masculinity. They will do anything to regain those things if the boundaries break down: withdraw, fight, have an affair, leave, work more—whatever it takes. Anything seems like a solution if it helps them regain their power and separateness.

They see the "controlling woman" as the problem and fail to deal with their own flimsy boundaries. If they had established good boundaries with their mothers, they would not fear being controlled by their wives or girlfriends. "Stop controlling me!" would turn into "No, I don't want to." They see their wives and girlfriends as the controlling mother they are not strong enough to deal with, and so they leave.

THE PERFECT WOMAN

Ann sat in my (Dr. Cloud's) office enraged at Tom. "I am sick and tired of being his hood ornament. 'Change your hair. Dress this way. Join this club.' He is always so concerned about how I look and the image I portray. I can't stand it anymore." I could see why. Tom's expectation for her was so high, she could not possibly stand it for very long and be sane. He harped at her imperfections constantly. I wanted to scream, "Who do you think you are, Don Juan?"

It soon became clear, as we got further into it, that Tom had the unresolved integration of his own imperfections that we discussed in chapter 8. He had not gotten to a point where he could accept all of himself, both good and bad, and so therefore he could not accept imperfections in others.

This search for the ideal woman keeps many men from finding true intimacy. If they do marry, they do not really get close to their wives, for they always fantasize a relationship that is better than the one they have. Sometimes they act out their fantasy in an affair. They forget that their wife or girlfriend seemed that wonderful to them at one time, until they actually had her. Then, the distance and the ability to idealize is gone, and she goes "bad" in their mind. Others seem prettier, smarter, nicer, kinder, more fun, or whatever.

The flip side of this dynamic is when men require their women to mirror their wishes to be ideal. Any criticism from their significant other is taken as "you're all bad." They demand worship and idealization instead of real love that includes their imperfections. When they are criticized, they withdraw or fight. And then they run to their fantasy person who sees them as wonderful. The affair can meet this need for adoration because it is not lived in day-to-day reality. It is secret, compartmentalized, and romanticized; the woman never has to deal with the reality of imperfections in these men. So, they see their mistress as good and their wife as a nagging witch.

AMERICAN EXPRESS PAYMENTS

If you are a man and have never done the "leaving home" thing, you will not find a truly satisfying relationship with a woman or fulfill your career aspirations. You still have too many control and security issues.

In the control sense, you still feel like your mom is the hub of the universe. You haven't established your own sense of adulthood separate from her. Psychologically, even though you might have your own place, you still live at home with mom. So she still, at some level, has control. If you don't have your own life apart from her, whatever life you do have you are renting from her. Ultimately, you lack control of yourself (see the symptom list in chapter 12).

To the extent that this is true, you may have difficulty directing your career, and you will have control issues with women. When they assert themselves, you will probably either resent them as "controlling mothers," or give in to their control and remain a little boy. And little boys over eighteen are never satisfied with either their partners or themselves.

When it comes to security, you probably still look to women to provide basic security instead of feeling secure in yourself. Therefore, you are forced back into a dependent mode with women and in your career, and you will never find one or the other ultimately fulfilling. For instance, we are motivated to work in part out of security needs, as well as actualization needs. If mom or mother substitutes are still your security, you will lack the motivation and drive to take the risks and tolerate the frustration necessary to find your own sense of accomplishment. You will continue to depend on mom security and your sense of accomplishment. This can happen whether you are single or married. If you haven't emotionally left mom, you aren't ready to either love a woman correctly or succeed on your own.

STILL-THE-BOSS MOM ISSUES

The dynamics of still being "one down" to mom are similar. Bill, in the beginning of this chapter, had never become an equal with women. He still felt so "one down" to his own mother, that whenever he encountered assertive women, he could only fight. In his mind, it was either dominate or be dominated. So, when bosses or lovers would assert themselves, a fight ensued. When Bill finally learned to feel equal instead of one down or one up to women, he found some satisfying mutual relationships and stopped having authority problems with women.

SAY IT AGAIN

All of these issues really say the same thing over again: If you are not finished with mothering, you are going to have problems. If you are a man, those problems are going to get you into conflicts, particularly in your relationships with women.

The problem is ultimately one of *regression*. If you are not finished with mom or mothering, every woman becomes a potential mother or mother figure. You regress to a little boy or teenager and turn the woman you care about into a mom. You will use her to resolve old issues, but it never works unless you are doing it in a conscious, directed, and purposeful way and with her permission. This is why healing environments are so crucial. You are in a support group to be helped, and everyone acknowledges that.

But this is not so in a dating relationship or a marriage. You are there as an adult, not as a child. And when you turn a wife or girlfriend into a healer, you run into trouble, because she has assumed that you are going to perform and act like an adult. And so when she makes a request that adults should be capable of—intimacy, boundaries, confrontation, equality—she thinks she is making a reasonable request. But then she hears the message in one way or another, "Don't mother me!" What you have to remember is that *only a little boy can be mothered.*

So watch for how you turn adult relationships into childhood struggles or attempts to get childhood needs met. They can be met, but both parties must understand that this is a part of the relationship. You may need to say, "I feel small right now and need some nurture." Or, "I am feeling 'all bad' right now and need reassurance that you still think I'm okay." All of these things are fine, but they need to be explicit and not acted out in a convoluted fashion. Make sure you own and directly express your needs rather than act them out.

SPECIFIC STYLES OF AVOIDING RESOLVING MOTHER ISSUES

Men are very good at leaving mother issues unresolved. Too often mothers have enabled this pattern, or a woman can be found who will. The whole idea of resolving mother issues is to find good mothering and bring all of your different parts to the relationship appropriately, and thus integrate as a person. You must have supportive relationships in order to integrate all of those feelings and parts that you did not experience with mom and have them integrated: needy feelings, dependent feelings, assertive boundary setting, respect for others' boundaries, imperfections, forgiving others' imperfections, sexual feelings, talents, and thoughts and opinions. In other words, *learn how to be all of yourself with women.*

The Alternative

The alternative to being all of yourself with a woman is to be different parts of yourself with different women. This is called splitting. A man keeps the different aspects of himself separated and finds different relationships in which to act out those different parts. Here are some examples.

Love-Sex Split

Some men have women they love and other women they act or feel sexual toward. They have "love objects" and "sex objects." These men cannot bring both their loving parts and their sexual parts to the same woman. So, a husband may love his wife but have an affair. At times, the sexualized liaison is interpreted as love, until he makes the break from his wife and tries to make it with his lover. Caught in the same pattern, he becomes disillusioned and wants his wife back or begins to look for a third woman.

The single man may say, "I love you, but I'm not attracted to you." Certainly this is often true; we are not physically attracted to everyone we love. But if the woman with whom he connects and the one to whom he's attracted are never the same person, he has a problem.

Fusion-Unavailable Split

Sometimes those men who cannot get their boundaries together in relationships fuse with a woman who loves them and long for a woman who does not. They get close to the available one, but become compliant and codependent, lose their passion, and then long for a distant love object. The distance provides the boundaries they lack, and so they can feel the passion again. But what they need to do is to bring their aggressive sides and their boundaries to one relationship.

Use One-Respect Another

This man finds one woman to meet his selfish needs and another to respect and adore. Typically, the used woman has limited boundaries and self-respect and does not require him to respect her. He simply uses her to regulate his different moods and appetites. She obliges, hoping for love, but then he goes away until he needs her again. At the same time, he pants after the second woman, doing everything he can to please her, until he has her.

This man needs boundaries put on his self-centeredness. He must learn that he cannot use women and receive anything in return. He also needs self-respect so that he doesn't act so adoring and sacrificial in a crazy way toward the longed-for one.

Moral-Immoral

Men sometimes have moral parts and immoral parts that are unintegrated. They are still hiding their "bad boy" side in shame from mom. They find different women with whom they can relate from their different parts. They may respect a wife with their moral side and have an affair where they let their "badness" show. Many religious leaders who have affairs are in this kind of good boy/bad boy split. They are good in the pulpit and to the wife and then find someone with whom they can live out their badness. All this to avoid integrating and bringing all of themselves to the same person.

Extremes

In trying to prevent the regressive experience we have described in this chapter, men usually revert to one of two immature styles: aggression or pleasing. They become hostile and aggressive with women to ward off the conflicts, or they comply and fuse with women, acting like little boys. Be aware of both of these tendencies. Neither is the way to be a grown man with women.

The Answer

The answer to splitting is to learn to be *all* of yourself with women. Bring your needs, your strengths, your skills, your weaknesses, your

bad parts, your grief, your sexuality, and all of the rest of you into relationship. This is how integration takes place.

You can begin to do that where you are. Find some safe relationships and bring all of yourself to them—from your dependent
parts to your independent ones. To be known is the beginning of
being made whole. Talk about all of these parts.

What About Dad?

Some men who have not finished with mom have a father problem. Men are designed to identify with dad for gender and sex role
identification, so that they might separate from their mothers. But if
dad is unavailable, they are left fused with mom, in conflict with her,
or pulled into the spouse position in some sick way. The fused version
can leave men with fears about their masculinity or sexuality. The
combative version leaves them empty inside, and when a boy must
play the role of spouse in any way, he will have difficulty separating
as well as have extreme narcissistic problems.

If you are ever to work out some of the more aggressive tasks
with women, you will need some men with whom to identify. A boy's
attachment to his male role models gives him strength to stand up to
women. If you lack male strength, you will continually be controlled
or fear being controlled by the women in your life. Grown men love
women; they are not controlled by them. Use the men in your support systems as role models to help you in your healing process with
mom.

Being a Nurturing Father

If you are grown and a father now, the more you can make yourself emotionally available to your wife and children, the fewer mother
problems they will have. A loved wife makes a better mother. And
children whose fathers love them are better able to separate from
their mothers and establish their own identity. If they can see good
modeling between the sexes, they will appreciate, and not resent or
avoid, the differences. Be a good dad, and you will add to the number of good moms in the world.

GROW UP

Men, there is only one way to summarize all of this—grow up. If you still have unfinished business with mother, you would do well to begin working on those issues so that you can treat your woman well and succeed in your career.

You will need a good counselor or support system to help you. If gender issues are involved, make sure that you avail yourself of some good male models, and find good women who will stand by you as well. You will need both to cure your mothering issues.

If you can get the mothering you need, work out the issues with your real mom, leave the dependent stance, and return to women as equals, you will find true fulfillment at the end of your journey. As God said, "It is not good for man to be alone."

Chapter Sixteen

What About Now?

When we began writing this book, my (Dr. Townsend's) wife, Barbi, liked the concept, but she voiced a concern. "I believe this book needs to be written," she said. "But now that I'm a mom myself, I have a lot more empathy for the job. Be gentle with mom." We tried to follow her advice.

We sincerely hope that we have communicated our respect for both the role and persons of motherhood. We are "pro-mother." In fact, we have spent, and still spend, a great deal of our own clinical training and growth emphasizing the study of the mothering process. We believe that mothering can make the difference between wasted lives and full lives, and we support and honor all the mothers who enter into this process to make a difference in the right direction.

We hope we haven't "mom bashed," but rather have helped you become aware of and take responsibility for the following:

- your own childhood
- your present character growth issues and tasks
- your present relationship with mother
- your present relationships with others
- your own parenting issues

Believe it or not, both of us have moms! They are human, and we ourselves gave them their share of headaches. But today we enjoy friendships with them that bring us much fulfillment and joy.

However, if we were to describe our intent in this book with one word, it would be *reconciliation*. When people are reconciled, they are restored to those from whom they were alienated and they are able to reconnect.

Reconciliation is one of our primary needs. God created us to reconcile relationships of all kinds. As we enter the process of growth and repair, especially concerning our moms, we are then able to bring peace to those who are alienated.

You may be facing one or more of the following types of reconciliation:

Reconciliation between yourself and mother. As an adult, you may now need to invite mom into the reconciliation process, if she is willing. You may need to forgive her for her mistakes. Or you may need to ask her forgiveness for your responses to her. When you reconcile with a willing mom, you don't forget the past; you *redeem* it. In other words, you bring the hurtful issues from your childhood to the present, get the unmet needs met by other people, and move into a mutual friendship with mom. You set limits and develop the relationship the way friends do.

Reconciliation within yourself. You need to deal with any alienation within your own character. This might mean healing a hurt from your childhood. It might mean accepting realities of the past and grieving them now in the present in the comfort of your safe people. It may mean giving up your own desires and wishes for that which can never be—things like

- Mom's refusal or inability to have a close relationship with you
- Mom's encouraging you in your own God-given separate identity
- Mom's acceptance of the "real you"
- Mom's viewing you as a grown-up
- Mom's owning and taking responsibility for her character limitations

This type of reconciliation involves you, God, and your support network. It doesn't really have much to do with mom anymore if she declined to be a part of it. Therefore, you accept the pain of these realities and get these needs met by others.

Reconciliation with your safe relationships. You'll want to stay connected to, and be on short accounts with, your remothering people. They are the ones who will help you finish what was undone or injured in the past. They are the ones who are now assigned to help you grow. Value them, let them love you, love them, be open to them, and heed them.

Reconciliation to responsibility. We've emphasized throughout this book that who we are today is largely the result of two factors: our significant developmental relationships, of which mother is most important, and our response to those relationships. We always have some responsibility in choosing love or isolation, life or death, light or darkness, and truth or deception. The older we are, the more responsibility we bear. We need to embrace that responsibility and not be afraid of the task. How we conduct our lives is our affair. The buck truly does stop with us. We must stop denying our issues and blaming mom, God, circumstances, or others. We must begin the long journey of repair for ourselves.

Reconciliation to God. Finally, we need to be reconciled with the Reconciler. God is the one who can't be proven, but is always there. He loves you personally and by name. When we all sinned and became disenfranchised and isolated from his love, he took the initiative, by his Son's death on the cross, to reconcile us back to relationship with him: "God was reconciling the world to himself in Christ, not counting men's sins against them."[1] If you have never asked Christ to come into your life, forgive you, and let you start anew with God, we invite you to do so. If you're a Christian who is alienated from God, we urge you to reconnect with him and his love.

This reconciliation forms the very foundation for our ability to forgive and to reconnect, not only with God but with mom, others, and ourselves. Reconciliation transforms us into the loving and working people we were intended to be. God bless you and your future growth.

Henry Cloud, Ph.D.
John Townsend, Ph.D.
Newport Beach, California 1995

For information about tapes, speaking engagements, a resource catalogue, or a Cloud-Townsend seminar near you, call 1-800-676-HOPE, or write

Cloud-Townsend Communications
260 Newport Center Drive, #430
Newport Beach, CA 92660

Notes

Chapter One: What About Mom, Anyhow?

[1]Daniel Goleman popularized the concept of emotional IQ in his book, *Emotional Intelligence* (Bantam Books, 1995).

Chapter Two: The Phantom Mom

[1]Psalm 22:9 NASB.
[2]Ephesians 3:17.
[3]Psalm 22:9.
[4]1 John 4:20.
[5]Matthew 22:39.

Chapter Three: Rebuilding Your Connection

[1]Matthew 7:18.
[2]Matthew 12:48–50.
[3]Luke 10:42.
[4]Also see chapter 11 "Where Are the Safe People?" of our book, *Safe People* (Grand Rapids: Zondervan, 1995).
[5]Psalm 116:5.
[6]2 Corinthians 5:10.
[7]For more information on these tasks, also see *Changes That Heal* by Henry Cloud (Grand Rapids: Zondervan, 1994).
[8]John 15:9 NASB.
[9]1 John 4:8.
[10]For more information on defenses, see *Hiding from Love* by John Townsend (Grand Rapids: Zondervan, 1996).
[11]Matthew 6:12.

Chapter Four: The China Doll Mom

[1]Matthew 23:37.
[2]Job 6:14 NASB.

Chapter Five: Getting It Together

[1]John 3:4.
[2]1 Peter 4:10.

³Job 6:14.
⁴Colossians 3:12.
⁵1 Corinthians 4:7.
⁶See *Safe People* (Zondervan, 1995).
⁷Proverbs 19:11 NASB.
⁸1 Peter 4:8.

Chapter Six: The Controlling Mom

¹Proverbs 18:14 NASB.
²Hebrews 12:11 NASB.
³Galatians 6:5.

Chapter Seven: Becoming Your Own Person

¹2 Corinthians 1:4.
²Proverbs 27:5.
³Galatians 6:5.
⁴For more information on setting limits, see *Boundaries* by Cloud and Townsend (Grand Rapids: Zondervan, 1992).
⁵Matthew 7:2.

Chapter Eight: The Trophy Mom

¹Romans 8:1.
²Romans 15:7.
³Matthew 5:3.
⁴Ephesians 4:32.
⁵Zephaniah 3:5.
⁶Romans 12:3.
⁷Psalm 139:14
⁸Philippians 4:8.
⁹Proverbs 13:12.
¹⁰Jeremiah 31:3.

Chapter Nine: Getting Real

¹Genesis 3:22–24.
²Matthew 5:4.
³James 5:16 KJV.
⁴Psalm 103:8–14.
⁵Romans 12:3.
⁶Psalm 100:3 NASB.
⁷Psalm 139:24 NASB.
⁸See Romans 12:6–8.
⁹Proverbs 19:11 NASB.

Chapter Ten: The Still-the-Boss Mom

[1]Proverbs 22:6.
[2]Ephesians 4:15.
[3]Deuteronomy 6:6–7.
[4]For more information on how to deal with destructive spiritual teachings, see *12 "Christian" Beliefs That Drive People Crazy* (Grand Rapids: Zondervan, 1994).
[5]1 Peter 4:10.
[6]Matthew 6:33.

Chapter Eleven: Rebuilding Your Adulthood

[1]Ephesians 4:31.
[2]Proverbs 15:31.
[3]Proverbs 25:28.

Chapter Twelve: The American Express Mom

[1]Galatians 4:1–2 NASB.
[2]See Genesis 2:23–24 NASB.
[3]See 1 Timothy 5:4.

Chapter Thirteen: Leaving Home the Right Way

[1]Proverbs 27:6.
[2]Genesis 1:28.
[3]Mark 7:13.

Chapter Fourteen: For Women Only

[1]Psalm 103:13–14.
[2]1 John 4:19.
[3]John 3:21.
[4]Luke 1:45.

Chapter Fifteen: For Men Only

[1]Genesis 2:18.

Chapter Sixteen: What About Now?

[1]2 Corinthians 5:19.

The Mom Factor is also available in audio from
ZondervanPublishingHouse
Audio: 0-310-20453-4

Discover the path to true inner healing and spiritual growth
through these additional titles from Drs. Henry Cloud and
John Townsend.

*Boundaries: When to Say Yes, When to Say No, to Take Control of
Your Life*
Hardcover: 0-310-58590-2   Workbook: 0-310-49481-8
Audio: 0-310-58598-8   Curriculum: 0-310-58599-6

*Safe People: How to Find Relationships That Are Good for You
and Avoid Those That Aren't*
Softcover: 0-310-21084-4   Audio: 0-310-59568-1
Workbook: 0-310-49501-6

*Twelve "Christian" Beliefs That Can Drive You Crazy: Relief
from False Assumptions*
Softcover: 0-310-49491-5   Audio: 0-310-59578-9

Also by Dr. Henry Cloud

*Changes That Heal: How to Understand Your Past to Ensure a
Healthier Future*
Softcover: 0-310-60631-4   Audio: 0-310-20567-0
Mass Market: 0-06-104345-1   Workbook: 0-310-60633-0

Also by Dr. John Townsend

*Hiding from Love: How to Change the Withdrawal Patterns
That Isolate and Imprison You*
Softcover: 0-310-20107-1

For information about books, speaking engagements,
or referrals for counseling, call 800-676-HOPE
or 800-NEW-LIFE.

ZondervanPublishingHouse
Grand Rapids, Michigan

A Division of HarperCollinsPublishers